The Heartmost Desire

J. Neil Schulman

Books by J. Neil Schulman

From Pulpless.Com™

Novels
Alongside Night
The Rainbow Cadenza
Escape From Heaven

Nonfiction
The Robert Heinlein Interview and Other Heinleiniana
The Frame of the Century?
Stopping Power: Why 70 Million Americans Own Guns
The Heartmost Desire

Short Stories
Nasty, Brutish, and Short Stories

Omnibus Collection
Self Control Not Gun Control

Collected Screenwritings
Profile in Silver and Other Screenwritings

The Lord ain't my shepherd

Cause I ain't no sheep.

I'm a god in a body

Not Little Bo Peep.

PULPLESS.COM

150 S. Highway 160, Suite C-8, #234
Pahrump, NV 89048, U.S.A.

(775) 751-0770

http://www.pulpless.com

Inquiries to jneil@pulpless.com

The Heartmost Desire

by J. Neil Schulman

Copyright © 2013 The J. Neil Schulman Living Trust.

All rights reserved.

All rights reserved. Published by arrangement with the author. Printed in the United States of America.

The rights to all previously published materials by J. Neil Schulman are owned by the author, and are claimed both under existing copyright laws and natural logorights.

All other materials taken from published sources without specific permission are either in the public domain or are quoted and/or excerpted under the Fair Use Doctrine. Except for attributed quotations embedded in critical articles or reviews, no part of this book may be reproduced or utilized in any form or by any means, electronic or mechanical, including photocopying, recording, or by any information storage and retrieval system, without written permission from the publisher.

Trade Paperback Edition ISBN: 1-58445-207-2
PDF Edition ISBN: 1-58445-208-0
Amazon Kindle Edition ISBN : 1-58445-209-9
ePub edition for iTunes Edition ISBN: 1-58445-210-2

Contents

Part I   9
Unchaining the Human Heart
— A Revolutionary Manifesto   9
The Scandal of Liberty   13
Introduction by
J. Neil Schulman   17
Chapter 1: Forbidden Passions   21
Chapter 2: Romeo and Juliet   26
Chapter 3: Pirate Radio   29
Chapter 4: Selling Your Soul   32
Chapter 5: Stomping Out Dancing   35
Chapter 6: Go Kuck Yourself!   40
Chapter 7: Eat Your Veggies!   46
Chapter 8: Thank You For Smoking!   51
Chapter 9: Risky Business   58
Chapter 10: High Times   62
Chapter 11: Man and Superman   67
Chapter 12: Escape Artists   71
Chapter 13: Science versus Omniscience   76
Chapter 14: Sex for Money   82
Chapter 15: For Love or Money   88
Chapter 16: Moonshiners, Medicine Men,
and Merchants of Death   93
Chapter 17: Banned In Boston   98
Chapter 18: Wash Your Mouth Out!   107
Chapter 19: Don't Look Now   114
Chapter 20: Fun and Games   120
Chapter 21: The Hand Is Quicker Than The Eye   125
Chapter 22: No Secrets Allowed (Except Ours)   129
Chapter 23: Don't Even Think About It!   136
The Laughskeller   142

Part II 151
I Met God
— God Without Religion, Scripture, or Faith 151
Preface by
Brad Linaweaver 155
Foreword
By J. Neil Schulman 157
Introduction
By J. Neil Schulman 161
Chapter 1: Kid Atheist 165
Chapter 2: First Doubts 181
Chapter 3: Contact 197
Chapter 4: No Religion, Too 219
Chapter 5: *Escape from Heaven* 226
Chapter 6: Mind Meld 243
Chapter 7: Revelations 255
Chapter 8: Aftermath 271
Chapter 9: Collaboration 287
Chapter 10: Heresies 305
Chapter 11: Doctrines 323
Chapter 12: Supernatural Law 329
Chapter 13: Heaven 333
God's Libertarian Prophet? 341
----------------I Met Ayn Rand---------------- 362
----------------*Escape from Heaven*---------------- 366
----------------*Lady Magdalene's*---------------- 369
----------------How to Talk to God---------------- 372
----------------Religious Do's and Don'ts---------------- 374
--------------------Abortion-------------------- 377
A Non-Christian's Prayer To Christ 379

Supplement
Who Is God and What Was He Thinking,
Anyway? 387
MY AMAZON.COM REVIEW OF THE GOD
DELUSION BY RICHARD DAWKINS 396
ESCAPE FROM HEAVEN A Novel Proposal 398
ESCAPE FROM HEAVEN Outline 399
ESCAPE FROM HEAVEN Writing Samples 407
WHEN DUJ JUST DIES 408
RETURNING TO A HEAVEN UNDER ATTACK 412
DUJ CONTEMPLATES HIS UPCOMING
MEETING WITH GOD 413
DUJ'S INTERVIEW WITH GOD 416
DUJ GOES ON A DATE 423
SATAN HAS A DIFFERENT OPINION 426
GOD MEETS DUJ AT A 7-11 429
WHAT DUJ HAS LEARNED BY THE END
OF THE STORY 430
About J Neil Schulman 433

Part I

Unchaining the Human Heart — A Revolutionary Manifesto

To Soleil

The Scandal of Liberty

Foreword by
Brad Linaweaver

I'm writing this in 2013. It's after April Fool's Day, and shortly before Tax Day. Just finished reading a book by J. Neil Schulman that he wrote when he was a young man of 56. And I've been watching what is euphemistically referred to as the alternative media; you know, the Fox Outrage Channel.

Thank God that *Unchaining the Human Heart* is not fair and balanced.

A lot has happened since Neil wrote this some years ago, his most ignored work. It seemed slightly important at the time. Now it is essential. The evidence of its relevance is all around us.

Because of what happened on FNC tonight, I think Neil's book should be required reading at all future "freedom" events. How unlibertarian of me.

Neil once appeared on FNC when he was being interviewed about his book on O. J. Simpson. One thing is certain. He will never be on Fox to discuss the book you hold in your hands, or currently view onscreen.

Returning to tonight's spectacle, Bill O'Reilly often has libertarians on his show for comedy relief. He prefers libertarians under FNC contract. He'd never have the author of *Unchaining the Human Heart* on his show.

Tonight, O'Reilly came out for nationwide stop and frisk laws that would make any sane person never, ever go out in public with a gun. Then he supported Martial Law for Detroit. Then he continued his support for the utterly mad War on Drugs.

What does this have to do with Neil's book?

A lot.

O'Reilly is representative of the majority of people who vote Republican. He is an independent populist. He is looking out for the Volk, if you know what I mean.

He is an enemy of libertarians, as much as any liberal/progressive at MSNBC is an enemy of libertarians. O'Reilly stands out from the crowd, however, because he is unusually honest.

Many right wing police state guys were only going to show their true colors if Romney had been elected to the Presidency. Well, O'Reilly is better than that. He comes out against the Constitution even when Obama remains in office. You gotta respect that. O'Reilly has never had a problem with the Obama kill list for the government killer drones. Guess that makes him a Liberal over at Fox.

Just kidding. O'Reilly is not a liberal. He is not a neo-con. There is an older word to describe him, if you know what I mean.

The point is that this man who puts the "F" into Fox is the most popular thing over there. That means Fox is really as statist as the liberal biased media, whenever it really matters.

Libertarians are crazier than usual if they think the American right or left has any use for them, except as a club to be wielded in partisan politics.

The time has come to unchain libertarian passions from psychotic partisanship. The libertarian heart has been broken enough times already.

Never again.

Before going on, full disclosure rears its persistent head. I am an agnostic and a minarchist. Most of my colleagues in Libertarian Land are atheists and anarchists. There are libertarian Christians (and other faiths) in the minarchist camp. There are even religious anarchists.

Neil is unique. He is not religious, but he is an anarchist who believes in God.

The Heartmost Desire

That seems fine to me.

What I don't understand is an anarchist who believes in Fox News, or MSNBC, for that matter. Equally bizarre is an anarchist who panders to Marxism on the web. A spectre is haunting the Internet.

I'm sixty years old, and I've never seen so many fake anarchists in my life!!!

What has happened?

Did America fall down the rabbit hole after 9-11?

Did single issue politics destroy the libertarian movement?

Whatever went wrong in this country, it never touched J. Neil Schulman. He has worked on Second Amendment issues for years. He has been effective. But he never let his steadfast defense of self defense blind him to other issues.

He sees the big picture.

Unchaining the Human Heart is his sermon to the totality of human liberty.

Why do some of us want to be free? His book answers that question. It does not address liberals or conservatives or the ever popular fascist center. This book is for us.

Neil crams more into single paragraphs than other libertarians put into entire boring tomes. He can rattle off more limitations on our supposed free speech that most of us ever consider. He can recite a list of cultural taboos to frighten the staunchest social conservative.

Neil is a libertarian.

So why is he so often in hot water with other libertarians, the natural audience for this book?

It's for the same reason that he would never be a guest on Bill O'Reilly. The host of *The Factor* is a thorough going statist, but he also loves American culture. Bill loves it more than many of the recalcitrant conservatives at FNC.

J. Neil Schulman is a radical libertarian who loves American culture as much as Bill O'Reilly. So there is a problem for a patriotic statist encountering a patriotic anarchist.

As Lenin might say, "What is to be done?"

A libertarian defends the right to be wrong. It takes a lot of effort to initiate force or fraud. Short of that, the libertarian is tolerant of actions that liberals and conservatives cannot understand.

But a libertarian also has the right to judge the value of values. A libertarian can have common sense. He can weigh the good and the bad in the shadowlands where ideas have yet to be put into practice.

There is one kind of libertarian who will derive no benefit from the words that follow. That is someone who has no heart.

Brad Linaweaver,
April 11, 2013

Introduction by J. Neil Schulman

I'm 56 years old and I've been self-consciously libertarian for all but the first eighteen.

I now have an eighteen-year-old daughter, for whom I am writing this, but it's not my intent to use this essay to convert her to being a libertarian.

Obviously, since I talk about my daughter in the third person, I'm not writing this only to her.

My daughter shares one characteristic with many younger people that made me think of her as the audience for this when the idea of writing it came to me.

My daughter thinks I spend too much of my time ranting about politics. She doesn't understand why I shout back at the television.

She considers most of what I've written — my books, scripts, stories and articles — dominated by my interest in politics, and that discourages her from reading them.

When I say I'm libertarian, I don't mean that as a partisan affiliation. I'm not a member of the Libertarian Party. Neither do I mean it in the ideological or movement sense. While I'm well-read in what libertarians consider the primary sources for the libertarian movement, and am in debt to many of them for ideas I regularly use, I no longer consider myself part of any organized movement. I've come to abhor ideology, itself, as a distraction from my own contemplative thinking.

Years ago I wrote a play titled *"Cult of the Individual."* I wasn't just being ironic.

When, in Monty Python's *Life of Brian*, Brian tells a crowd of unwanted acolytes, "You're all individuals!" — prompting a shout from one voice in the crowd, "I'm not!" — the humor wasn't only the oxymoron. Adherence even to individualism, because it has become an ideology, prevents one from being a free individual.

The problem with ideology is that it reduces everything to ideas. Oh, my dear daughter, how I spent much of my life being guilty of that!

As I've matured, I've come to appreciate the more non-cerebral parts of my life. Yes, I still appreciate intellect and wit. That's how I make my living! Nonetheless I've become both more self-aware of, and less alienated from, allowing myself to respond first with feelings, and not instantly shut down those feelings with thought.

I grew up reading science-fiction. So when — also around age 18 — I first met other science-fiction readers, I met many others who, like me, led with our brains. If feelings were even spoken of, they were channeled into trivia.

It's no accident that emotion-challenged scientists, robots, and aliens are staples of science-fiction. Science-fiction writers knew who their fans were and appealed to us with psychological mirrors.

After I peeled away at layer after layer of politics and ideology, I found an emotional core that explained to me not only why I was attracted to libertarianism, but why this particular ideology — as hostile as its advocates were to using feelings as the means of choosing pursuits — is the one that at its core is devoted to protecting human loves and human dreams.

Paradoxically, the ultra-cerebral philosophy I've spent a lot of my life talking about is the one that's best suited for those who lead with their hearts and care about others' feelings.

To put it simply: the politics, movements, and ideologies that value and seek liberty for the individual over the interests of all groups — starting with the family — have been attempts to protect those things which make life meaningful and pleasurable. They have tried to protect whatever it is that you love ... whatever are your aspirations ... whatever you dream about as your passion.

For all my Spock-like arguments — my geekiness and wonkiness — my devotion to liberty is about protecting your hopes, dreams, and passions.

I've come to understand that libertarianism as a movement has been a failure not only because we have preached it as a set of abstract ideas, but because when we have shown strong emotion it has primarily been hostility to values strongly felt by others.

We've failed because we didn't get that it's not about what we're against but what it is that we're for.

When we've won support it's because we managed to connect with something specific that people cared about in their own lives. When we lost it's because we couldn't connect to people's lives.

Again, my dear daughter, this came as a revelation to me. I finally understood that when movements toward liberty have been successful it was because there was something specific and tangible that people loved and were fighting to protect.

This book will be giving examples of that. I'll detail how other political movements are based on spreading hate and fear — and appealing to the greed of human beings who want to get something for nothing — but neglect to mention that what you have to give up to join them is any possibility of remaining faithful to your own true loves and reaching for your own highest dreams.

What you have to give up to join them is you.

This has led me to a thought that I hope will transform my life as much as it does yours:

Even if I don't love what other people love — even if their hopes and dreams seem ridiculous or even offensive to me — I must start by respecting what they love, what they hope for, what they dream.

The beginning of liberty is when I respect — and pledge to protect — what others love, if — and this is a big "if" — they also respect and pledge to protect what I love.

For you wise acres reading this, I'm not falling for the tricks I see coming. No, respecting what you love doesn't mean that if you "love the earth" I can't put my carbon footprint up your global ass, or if you "love God" I can't make fun of your end-of-the-world cult, or if you "love animals" I have to sign onto your campaign to get dolphins the right to vote.

But for my daughter, who is reasonably sane, how this can work in practice, and liberate the world, is a journey I hope you'll take with me.

J. Neil Schulman, November 20, 2009

Addendum:

No changes.

J. Neil Schulman, April 11, 2013

Chapter 1: Forbidden Passions

Just what is it in your life that makes it worth getting out of bed in the morning?

For me, my best days are being an explorer.

I don't have to put on a pith helmet, sling an elephant gun over my shoulder, and trudge into the heart of Africa or through tropical rain forests deep in South America.

What gets me out of bed is finding an idea new to me and following where it leads, whether that journey is writing a new book chapter or story, entrepreneuring a new business, or walking onto a movie set and trying to figure out how I'm supposed to watch other actors in a scene I'm directing while I'm also on camera playing dead.

But what if I wasn't allowed to write or make movies or pursue new business ideas? What would my life be like then?

I don't have to time-travel back many years to find authorities that despite a constitutional guarantee of my freedom of speech and freedom of the press would have charged me with a crime because my writing or filmmaking could be interpreted as obscene, blasphemous, seditious, or otherwise contrary to public morals and safety.

The 1961 obscenity trial of novelist Henry Miller is within my lifetime, and had Miller lost I would have had to remove sexually-explicit scenes from my novels *Alongside Night*, *The Rainbow Cadenza*, and *Escape from Heaven*.

The Hays Code for making movies is within my lifetime, and had it not been overturned by free-speech activists the Hays Code would have forbidden me to show my film *Lady Magdalene's* in which I portray a house of prostitution as a legal employment opportunity, or the scene in which — playing an al Qaeda trainee — I pull down an American flag and throw it to the ground.

I don't have to travel very far to find foreign countries that would consider my writing and filmmaking to be libelous to their government or officials, or violating their local laws ... and in today's multinational trade environment could issue an arrest warrant for me that could prevent me from traveling to their country.

But even in the United States, today, my freedom of expression is still controversial.

Recently I wrote a piece for my Facebook friends called "Thank God we still have free speech!"

It read:

> Thank God we Americans still have free speech!
>
> You can still say anything you want (unless what you say threatens National Security or public safety, or is hate speech against a protected minority or interest group, or threatens the President of the United States or his family, or reveals the contents of a Grand Jury investigation, or reveals information that might expose the identity of a clandestine field agent or violates insider trading laws or is in opposition to universal health care or is in communication with an extraterrestrial, or is sexual harassment in a workplace, or attempts to fully inform a jury about their right to rule on the law as well as the facts, or violates a non-disclosure agreement, or falsely declares information to the Internal Revenue Service or is crying fire in a crowded theater or is electioneering near a polling place or is a statement in favor of a candidate which hasn't been declared as a campaign contribution or otherwise violates election laws or threatens the well-being of a minor or incites a riot or reveals information about the location of a person

relocated under witness protection or violates a judge's gag order or is a communication to someone who's got a restraining order against you or represents an implied threat to a school or its students and teachers or obstructs justice or is deemed to be lying to a federal or police officer during a criminal investigation or promotes the use of tobacco or illegal drugs or is lying to a census taker or is in contempt of court or contempt of Congress or slanders or libels someone or is contemptuous of Muhammad or Allah or is obscene or pornographic or violates someone's copyright or trademark or is a prayer or statement in favor of a religion within a public school or at an event organized by a public school or violates Facebook's, Twitter's, Myspace's, or YouTube's terms of service.

So speak up! You have the God-given right of free speech!

(But don't quote me at a public school.)

For much more of human history than my life — and much more of the world than my country — every time I sat down to write, or tried to make a movie, I'd have to be looking over my shoulder to make sure that some cop or political officer — or some snitch — wasn't looking for an opportunity to turn me in to the authorities because they disapproved of what I wanted to say.

My creative freedom is one of my passions and is one of the things that makes me libertarian in my views.

Free expression is something I will fight for ... and that is not a metaphor. In the extreme necessity I would fight for my right to write.

Yes, it's that important.

At various times and places other kinds of passions have

been outlawed, and only outlaws could express these passions: forbidden love, forbidden sex, forbidden friends, forbidden imagination, forbidden music, forbidden lyrics, forbidden jokes, forbidden words, forbidden poems, forbidden reading, forbidden books, forbidden stories, forbidden movies, forbidden comics, forbidden dancing, forbidden art, forbidden science, forbidden math, forbidden buildings, forbidden faiths, forbidden foods, forbidden drink, forbidden plants, forbidden sports, forbidden travel, forbidden smoke, forbidden games, forbidden toys, forbidden professions, forbidden knowledge, forbidden speeds, forbidden skills, forbidden medicine, forbidden risk, forbidden thoughts, forbidden fantasies, forbidden privacy, and even forbidden colors.

If anything has made someone not willing to do what they were told because something was more important to them, the people to whom the only passion is a death grip on other people's throats have tried to outlaw, control, or at least tax it. The passion for power over others is one I will not be defending. Nor will I be defending passions which depend on molesting or exploiting the innocent and the powerless.

But for those pleasures which make life beautiful and worth living, whatever they are, someone wants to forbid it. Megalomaniacs are a jealous lot. They want no competition. They want no gods before them. They want all attention on them.

As Groucho Marx sang as Rufus T. Firefly in the 1932 movie *Duck Soup*, "If any form of pleasure is exhibited, report to me and it will be prohibited! I'll put my foot down. So shall it be! This is the land of the free!"

Thomas Jefferson wrote in the Declaration of Independence that "We hold these truths to be self-evident, that all men are created equal, that they are endowed by their Creator with certain unalienable Rights, that among these are Life, Liberty and the pursuit of Happiness."

But what Jefferson didn't have the space to explain in his wartime requirement for eloquence and brevity was that Life, Liberty and the pursuit of Happiness is a diagram of necessity shaped as a pyramid. Life is at the base of that pyramid and Happiness is at the apex.

Without Life there can be no Liberty.

Without Liberty there can be no Happiness.

Life and Liberty are the rainbow. Happiness is the pot of gold at the rainbow's end.

Chapter 2: Romeo and Juliet

If I had to take a quick guess about whether governments, churches, or families have been most oppressive to the romantic desires of lovers, my money would be on families. But it's definitely a horse race.

Throughout much of human history — and in much of the world today — romantic love is an idea subversive to an established order in which marriages are arranged by families for reasons of finances or politics. It's not only daughters who are treated like commodities when families arrange marriages, either. A potential husband has to be financially stable and of a character likely to remain that way. Beauty and sexual attraction hardly register at all when marriage is handled by a family's mergers and acquisitions department; wealth, social standing, power — and of course not being a dreaded outsider from the wrong caste, clan, color, church, club, job, language, politics, or place of origin — are infinitely more important.

So it was in the 1590's when William Shakespeare adapted to the stage Arthur Brooke's poem *The Tragical History of Romeus and Juliet* into his most famous play about two feuding families whose teenage children fall in love and seek a marriage forbidden to them by custom and power. Romantic love was still a novelty when Shakespeare wrote about it, and Romeo and Juliet — first staged when it wasn't even socially acceptable to have the role of Juliet played by an actress — was as subversive in its day as *Tea and Sympathy* was in 1956 when it portrayed a romance between a 17-year-old boy and a married woman twice his age, or *Guess Who's Coming To Dinner* was in 1967 when it portrayed an interracial couple, or 1973's *La Cage aux Folles* was in its portrayal of homosexual lovers.

Readers familiar with my articles critical of the politics of gay marriage might be surprised to learn that I am as absolutely supportive of the rights of same-sex couples to fall in love and spend their lives together as I am for opposite-sex couples. My problems with the semantics of calling such couplings "marriage" — and populist defense of congregations' and voting populations' rights to decide on a definition for their church and polity that restricts the definition of marriage to couples with "one-each penis and vagina" — do not in the slightest mean that I wouldn't place myself as an armed citizen in between any bigot seeking to interfere with a bonding ceremony between a same-sex couple, or dissociate myself from lowlifes who can't find it in their heart to accept same-sex couples as respected members of their community, workplace, or social set.

But the news and entertainment media's over-exertions to defend one underdog aside, there are still many, many more opposite-sex lovers on planet Earth whose romantic desires are being foiled by family, religion, or law, than there are same-sex lovers ... and it's not my intent in this book to succumb to special pleadings.

The freedom to fall in love and commit oneself to that person will never be entirely non-controversial. My grandfather, Abraham Schulman, was 26-years-old when he married my grandmother, Anna Rosen, who was 13. Even then, at the turn of the nineteenth to twentieth centuries, the age difference was shocking enough that my grandmother added several years to her "official" age. I never would have learned the truth if later in life my grandmother hadn't been afraid to lie about her real birth date as beneficiary to my father's life insurance policy. But by today's standards, my grandfather was a child molester who would have been sent to prison. Had today's laws been applied back then, I could not be writing this since my father was their fifth child.

There are still parts of the world today where arranged marriages are the rule and marriage for romantic love is discouraged, if not forbidden.

Customs vary, even today, such that the definition of an

"incestuous" relationship might forbid relations between stepchildren or adopted children with no biological consanguinity; on the other hand, in other parts of the world brothers and sisters may still marry.

Even leaving out "one-each penis and vagina" as the minimum needed for natural human reproduction, both multiple-participant marriages — and all variations of coupling outside state- or church-sanctioned monogamy — allow for far more variety of human romantic passion than is customarily approved of in the average rectory or county clerk's office.

And here's where I shall sound as quaint as did the fictitious version of H.G. Wells in the 1979 movie *Time After Time*. I'm here to defend Free Love.

The decision to follow one's heart — damn the local customs, full speed ahead! — has to be a hallmark of human liberty.

No, I won't defend relations between adults and children. Biology, and thousands of years of customs derived from biology, have long established puberty as the dividing line between childhood and adulthood, and most cultures when not invaded by imperialists have rituals making it clear who is marriageable and who is not according to whether an individual has grown into the physical capacity to reproduce. Pick up a book by any honest and non-judgmental anthropologist. Or just find the nearest Bar Mitzvah. Some customs, merely by not going away, become subversive to piety and its secular edition, political correctness.

But between or among consenting adults, the right to love whom one does love is one of the pillars of freedom.

That is why this freedom — the right to love — is at the top of the list for tight controls by those among us whose main passion is to be your ruler.

Chapter 3: Pirate Radio

On April 1, 2009 in the UK, and on November 13, 2009 in the U.S., a movie originally titled *The Boat That Rocked* and retitled *Pirate Radio* for its American release, told a fictionalized and somewhat fanciful story of a boat in the early 1960's, anchored just far enough off the British coastline that it was in international waters. Consequently — at a time when the government-owned British Broadcasting Company monopolized British radio broadcasting and had no pressure to respond to its listening audience's desire for pop music — "the boat that rocked" broadcast rock and roll to an eager British listenership, and sold commercial advertising to pay for it.

Historical anachronisms in this wonderfully enjoyable movie are beside the point for me. There really were commercial pirate radio stations broadcasting rock into the UK in the 1960's for the precise reason the movie portrays. The BBC had a government monopoly, were not subject to any incentives or penalties if they failed to attract an audience, and thus had no reason to seek popularity. Elitism requires either tax subsidies or wealthy benefactors in order to survive. The BBC operated by taxing the public but its elitist operators felt no accountability to broadcast to the taxpayers what they wanted. Seeking popular approval — known as box office, sales, rentals, ratings, impressions, circulation, subscriptions, or eyeballs — is survival for any enterprise that hopes to pay its bills by satisfying a customer base.

Pirate Radio is a classic object lesson contrasting the difference between government and privately run enterprises.

But an economics lesson isn't my point here.

In the movie *Jurassic Park*, Jeff Goldblum's character, Dr. Ian Malcolm, is skeptical of the idea that breeding reconstituted dinosaurs is a sound business plan for a theme park. He makes compelling arguments that small variations in complex systems can result in unintended consequences, especially when dealing with biology. When Malcolm is told that the dinosaurs can't reproduce on their own because they were bred all female, he retorts, "Life will find a way." The plot of *Jurassic Park* proves Malcolm correct, as a spliced DNA sequence used to bring back the dinosaurs allows for spontaneous sex change — and the dinosaurs do start breeding on their own.

As it is with forbidden dinosaurs it is with forbidden music: life will find a way.

I grew up in a household devoted to classical music. My dad made his living as a classical violinist. My parents were of a generation that never heard rock and roll until they were adults ... and when they finally heard it they didn't like it.

My older sister and I were a different story. We came of age in the era of rock and roll. One of the first songs I remember hearing on the radio was Elvis Presley singing *"Hound Dog."* I was ten when the Beatles first played Ed Sullivan ... and within a few years I had my own electric guitar and amplifier (a Bar Mitzvah gift from my grandmother) and I was playing nothing but rock and roll — the Beatles, the Stones, the Animals ... and my own attempts at songwriting.

Still, whether coming from the radio, or a record player, or a tape recorder, or my own electric-guitar amplifier, the only words I ever heard from my classical parents about the rock and roll music my sister and I loved was, "Would you please turn down that noise?"

Rock and roll wasn't the first music to provoke fanatical passion from its audience. Teenage girls swooned over crooner Rudy Vallée in the 1920's and over Frank Sinatra in the 40's and 50's. By the time teenage girls were straining their larynxes over the Beatles in the 1960's musically-generated hysteria was a well-known phenomenon, reliable enough to write it into business plans. But even crassly commercialized and packaged, the passion of musicians to be true to their muse, and of audiences to follow the geniuses rather than be herded toward plastic imitations, meant that even if Jimi Hendrix was an opening act for the Monkees, it was Jimi Hendrix who was making the musical history.

Rock and roll was hardly the first forbidden music, either. Long before rock and roll was forbidden ragtime was; and long before ragtime was forbidden "consecutive fifths" were disallowed in musical composition that we today would regard as classical.

Over and over, passion prevailed, rules were broken, and the silly control-freaks were overcome.

But with each new generation of musicians came a new generation of self-appointed guardians of the public morality, jealous no-talents who considered that if they couldn't create anything great at least they could put their jackboots on top of it.

I hope my repeated examples in this book of power-grabbers targeting anything that makes life worth living doesn't get to be tiresome.

So to avoid making this book a mere litany of passions and their oppressors, let's change things up and talk about just what it is They want from you, and what They will offer you to get their slimy hands on it.

Chapter 4: Selling Your Soul

It's an old story told many, many times. Hollywood (they should know!) loves it. *The Devil and Daniel Webster. Bedazzled. Oh God, You Devil!*

The Devil comes to some poor loser when he's at the lowest point of his life — when everything's gone to crap, when all seems lost, when hope has given way to despair — and makes him an offer he can't refuse.

"I'll give you everything you want," says the Devil. "Just tell me and I'll give it to you. And all I want is your useless, worthless, good-for-nothing soul."

Somehow it just never seems to work out as advertised.

Guess what? It's not just Hollywood that knows this story by heart. It's also Washington D.C., Sacramento, New York City, and Juneau.

Every politician –every politician, even the ones with principles — has a little of Old Nick in him. Or — as Elizabeth Hurley in the 2000 remake of *Bedazzled* would point out — in her.

Just give us your useless, worthless, good for nothing freedom — you'll never miss it! — and we'll give you whatever you want. Anything you want.

You want a new shopping center for your run-down city? You got it! Oh, we might have to knock down a few houses and some mom-and-pop stores — not yours, nobody you know! — and that Hometown Buffet, thirty-screen multiplex, and Whole Foods Market is on its way. Not into consumerism? It can just as easily be a shiny new middle school, an endangered species habitat, a Gay and Lesbian Medical Marijuana Clinic, or a carbon-neutral performing arts center.

Let's not forget the basics. Beef, peanut butter, and lettuce without E coli. Free health care — make sure to get that H1N1 shot! A minimum-wage job in a nice air-conditioned office and a four-day work week. A government guaranteed 30-year-fixed 4% mortgage so you can have that kitchen with the island and the swing set in the back yard for your kids. Don't worry about your old age — we got your back ... unless it needs surgery. And don't worry — we promise not to tax you for any of this. I mean, you'll never make enough to have to pay much income tax, and you shouldn't be buying cigarettes, gas guzzlers, sugary soft drinks, fatty foods, or big-screen TVs, anyway.

And those silly dreams you had of making it in show business, or starting your own bookstore café, or dojo, or art gallery, or holistic health center, or living off food you raise on your own land. Have you looked at the statistics of how few people actually make a living as an actor, and how many small businesses go under in the first two years, or how the family farm is history? Grow up! You need to stay in school, and stay in college, and stay in graduate school — don't worry, we'll loan you the money at a reasonable interest rate — or you'll never get a good job at General Motors — I mean Circuit City! — I mean TV Guide! — I mean MySpace! — I mean Walmart!

You know you're making a deal with the Devil when at the end of the day you feel whipped, trapped, defeated, swindled, and just beat. And when all that's left is getting off your feet and leaning back in the La-Z-Boy, snapping open a Bud and a box of Oreos, catching the scores, and wondering why you can't see your dick when you pee anymore, you know it was a bad deal.

Don't do it! Look that gift horse in the mouth — if the Trojans had, the Greeks wouldn't have made it into Troy! If it seems like it's too good to be true, it probably is! A sucker is born every minute. Be the genius who's born on the half minute!

Above all, don't let anyone tell you not to pursue your dreams. If at first you don't succeed, try, try, again! Don't break the Ten Commandments, but if you have to break the law to keep the tyrants off your back remember that Moses, Jesus, Jefferson,

Thoreau, Gandhi, and Martin Luther King, Jr., broke the law, too!

Now let's get back to looking at some more of those life-enhancing passions that the Devil doesn't want you to have.

Chapter 5: Stomping Out Dancing

When I was a small child — through around age seven — I was as physically active as most normal children. I ran, jumped, played outdoors with my friends. I was not overweight and I don't recall having any less physical energy and stamina than the friends I played with. But just a few years after that I was overweight, had no physical stamina for running, and compared to the kids around me I had little upper body strength. I've never been able to do push-ups, pull-ups, climb ropes, and my one attempt to do overhand bars resulted in my falling, hitting my head, and losing consciousness. Frankly, I don't know how to account for what happened to me, but I do know that for most of my life physical activities that require stamina and wind have been challenging for me.

No, I've never been diagnosed with a breathing disorder such as asthma.

Ironically, I'm otherwise gifted at physical coordination. I have good hand-eye coordination. I'm a good shot with both rifles and handguns, and the first time I had a shotgun in my hand I hit four out of five skeet clays launched for me.

When in ninth grade I tried out for my junior-high-school's basketball team, I was as good or better than anyone else in the try-outs at sinking baskets. But I couldn't make the team because after only a few seconds into court play I didn't have the wind to continue.

I did a little better at boxing because I could learn and use combinations effectively. But if I couldn't beat my opponent quickly it was over for me: I'd simply run out of breath and have to give up.

These limits on my capacity for physical exertion meant that I could never become an expert dancer. When I think about this it's painful. It may be one of the few actual regrets I have in my life. Because of this, if there has been any envy in my life, it has always been for dancers even more than for accomplished musical instrumentalists.

Because my father was a violinist, classical ballet music became some of my favorites; but I always hated watching ballet on TV. I thought it was ballet dancing I hated. It took me years to discover — and only when in my thirties I first attended a live performance at the New York City Ballet — that the reason I hated watching ballet on TV, and thought it was ballet itself that I hated, was that TV directors told the camera operators to stay close on the dancers and track them across the stage. In other words, all the choreography was lost to me because I couldn't see the full stage. It was probably the low-resolution of American television which made this necessary, but in my opinion only large-screen HDTV can show ballet the way it needs to be seen: by locking a single camera on the whole stage and simply televising what someone seated in an orchestra seat would see.

So, I discovered late in life that, despite it largely being a spectator sport for me, I love even ballet dancing. Including figure skating.

And, for the record, I also love show tunes. If it weren't for the fact that I have zero interest in sex with other men and am obsessed with wanting to have sex with women, I'd make a pretty good gay man. I think this makes me what lately has been called metrosexual.

I passed through puberty in the early 1960's, close enough to the 50's that it was still expected that a young man should learn ballroom dancing. In seventh grade, after school, I attended a class in which I was taught — among others — the Foxtrot, the Waltz, the Tango, and the Mambo. In fact, on the day of the big Northeastern Power Blackout on November 9, 1965, I was in my dance class when the electricity went out.

But the 60's was also the decade in which traditional ballroom partner dancing was largely replaced at social functions by

The Heartmost Desire

free-form solo dancing: the Twist, the Frug, the Swim, and the Hully Gully. I never warmed much to the change. It was the romantic in me. Why would I want to be on a dance floor by myself instead of holding a girl in my arms?

Which brings us to the recent case of high-school senior, Tyler Frost.

In May, 2009, Tyler Frost, a senior at Heritage Christian School in Findlay, Ohio, was suspended from his school because, after being warned not to, he defied his school's ban on dancing and took his girlfriend, Rebecca Smooty, to Findlay High School's prom.

Heritage Christian School is a private Baptist school that bans dancing, rock and roll, and hand-holding.

Suspended for going to another school's prom. The Baptists running the Heritage Christian School might as well be the Taliban.

I'm a solid believer in God, but self-righteous Christians and Muslims who make music and dance their nemesis are my enemy and should be the enemy of all freedom-loving Americans. Just because they conduct their jihads without taxpayer funds doesn't make them any less vile.

The fanatic Baptist hatred of music and dancing isn't new. The wonderful 1984 (1984!) movie *Footloose* fictionalized a story of Baptist-controlled Elmore City, Oklahoma, which through 1980 had a city ordinance banning dancing. This wasn't just a private school enforcing its dogmatic policies on one of its students. This was an actual American city whose tyrannical blockheads used the police power of government guns to enforce their theocratic prohibition of a major form of human self-expression.

Oh, but surely the federal courts will protect us from such theocratic laws?

Guess again. The town of Purdy, Missouri also banned dancing. A lawsuit was filed against the town in federal court

— Clayton v. Place — which reached the United States 8th Circuit Court of Appeals. That court upheld the town's right to ban dancing — and both a request for a re-hearing and an appeal to the Supreme Court of the United States were denied.

The right of a town to ban dancing is established federal law in the United States of America.

And some might wonder why I consider the religious right just as much a threat to human liberty as the secular left.

No, the Baptists weren't the first to ban dancing, nor are they the last.

If you watch another 1984 movie *Amadeus* — 1984 again? Hmmm! — you learn that 18th-century Habsburg Holy Roman Emperor Joseph II — a secular autocrat considered hostile to papal authority — nevertheless had to be convinced by Mozart (and possibly in real life by Salieri) to rescind his ban on ballet dancing within operas.

But it wasn't just ballet that has inflamed the guardians of public morals. It was also ballroom dancing.

When the Waltz spread from Austria and Germany to England and France in the early 19th century, The Times of London in 1816 wrote, "'National morals depend on national habits: and it is quite sufficient to cast one's eyes on the voluptuous intertwining of the limbs, and close compressure of the bodies, in their dance, to see that it is indeed far removed from the modest reserve which has hitherto been considered distinctive of English females. So long as this obscene display was confined to prostitutes and adultresses we did not think it deserving of notice; but now that it is attempted to be forced upon the respectable classes of society by the evil example of their superiors, we feel it a duty to warn every parent against exposing his daughter to so fatal a contagion."

The reason dancing is threatening is that dancing is sexual. Oddly enough, the sexuality of dance was used as a substitute for sex, itself, by the 19th century Christian sect, the Shakers.

I've visited Shaker Villages in New England. These are historical preservations because there aren't any Shakers anymore. They refused to have sex and died out. In my view that's taking the love of dancing just a dance step too far.

Other ballroom dancing — particularly the Tango and the Lambada — have provoked similar reactions.

Islam doesn't allow dancing between unmarried men and women, nor dancing intended to arouse sexual passion.

So the banning of dance is just one battle in the War on Sex. Which I'll discuss further in my next chapter.

Chapter 6: Go Kuck Yourself!

Robert A. Heinlein, whose 1961 science-fiction novel *Stranger in a Strange Land* is considered one of the classics of the sexual revolution, packed more practical advice into any of his novels than most self-help books published before or since. Take, for example, a mini-essay of his on the best way to lie. An amateur liar — Heinlein informed us — just tells falsehoods. A better liar tells the truth but only part of the truth. An expert liar, Heinlein taught me, is one who tells the truth, the whole truth, and nothing but the truth — the requirements for being able to swear under oath without committing perjury — but he tells the truth so unconvincingly that everyone is convinced he's lying.

Bill Clinton was only a moderately good liar when he told the world, "I did not have sexual relations with that woman, Miss Lewinsky." If you look up the meaning of "sexual relations" in a dictionary suitable for use in a court of law, it has the specific meaning of "sexual intercourse." That definition doesn't cover blow jobs, which is of course why getting a Lewinsky became, for a while, a synonym for that sexual practice which by dictionary definition is not actually sex.

There is a good reason to consider "sexual relations" sex and blows jobs not sex. Sexual relations can effect a pregnancy. A blow job — unless a woman has a hither-to-undiscovered gastroenterological tract — can not.

So for the purposes of discussing human sexuality, we need to start by distinguishing behavior which can make a baby from behavior that can make an orgasm.

Bringing out the old Venn diagrams, you have your A Circle containing all behavior that can make a baby. The B Circle contains all behavior that can make an orgasm. The A and B circles overlap. Our professor of symbolic logic then asks us to make some true statements. 1. Some babies can be made without orgasms. 2. Some orgasms can happen without making a baby. 3. Some orgasms make babies.

It's somewhere between mildly amusing and astonishing to me that in writing a chapter on sex intended for grown-ups — that is, humans past puberty, many of whom reading this have engaged in both sex and sexual practices, and have even made babies — that I have to start by giving an elementary-school health-class lecture on the Birds and the Bees. But the sad fact is that all of our language today has become so polluted by political spin that if I don't provide clear definitions I can't speak truth to power.

To begin with, same-sex couples can't fuck. Heterosexuals have a monopoly on fucking. Fucking, for all its extra definitions, has a core definition — like sexual relations — of sexual intercourse. Sexual intercourse, being the biological process by which terrestrial mammalian primate human beings reproduce, requires one-each penis and vagina, with the penis ejaculating sperm-rich semen into a vagina leading to an ova-rich uterus. If the penis's ejaculation is directed into any other passageway or container — a mouth, an anus, a condom, or a Kleenex — it's not sexual intercourse. It may get very close to being sexual intercourse — particularly in the case of fucking with a condom, which only has a 90% success rate of preventing the semen from entering the vagina — but if we're not going to fuck around with language, it's not fucking.

It's paradoxical that today's Religious Puritans agree with their political nemeses, the Gays — that Circle B activities are sex.

It's also ironic that the old Soviet Communists were just as puritanical.

Now, I'm a lucky guy. Truly blessed. God made me so my passions — my desires, my obsessions — match up with my biological architecture. I want to stick my penis into vaginas.

I can understand why some gay men might feel God fucked

them over. They want to stick their penises into the mouths and anuses of other men, but women's vaginas have no appeal for them. They're full of sperm, all dressed with no place to go. This mismatch between soul and body has got to just suck.

I have a news flash for gays, both male and female. God isn't the only Player. And since God is Good, you might start looking around for some other Player — known for being Not Good — to blame for fucking up the soul-body connection.

But speaking for myself — and leaving God way the fuck out of it — I'm more than a little envious about the whole gay pride thing.

Let me start by admitting that my passion for women doesn't just involve wanting to fuck them. I also want to engage in other sexual activities with women that doesn't always involve my inserting my penis into their vaginas. Or at least not only inserting my penis into their vaginas. Or before I insert my penis into their vaginas.

These are activities which fall on the Venn diagram not into Circle A but into Circle B.

We need a new slang term other than "fucking" for the activities in Circle B. The word "fetish" might work, but fetish has bad connotations of men in dark raincoats. When it comes to rain gear I've always been the Philip Marlowe light-colored Burberry trench coat sort of guy.

I think the two closest terms for Circle B activities I've been able to come up with — and keep in mind that I'm close to four decades in as a professional writer — are "sex play" and "love play."

You need a new slang term for Circle B activities other than fucking? Going through the alphabet looking for null English rhymes, how about kucking?

Works for me.

I'm here to defend the rights of all post-pubescent biological adults to engage not only in Circle A baby-producing activities

— fucking — but also to defend all Circle B consensual adult sex play and love play — kucking.

So Gay Men, please feel free to go kuck yourselves. I've got your back. Just not too close, thanks.

But I also feel that gays have precisely no more and no less right to feel pride in their Circle B lifestyles than do any other practitioners of Circle B sex and love play.

I want equal pride for my non-gay fetishes!

In this book so far I've given some examples of human passions that authoritarian tyrants work to suppress. I believe the reason they suppress these passions has nothing to do with what the passions are for, but merely because — being pleasurable — it provides a means of getting leverage over human beings that can be used to control them, make them do things for you, and to take the fruits of their labors and transfer wealth from your pockets into theirs.

Controlling both fucking — through marriage and age-of-consent laws — and kucking — through laws and codes regulating sex play and love play — may have competition only from dietary codes (my very next chapter!) when it comes to tyrannizing human beings.

The default position for orthodox or fundamentalist cultures based on the Jewish, Christian, and Islamic religions is: no kucking allowed. Some cultures based on Jewish, Christian, and Islamic religions have attempted even to restrict fucking to a single sexual position — the so-called missionary position — and even to prohibit nude bodily contact between husband and wife during sexual intercourse.

These are some crazy muthahs!

I believe in God but few people believe in me when I state that I am just as hostile to dogmatic religion as I was when for the first three decades of my life I was an atheist. I recently found myself on lists of libertarians who are "religious."

You have got to be shitting me.

If you learn nothing else about the author of this book, learn well the following: I am not religious.

I pray because it's a convenient way for me to uplink with God.

A couple of times a year — Passover and Channukah — I celebrate observances of my family's Jewish traditions.

I eat ham and lobster.

I don't fast on Yom Kippur — it screws up my dieting.

I find some religious scriptures to contain stories seminal to my cultural matrix, and use them when useful. But I accept no religion's orthodoxy as authoritative, no scripture as infallible.

When it comes to the sexual and dietary codes deriving from Jewish, Christian, and Muslim scriptures I consider them nothing less than psychotically demented: Unfit for Human Consumption.

Keep in mind that you're getting this statement not from an atheist or an agnostic but from a man who publicly asserts that he has had a direct revelation from God and who considers that most adherents of organized religion would discard God — including their Savior — in a New York minute if upon his personal appearance he challenged their church's dogmas or their scripture's inerrancy.

My reading is that from God's point of view scripture is a record that over and over and over every time God has gifted men with a messenger, the message has initially been rejected in preference to previously adopted human writings. Then the revised message becomes a new dogma, as blindly followed as the old. Much of modern religious practice strikes me as idolatry: worshiping writings over God.

I'm a writer. I know the difference. I choose God.

Whether you agree with the back story for our Comic Book that God designed our biological matrix — and by the way that doesn't preclude anything Mr. Darwin, Mr. Spencer, or Mr. Dawkins have written if you believe launching a new space-time continuum can contain the DNA to evolve an entire universe — or you believe we're all just lucky to be here, our ability to experience physical rapture in almost infinite variation is the greatest perk of being born human.

Whatever gets you off — so long as all players are biologically mature and conscientious consenters, and doesn't spread plagues — is your business.

Chapter 7: Eat Your Veggies!

As the Danish Ham, Omelette, said in his famous soliloquy, "To eat, and what to eat — that is the question."

If Jimmy Durante thought "Everybody wants to get into the act!" when it comes to show biz, wait until it comes to what's on your plate. Hoo boy! Everybody wants to tell you what you should and shouldn't eat.

Muslims don't want you to eat pork because it's unclean. Jews say not only is bacon not kosher, but it's a no-no to eat lobsters, and you can't eat a cheeseburger because — and I'll never figure out the logic in this — it's sinful to eat baby goat meat that you boiled in its mother's milk. And for a week every year you have to eat crackers because Moses was on the lam from the Pharoahs, and if it wasn't for Matzoh there would still be Pharaohs enslaving us ... three-thousand-odd years later. Yeah. I wake up shivering that King Tut's gaining on me. Oh, and one whole day a year — nothing! Eat nothing for a day and God will forgive all the shenanigans you've been up to for the previous 365 days. (Rabbi, Rabbi, if I'm on Mars, how do I convert the Jewish calendar to Mars' 687-day year?)

Hindus say no problem if you want to eat baby goat boiled in its mother's milk, but cows are sacred so no roast beef for this little piggy!

When I was growing up Howard Johnsons had a 99 cent all-you-can-eat Fish Fry Day because Catholics were supposed to eat fish Friday. And being Jewish I never got the hang of Lent. You're supposed to give up something, but who were you supposed to lend it to?

Of course there's always your parents. "Don't you know there are children starving in Europe? Eat everything on your plate — including the canned spinach — because there's no chocolate pudding for you if you don't!" Canned spinach? Haven't you cretins ever heard of a wok?

And the vegetarians. Here it comes. Meat is murder! Didn't you ever see Bambi? You know what they did to that chicken before it got to the supermarket? And how would you like it if you're swimming around, minding your own business, spot a tasty-looking worm, and — Bam! — you got a hook stuck in your throat?

Mommy, mommy — how come it's okay for a fish to eat a worm but it's not okay for me to eat a fish?

We're not done.

You're fat and it's because you're eating all the wrong things. Saturated fat will give you high cholesterol and will kill you — so no butter. Eat margarine instead. Wait, wait, wait! We just figured out that margarine has partially hydrogenated oils that clog your arteries even worse than butter. Of course we didn't figure this out for fifty years and we're so very sorry for all the millions of people our dietary advice gave heart attacks to.

Fat will make you fat. What could be more obvious?

No, wait a minute! Now there's new evidence that carbohydrates, not fat, have been the problem all along. And all the fat we've been forcing the food manufacturers to take out of their products — making them replace the fats with carbs — might be the reason the rates of heart disease, obesity, and Type-II Diabetes are skyrocketing.

Grrrrrrrrrrrrrrrrrrrrrrrrrrrrrrrrrrrrrrrrr!

Woody Allen got this in his 1973 science-fiction movie, *Sleeper*:

> Dr. Melik: This morning for breakfast he requested something called "wheat germ, organic honey and tiger's milk."
>
> Dr. Aragon: [chuckling] Oh, yes. Those are the charmed substances that some years ago were thought to contain life-preserving properties.
>
> Dr. Melik: You mean there was no deep fat? No steak or cream pies or... hot fudge?

Dr. Aragon: Those were thought to be unhealthy... precisely the opposite of what we now know to be true.

When my daughter was little I made a treaty with her. If I promised not to tell her what she had to eat, she promised not to tell me what I shouldn't.

Listen. Food is one of the great pleasures in life. The five most beautiful words in the English language are "All You Can Eat Buffet."

It's almost worth it to get hit by a bus if you can try out the all-you-can-eat, best-food-you've-ever had in Judgment City.

Forget roulette — that's what Vegas is about, baby!

Lobster in butter sauce. Heavenly!

Spinach thrown into a wok with olive oil and garlic, and left there just long enough to crack it. Wow!

Have you ever had blueberry pie made with fresh blueberries? Peach pie made with fresh peaches?

Did you know there are experts on meat that when you get to the steak house the waitress asks you whether you want your Porterhouse aged "wet" or "dry"?

Have you ever done a search for the world's biggest burrito? There's this little place called El Abajeno on Inglewood Boulevard just south of Culver Boulevard in Culver City, California ...

You really shouldn't call yourself a critic of American cooking if you've never sampled the menu at the Publick House in Sturbridge, Massachusetts — don't miss the Indian Pudding for dessert — or tried the Shoo-Fly Pie at the Plain & Fancy Farm House in Lancaster County, Pennsylvania.

The search for the world's best hamburger. It used to be so much easier before the goddam government decided that because e coli can travel on raw beef — it can travel as easily on raw lettuce and spinach — hamburgers had to be overcooked to the consistency of shoe leather. And restauranteurs —

probably on the advice of their lawyers — started lying to their customers, claiming it was illegal for them to serve you a rare hamburger.

Yes, it's a lie. I looked it up. You should have known it was a lie when they said you could still order the sashimi and the rare steak.

Once in a while I can still find a restaurant to make me a rare hamburger.

But that's why all the fast-food-hamburger-chains — McDonalds, Burger King, Wendy's, Jack in the Box, Carl's, Jr., In-N-Out Burger — are all traitors to the American Dream. If their kitchens truly aren't clean enough to make a rare hamburger, their kitchens deserve to be sterilized with napalm.

Bacon-cheeseburgers with avocado are sensational. Try it, Rabbi. You'll see the Face of God. And remember that the reason Cain slew Abel is that Cain got jealous that God preferred the smoke from Abel's meat barbecuing to the stench of Cain's burning vegetables.

If the only tuna you've had is out of a can and not served uncooked, you've never tried tuna at all.

The best pizza I ever had was the double-stuffed I had at a long-gone eatery called Ambrosia in the suburbs of Chicago.

My Aunt Lena's pot roast and noodle pudding.

The Eggplant a la Russe at the Russian Tea Room, and the can't-get-them-in-your mouth sandwiches at the Stage or Carnegie Delis.

Carvel Ice Cream.

Freihofer's chocolate-chip cookies.

Friendlies, back when the Fribble was still called the Awful Awful — "Awful Big, Awful good!"

Howard Johnson's Tendersweet Fried Clams or Welsh Rarebit — and their Indian Pudding with vanilla ice cream was pretty good, too.

Then there was the eatery in the 70's/80's on Motor Avenue

in Los Angeles that served this fantastic fusion cooking — I think its name was Epiphany, or Serendipity, or something like that — and it had a signature ice-cream dessert called "the Scrunch."

And I remember Mamma's Buffet, corner of Wilshire and Lincoln. All their Asian food was orange.

The point is that the variety of food pleasures are near endless and every busybody wants to tell you what you must and must not eat. Some of them — not many — may actually have your health on their minds. The rest are vicious misanthropists whose palates were crippled by various dietary cults who insist they're entitled to impose their narrow food bigotry on everyone else.

They are the very Devil.

An old friend of mine, Clive Amor — my father's assistant concertmaster in the San Antonio Symphony Orchestra — was born in India, raised in London, and studied violin with Jascha Heifetz in the U.S. I knew him in Texas. Clive and I went out to eat a lot and he'd order far more than he could eat, leaving more than half over. I'm into doggie bags to take uneaten food home for later; Clive wasn't. Jokingly, once, I said to him, "Don't you know there are kids starving in India?"

And Clive said these golden words to me, God bless his soul: "I got out of India. I don't have to eat that."

Freedom begins when the child tells his parents to take these lima beans and shove them.

The spanking is worth it to remember the price of liberty.

A musician I know who lives in the mountains of Colorado puts it this way: "Vegetables? That's what food eats!"

Putting it my way: I eat vegetarians.

As for PETA: I respect their right to eat or not eat whatever they like.

The problem with PETA is that they don't respect mine.

Chapter 8: Thank You For Smoking!

Thank You For Smoking is a 1994 novel by Christopher Buckley, son of National Review founder, novelist, and Firing Line host William F. Buckley, Jr.

It was made into the 2005 movie *Thank You For Smoking* by Jason Reitman, son of *Ghost Busters* director, Ivan Reitman.

But the phrase "Thank You For Smoking" didn't originate with Jason Reitman's screenplay or Christopher Buckley's novel, nor did it originate with either of their famous fathers, though Christopher Buckley's father was possibly a conduit.

"Thank You For Smoking!" was a campaign-style button made up possibly as early as the 1970's by Samuel Edward Konkin III, publisher of *New Libertarian Notes*, author of *The New Libertarian Manifesto*, and an inveterate pipe smoker. It's possible that he was wearing that button, or uttered the slogan as he habitually did when anyone else lit up, when he met the elder Buckley.

Now, "Thank you for smoking!" wasn't the only button that Sam liked wearing. He also wore one made up by National Review writer, Timothy J. Wheeler, that read, "Every joyous calorie cries Yea! to life!"

So, honesty compels me to report that Sam was both still a pipe-smoker, and overweight, when in February 2004 he collapsed and died in his Beverly Hills apartment at age 56 of causes that will never be known, since there was no autopsy and since in the three decades I knew him Sam never once saw a medical doctor — not even when he was stabbed by a mugger.

I don't know what caused Sam's body to cease sustaining his life. I don't know if his smoking or eating habits had anything to do with it. But I do know that Sam enjoyed smoking and eating and if you had told him with a seer's certainty that one or the other would end his life prematurely he would have replied, "So what?"

Sam emailed a friend on his last birthday, "I never expected to live this long."

Samuel Edward Konkin III was uncompromising when it came to living a lifestyle based on personal liberty. He was a Canadian who came to the United States on a student visa to attend graduate school ... and overstayed his welcome by twenty-nine years. He easily could have satisfied any employment requirements for permanent residency — he counted dozens of American businessmen among his acquaintances, and a United States Congressman spoke at his memorial service — but complying with United States immigration law would have taken the fun out of it for him, and if Sam lived for anything, it was for fun.

Sam's education was in science. He held a Master's Degree in Theoretical Chemistry from New York University and completed everything needed to receive a doctorate ... except for writing up his completed research into a dissertation and turning it in. So if you talked to Sam about the statistical correlations that suggested cigarette smoking increased the odds of contracting life-threatening diseases such as heart disease, various cancers, or emphysema, Sam would argue right back that correlation did not equal proof of causation; and that even if the data were correct all smoking did was increase the odds of contracting a disease. Sam had conducted a risk-benefit analysis for pipe-smoking, and he had decided that the pleasure he obtained from smoking a pipe outweighed any risks to his health.

Speaking for myself, I came to other conclusions. At age sixteen I started smoking cigarettes. I smoked cigarettes for several weeks until I was mugged in Boston Common by a man who, at knife point, robbed me of all the cash I had on me — less than three dollars — and a pack of cigarettes. I decided that if my cigarettes were worth mugging me for, it wasn't worth it.

I didn't buy another pack.

Judging from Sam's and my common experience of being mugged at knife-point, knife-wielding muggers represented a greater risk to our health than smoke.

I did smoke cigars and a pipe on occasion for many years — not very often because if I smoked two days in a row I got a sore throat. Nonetheless, I've never believed smoking outdoors — or the presence of second-hand smoke in a private restaurant, bar, hotel lobby, or office with an effective air-changing ventilation system — represented enough of threat to public health to justify smoking prohibition.

In the name of public health tobacco products are forbidden to be sold to anyone under 18, cigarettes are heavily taxed — with money from these taxes being used to produce and proliferate government anti-smoking propaganda — and despite decades of warnings to smokers about the health risks associated with cigarettes, the tobacco companies were held financially liable for their products causing smokers' sickness and death. Authority has been given to the FDA to regulate cigarettes, on the grounds that cigarettes are a delivery system for the drug "nicotine." Hypocritically, the government encourages smokers to ingest nicotine delivered by skin patches and chewing gum as a means of quitting smoking, which clearly demonstrates that it's not nicotine the cigarette prohibitionists give a damn about — it's smoking. If a nicotine-free cigarette were marketed, the FDA would still have legal authority to control it.

In the movie *Thank You For Smoking* a tobacco spokesman testifies before a Congressional committee that if his son chose to smoke when he turned eighteen, he'd buy him his first pack. But in a deleted alternate ending on the DVD, this same spokesman is shown knocking a cigarette out of his son's mouth after the hearing. This scene was intended to denote if not the spokesman's hypocrisy, at least his sense of guilt.

I've never understood why smokers allow themselves to be treated as second-class citizens. It's clear that Sam's "Thank You For Smoking!" buttons never ignited a national smokers' rights movement. There's never been a mass rally on the Washington Mall by cigarette smokers in defense of their right to smoke. There has never been a mass-membership organization for cigarette rights, as the four-million-member NRA is for gun owners' rights. Of course there isn't a constitutional amendment that reads, "A well-smoked cigarette, being necessary after sexual Congress, the right of the people to keep and smoke Tobacco, shall not be infringed." The "pro Smoking campaign" Facebook Group has 24 members.

Let me come out solidly in favor of good health. I know it's a controversial position to take these days, when the Voluntary Human Extinction Movement is hoping the human race would just die off, but really, I think health is preferable to sickness.

But I think this would also be a good moment to quote the opening of my 2002 novel, *Escape from Heaven*:

> There's an old saying that everybody wants to go to Heaven but nobody wants to die.
>
> That's how it was for me, anyway.
>
> I drove a Mercedes because I was told it was the safest car in a crash. And it was a smart choice. I died of something else.
>
> I owned a handgun so I wouldn't die at the hands of a burglar. I was right about that, too. The burglar who broke into my bedroom ran like hell when he saw the .45 Government Model I was pointing at him ... and I died of something else.
>
> I quit smoking, did my best to keep my weight down and eat a low cholesterol diet, and practiced safe sex, because I didn't want to die of cancer, heart disease, emphysema or AIDS, and it paid off: I died of something else.

You see, that's the part they forget to mention. No matter what nasty ways of dying you avoid, there's always another one waiting for you. If one thing doesn't get you, another thing will. Everybody could have saved a lot of thought that went into bumper stickers and public service messages. All they would have had to say is, "Don't do that. Die of something else."

In a Cold War commencement address at American University in Washington on June 10, 1963, President John F. Kennedy said, "So, let us not be blind to our differences — but let us also direct attention to our common interests and to the means by which those differences can be resolved. And if we cannot end now our differences, at least we can help make the world safe for diversity. For, in the final analysis, our most basic common link is that we all inhabit this small planet. We all breathe the same air. We all cherish our children's future. And we are all mortal." Five months later, JFK showed us how mortal he was, and despite breathing the same air it wasn't a cigarette that killed him on November 22, 1963.

I've seen a lot of public service announcements warning kids not to take up smoking. I've never seen a single public service announcement warning kids not to let their parents drive them to school or not to commit murder — auto accidents and homicide being top causes for teenage deaths. Of the top twenty causes of teen deaths, cigarettes aren't even on the list. That's because smoking cigarettes is of little danger to teenagers. The serious health risks take years and years to materialize. The heavily tax-subsidized ad campaigns against teenage smoking make as little sense as spending millions of bucks each year to warn teenage boys about the dangers of prostate cancer.

If you smoke heavily enough for long enough, cigarette smoking can represent a significant threat to your health.

But cigarettes are also calming and many smokers will tell

you it helps them to think. And I can tell you as a non-smoker that — contrary to propaganda that kissing a smoker is like kissing an ashtray — kissing a smoker can be quite pleasant.

Anti-smoking propagandists always make fun of the old cigarette commercials showing doctors recommending cigarettes. But guess what? Cigarette smoking might actually have some health benefits after all.

Research shows that nicotine may delay the onset of both Parkinson's Disease and Alzheimer's Disease. I don't see why that little fact shouldn't be on *The O'Reilly Factor* and *Countdown with Keith Olbermann* alongside the debates on stem cell research.

Reports suggest that nicotine may also improve symptoms of Attention Deficit Hyperactivity Disorder (would passing out cigarettes to sixth graders improve their reading scores?) and Tourettes syndrome. Remember: cigarette smoking is of relatively little health risk to young people — not when a peanut butter sandwich is considered a lethal weapon in many school cafeterias. Oh, yeah. We're supposed to figure in the risk of long-term nicotine addiction. As if addiction doesn't mean any habitual behavior disapproved of by the power-freak using the term. As if "long-term" to Congress is further than the next election, less than two years away.

As if in the age of the Singularity anyone can make a scientific prediction about what the medical challenges will be forty years from now.

Nicotine enhances the release of neurotransmitters, enhancing a smoker's ability to focus.

And I believe there's an interesting correlation to be discovered between the overall reduction in rates of smoking and the overall increases in rates of obesity. But what's the chance of discovering politically incorrect facts like that once the government has a complete monopoly on funding for health-care research?

Health issues aside, for a lot of people smoking is pleasurable. The risk-to-benefit analysis of smoking versus health needs to take that into account.

Pleasure is important.

Pleasure enhances life.

Pleasure is good.

But pleasure is not even on the map for the legions of aggressive health Nazis obsessed with controlling you.

The adverse risks that come with the pleasures of smoking is your right to calculate free of their interference and burdens ... and I think any sort of personal pleasure is worth fighting for.

It's time for smokers to stop acting like whipped dogs and start standing up for themselves as a consumer's lobby. They've left the lobbying job to their suppliers — the tobacco growers and cigarette manufacturers — for too long. That's spineless. At the very least allowing someone else to tell you you're too stupid to calculate your own pleasures versus health risks shows no self-esteem.

If you let them get away with taking away your tobacco, the next thing you know they'll want to take away is your alcoholic beverages and firearms.

Alcohol, Tobacco, and Firearms. There's a federal bureau specifically to control those three things. And alcohol used to be prohibited completely.

Now that can't be a coincidence.

I absolutely support the right of non-smokers to have clean air to breathe. Before smoking inside was made illegal, you used to be able to find smoke-free air by walking outside.

Not anymore.

In the next chapter, let's talk in general about the risks we take to make life worth living.

Chapter 9: Risky Business

So you're probably thinking I'm going to start this chapter drawing wisdom from the 1983 movie *Risky Business* that launched Tom Cruise's career as a film star. But no. The text medium can't really do justice to the tighty-whitey air guitar dance Cruise did to Bob Seger's "Old Time Rock And Roll" and as hot as Rebecca de Mornay was in that movie, she really doesn't have much to do with what I want to write about. Except for this speech: "Sometimes you gotta say 'What the Fuck,' make your move. Joel, every now and then, saying 'What the Fuck,' brings freedom. Freedom brings opportunity, opportunity makes your future."

Okay, I guess I did start out with drawing wisdom from *Risky Business*.

But since I really wanted to start this chapter drawing wisdom from Albert Brooks' 1991 movie *Defending Your Life*, maybe this chapter has the wrong title.

In *Defending Your Life* — on my short list of movies I can re-watch endlessly — Albert Brooks plays Daniel Miller, a risk-averse Yuppie executive. When he's killed in a car accident, Daniel finds himself reborn into a cloned body in an afterlife realm called Judgment City. There Daniel finds himself having to defend himself in a life-review hearing, prosecuted for wasting his potential by being too timid to grab the opportunities offered him.

Now, if I ever find myself on trial on Judgment City, I think I'm going to be in Department B, where instead of reviewing all the times I was too afraid to say "What the fuck," I'll be looking at all the times I told self-important assholes who pissed me off to go fuck themselves. I'll be the guy who asks the judges where they get off thinking they have the authority to sit in judgment on my life, patiently explaining to them that they're too flat-headed even to start calculating what percentage of my brain I use, demanding to be taken directly to the office of my good buddy, God, and if they think I'm going to walk around in that stupid-looking robe they call a tupa they've got another thing coming.

Look. I'm not the bravest guy. As a kid I could never bring myself to dive into water. I never did, even though I later got a certificate in SCUBA diving with an underwater swim to a depth of fifty feet. I've never sky-dived or Bungee-jumped or hang-glided or driven race cars. I tried piloting a helicopter once; they don't tell you that, unlike driving, you can get sick to your stomach. I've always avoided fights because I don't like getting hit back. It hurts. I can talk about a handful of times in my life when I guess an objective observer might conclude I showed courage in the face of immediate danger, but I'm pretty sure I would have been useless in the invasion of Normandy.

Taking career risks has never been a problem for me. If I have any problem it may be that I've spent too much of my life on the edge of disaster. At various times in my life I've had my car repossessed, had all my credit cards go belly up, and been six months behind on paying the mortgage — all because I chose a career path as a self-employed free-lancer with no safety net, no unemployment insurance, no Plan B, nothing "to fall back on." I know what it's like to go for broke and end up broke. I know what it's like to be "all in" and lose the pot — not literally on a gaming table, but with equivalent stakes in the Game of Life. My financial life has been a roller-coaster that makes anything at Magic Mountain look like the Tea Cups at Disneyland.

But even as I sit here writing this — wondering where I'll find the money to make the health insurance payments this month — I wouldn't have missed this ride for anything.

I have friends who took what they thought was the sensible and safe path — college, graduate school, working their way up the corporate ladder — only to find themselves unemployed and in debt for years, in a situation not all that different from mine.

I invested half a million dollars of my family's money in producing and directing an independent film from my own script. After the housing market collapsed, eating our equity, this investment ended up being all the savings we would have had left. The movie hasn't yet begun to start recouping that investment. Yet, I lost almost as much in what was considered the safe policy of putting money into primary home equity ... and lots of people lost far more money for good by trusting Bernard Madoff.

I may yet sell my movie and get the money back.

Nor have I lived my life as one of those people who have been afraid to fall in love. I've fallen in love with several women, and married one of them.

Fear of heights is not one of my problems, and not only am I not afraid of public speaking, I get off on being in front of an audience. I used to think I was afraid of roller coasters until I realized that it wasn't fear. I just don't enjoy being body slammed by swift gravitational changes. You put me on a roller coaster I'd better be in earth orbit at the end of it or it's not worth it for me.

We live in a culture that is obsessed with safety and security. People's fears often have no relationship with the actuarial risks. I know for a fact, from years of research, that the widespread availability of privately owned and carried firearms decreases the risk of gun massacres; yet, as I write this, the "gun-free-zone" on a college campus — and incredibly even on the army base — is still the irrational, fear-based response to repeated cases where one madman with a gun can murder dozens and wound many more disarmed victims. Often in life fear makes victims and courage makes survivors.

Our society has institutionalized fear.

Many well-meaning parents advise their children not to

pursue risky professions — like the arts — without having something sensible "to fall back on," never realizing that the rigors of pursuing any risky profession almost guarantees that something to fall back on acts to undercut the courage needed to persevere and prevail. If you have something to fall back on ... you'll fall back.

Casino gambling is denigrated as a vice, even while hypocritical statists advertise Lotto tickets on bus ads and the evening local news. Nobody admits the truth that betting on a poker hand is just as much an investment as putting money down on a stock pick.

It's only the skills you master that can reduce the risks.

TV commercials advertising cars driven in dynamic action advise viewers that they're watching professional drivers on closed courses. The automakers are forbidden to notify their customers that it's the dangers of speeding over interesting roads which is the only thing making these boxes on wheels look sexy.

The safe path is the one always sold by the establishment: stay in school, get a good job. Never mind that learning on your own through reading and life experience — never regarding anyone else as your boss — may be the surest formula to come up with something great that the human race never had before.

As I quoted President Kennedy in my last chapter, "We are all mortal." Our days are the total capital we are loaned to invest, and sooner or later the banker calls in the loan. The only real risk is the possibility that we can waste our lives never using our life and liberty to pursue happiness.

Violin virtuoso Jascha Heifetz, in his master classes on TV, can be heard telling his students hesitating to strike out with originality, "Take a chance."

The only truth about taking risks in life is summed up in the cliché: if you don't bet, you'll never win.

Chapter 10: High Times

Let me start out by saying: I don't do drugs.

What a fucking liar I am!

I just had a travel mug of high-grade coffee. Okay, I cut it. I mixed dark Sumatra beans with decaf French roast. I do that because if I keep the amount of caffeine down per mug of coffee, I can do two or three mugs per day. But make no mistake. I'm mainlining the maximum amount of coffee each day that my body can tolerate without giving me heart palpitations, insomnia, indigestion, lower-intestinal distress, leg and foot cramps, and bouts of hyperventilation. I take both calcium and potassium supplements daily to balance my electrolytes and counteract some of the most harmful effects of caffeine.

But make no mistake. I'm a java junkie. The Mormons have caffeine alongside alcohol on their list of prohibited stimulants. And let's not forget George Carlin telling us that coffee is the low end of the speed spectrum.

One of the reasons I tend to believe that Native Americans may be the Lost Tribe of Israel is that we have in common not having a lot of tolerance for alcohol. I think I've been drunk only two or three times in my life, because my first drink makes me sleepy and a second drink just puts me out.

But I do enjoy drinking.

I like sipping twelve- or eighteen-year-old single-malt Scotch, or the better Jack Daniels called Gentleman Jack, or Tullamore Dew, or Knob Creek Bourbon Whiskey, or a decent Cognac. But this is a rare pleasure for me these days, because these are empty calories and I'm on a constant diet, and because alcohol is a contraindication for the oral Diabetes medications I take.

When I was writing my second novel, *The Rainbow Cadenza*, I had an almost-year-long writers' block after completing only the first three chapters. I received a letter from my editor — who had paid me an advance and was awaiting the manuscript's delivery — that read, "Your lateness is no longer amusing." I knew I needed to find a way to get past this and turned to drugs. I got into the habit of beginning to write late at night, and started each night's writing session by making myself a Kahlúa and coffee. The coffee woke me up. The Kahlúa anesthetized my fear of writing.

I finished the novel in less than three months.

When I was sixteen I was prescribed Ritalin by a doctor to help me with weight loss. All I remember is that a Ritalin and a cup of coffee was the greatest high I've ever had. But Ritalin also gave me excruciatingly painful leg cramps so I quit taking it pretty quickly.

Of course I've tried marijuana. I never bought any but I was in groups where joints were being passed around and I toked when it was handed to me. It was mildly pleasant but never really did much for me, and it gave me a hangover. I certainly don't need any more reasons to get the munchies. So I can't say, personally, that I'm a fan.

Years ago I was offered all the cocaine I wanted. I never tried it. I knew what drastic effects caffeine had on my metabolism and didn't feel I needed anything that would dump noradrenaline into my system any faster.

The only opiate I have any experience with is codeine. It never got me high but I still think Terpin hydrate with codeine is the most effective cough syrup my parents ever gave me as a child.

I've experimented with cognitive enhancing supplements like L-Phenylalanine — and the Omega-3 fish oil I take is supposed to balance out my serotonin levels — but the effects are so mild, and onset so slow, that none of them really belong in a chapter about getting high.

And that's all he wrote for my personal experience with mind-altering and mood-altering drugs.

Zoologists tell us that many animals consume plants and other substances that alter their behavior. Anyone who's lived with a cat knows how catnip works. If we lived in anything approaching a sane society, alongside the book *Everybody Poops* in the children's section of Barnes and Noble there would be another book called *Everybody Gets High*.

Getting high is, when broken down to basics, the pursuit of feeling good. There are people who either don't want anyone to feel good, or only to feel good with their permission.

If — at no time in your life — it has never crossed your mind that you need to go to a doctor to get a permission slip in order to buy a product that you will use on your own body, then it's my sad duty to report to you that reading this sentence, right now, is the very first time you have ever encountered the concept of freedom.

If having been awakened to that missing thought you are inclined to make excuses for that lapse of knowledge, or argue with me that it is in any way justifiable, I'd also like to suggest to you that you have been thoroughly brainwashed.

Or you may be one of the brain washers in which case, go fuck yourself.

Freedom starts with ownership of your own mind, body, and soul. Unless you are a child, incompetent, or convicted criminal who needs a keeper, anyone who stands in between you and your right to have absolute control over what does or does not go into your body is attempting to be your ruler.

Are there risks to taking drugs? Of course there are. Read back a chapter about risks and benefits. The question is not whether there are risks of bad outcomes from ingesting mind- and mood-altering chemical substances.

The question is who decides — you, or your Master.

Now, one of the things about having a mind that is subject to effects from living within a physical body is that the mind's ability to make decisions can be chemically impaired. Decisions made while impaired may well be irrational, irresponsible, and dangerous.

So what? There are lots of people who I'd trust drunk or stoned to make decisions that might affect me before I'd trust lucidly conscious people who are simply evil. If they represent a threat I suggest self-defense, in the same way one would protect oneself against an out-of-control machine or a wild animal. But a non-specific possibility of danger is not a sufficient reason to deprive adult human beings of their self-dominion. There needs to be an actual threat.

So, yeah, I don't have a problem with taking the car keys away from a drunk. But bringing back alcohol prohibition because there are drunk drivers isn't a solution you get from mothers. It's a proposal made by motherfuckers.

One shouldn't need a permission slip from a government-board-certified physician to smoke marijuana if you think it will help you survive chemotherapy, or help with your eyesight.

If you're in pain, the management of that pain shouldn't be in the hands of a doctor who's scared shitless he'll be the one making the perp walk if he gives his patient enough narcotics to make the pain go away.

If you believe Peyote or LSD will help you see the Face of God, no Narc should stand in your way with a devil's pitchfork.

And if meth labs were legal in industrial districts, we wouldn't have houses igniting neighborhoods in the suburbs.

Drug prohibition is responsible for empowering organized crime domestically and a Narcocracy on the United States' southern border so foul that the stench of corruption and death reaches hundreds of miles north. Then we wonder why Mexicans will endure unbelievable hardships just for the chance to exchange their bedeviled country for ours.

But I'm not here just to make a case for the freedom to take drugs.

I'm also here to make the case for the freedom not to take

drugs.

Nobody has the right to drug you without your consent and I believe that is one human right extending even to children. We have a priest class calling themselves psychiatrists who instruct parents to drug their children with psychotropics that have never even had clinical trials on children. Of course experimenting on children would be evil — so let's just give them the drugs untested, huh?

Then we wonder why some kids go crazy and try to kill as many people at their school as they can get in their sights.

Tyranny has at least as many dire consequences as freedom. That may be a hard comparison to make because freedom has so rarely been tried.

But that's one clinical trial, as far as I'm concerned, which is long overdue.

Chapter 11: Man and Superman

There's a popular bumper sticker you might have seen: "If You Can Read This, Thank A Teacher."

Here's another one for you: "If You're Reading 'Unchaining the Human Heart — A Revolutionary Manifesto,' Thank Superman."

I was born in 1953, in New York City. I don't remember a time we didn't have a TV set in our living room. I watched cartoons. I watched Rocky Jones, Space Ranger. But my favorite TV show was by far the 1952-1958 TV series, *Adventures of Superman*, starring George Reeves.

What made Superman super was his super powers. He had super strength. Bullets bounced off him. He had X-Ray vision. But the super power I cared about most was that Superman could fly. He didn't need an airplane or a helicopter. He didn't need wings. He could just jump up and keep on going — as high as he wanted to, as far as he wanted to — defying gravity, and propelling himself to whatever destination he chose, faster than a speeding bullet — which for a speeding rifle bullet gets Superman to supersonic speeds.

Adventures of Superman stopped producing new episodes when I was five years old, and the possibility of a new season died with George Reeves in 1959. But the end of the TV show didn't cut me off from my Superman habit, since a walk to the corner candy store had already revealed to me that there were *Superman* comic books, and other comic books in which Superman appeared as a character: *Superboy, Lois Lane, Jimmy Olsen, Action Comics, Justice League of America,* and others.

By the time I got to kindergarten I was already a proficient reader, although my vocabulary tended to be populated by words you didn't find in *Fun With Dick and Jane*, like "invulnerable," "stratospheric," and "telepathic."

I didn't know it at the time, but before I was a year old

a German-born psychiatrist named Fredric Wertham had written a book called *Seduction of the Innocent*, which argued that comic books corrupted youth and promoted juvenile delinquency. Beginning a few weeks after my first birthday, a subcommittee of the United States Senate Judiciary Committee — led by Republican New York Senator Robert Hendrickson and Democratic Tennessee Senator Estes Kefauver — held hearings to investigate claims that "crime" and "horror" comic books caused good kids to go bad. One of the witnesses was William Gaines, publisher of E.C. Comics, which published comic books in the genres of science fiction, military, satire, crime, and horror. The committee were really only interested in the last two genres, which they considered the most graphic and lurid.

The result of Wertham's campaign and the Senate hearings was a stirred up mob demanding censorship of comic books. The comic-book publishing industry did what any businessmen do when faced with the threat of government restrictions — they chained themselves first. The Comics Code was born which turned comic books, for the time I was reading them, largely into infantile pap — books like *Casper the Friendly Ghost*, *Richie Rich*, and *Archie*. That was fine when I was a baby just learning how to read. But by the time I was a teenager and discovered real science-fiction and fantasy in the library, I had outgrown these dumbed down comic-book stories and stopped buying them.

What I didn't know until it was much too late for me was that if I had switched from DC comics — which published *Superman* — to Marvel Comics — which published *Spider-Man* and *X-Men* — I would have encountered the subversive Stan Lee and Steve Ditko, who were finding ways to get around the Comics Code with plot-lines and character development competitive with the science-fiction and fantasy books I was reading by Robert A. Heinlein and C.S. Lewis.

Meanwhile, I became a fan of William Gaines anyway, since he had moved on to publish the most iconic humor magazine of my youth, *Mad Magazine.*

But why was Superman so important to me?

Psychiatrist Carl Jung wrote of the collective unconscious and archetypes which are universal to the thoughts of all human beings. Building on this, Joseph Campbell wrote of universal myths and of a spiritual "force" that bound all of us together. This "force" eventually found its way into the mythology created by a young filmmaker, George Lucas, who used it as the centerpiece of *Star Wars.*

But the idea behind Superman is firmly embedded in our culture, going back to the Genesis story which begins Judaism, Christianity, and Islam: a story that tells us our race was created to be immortals who fell to a mortal life on earth as we know it today. The primary Western religions don't just tell us what we lost; they promise us a New Eden, or Paradise, or Heaven, in which we get back what we lost.

Superman is the Jungian archetype embedded in our unconscious of what we were and are supposed to be again.

For many years I flew, like Superman, in my dreams, thinking they were only dreams. But even as dreams these were experiences as important to me as anything that happened to me when I was "awake."

Then, I learned that some of these flying dreams could arise to a level of self-consciousness called "lucidity."

I began to realize that, since I couldn't fly while I was awake, if I was flying it meant I had to be dreaming. But if I knew I was dreaming then I wasn't dreaming anymore — and if I didn't wake up right away, it gave me a measure of conscious control of where I was flying.

Eventually this conscious control allowed me to fly to places and see things that I could remember when I woke up. And, by checking details on Yahoo and Google of what I had seen while "dreaming," I found I could sometimes verify that what I saw while "asleep" was real.

Dreams had turned into astral travel or Out-of-Body projections.

At least while I was asleep — and no longer chained by my material body and the earth's pull on it — I had become Superman.

For real.

And how great a liberation is that?

Chapter 12: Escape Artists

"Who are the people most opposed to escapism? Jailers!"
–C.S. Lewis

I've written eleven books and this is my twelfth. Counting this one, seven of them are nonfiction.

I've also been a newspaper photographer, a songwriter, a boiler-room phone salesman, a campus activist, a meeting and conference organizer, a journalist, a magazine editor, a screenwriter, a pizza man, a literary agent, a book publisher, a film director, a poet, a philosopher, and an actor.

But more likely than not when I'm introduced to an audience — after the audience is assured that I need no introduction — I'll be introduced as a science-fiction writer.

Gee whiz, that's leaving an awful lot out of the introduction. But it's still the highest compliment I can be given.

The charge of escapism is made against movies, books, magazines, comics, TV shows, games, comedy, and any other entertainment medium that engages the imagination. I've spent a good deal of my professional career — and my personal life — doing nothing else.

The term "escape artist" is usually applied to stage magicians — like the immortal Harry Houdini — who bind and chain themselves in handcuffs, shackles, locks, and chains, sometimes with time pressures like drowning or suffocation to limit the amount of time they have to escape. I suppose to be fair we'll now have to add stage magic, itself, to the list of escapist entertainment since the audience knows the magician is somehow tricking them and are caught up in the suspense regardless.

The key to any sort of escapism is the audience member's "willing suspension of disbelief."

All consumption of narrative entertainment — and that does include games, jokes, and tricks — involves a conscious act of faith.

Guess what? I now get to add religion onto the list of escapist activities. Without imagination, there can be no religion.

That should not be either a surprise or an offense to anyone whose religion begins with the Book of Genesis. Are we not told by that story that we are made in God's image? The verb of image is "imagine." If we were indeed created by God, we were created by an act of Divine Imagination.

C.S. Lewis — both a Christian apologist in nonfiction and a writer of Christian mythopoeic fantasy in fiction — understood that without what he called a "baptized imagination" there can be no genuine faith. That's why Lewis defended even the science-fiction and fantasy written by atheists and agnostics against the charges of "escapism." All Lewis asked for was a level playing field with other purveyors of imagination to weave his narrative spells. Lewis believed that once the imagination was turned on, God would do the rest.

Which, of course, leads us to a seeming paradox: if there's a serious point behind the fantasy, just what is it that one is escaping from?

I think the escape is from the idea that life must be dull and routine. I assure you. The life of the dullest person you know — if you give a writer like me the chance to get to know them — is the stuff of legend.

Fans of fantasy and science fiction refer to those who don't share their passion for escape as "mundanes." But no one is mundane. There are only people who are afraid that if they dream, they will awaken into a nightmare.

I sometimes wonder whether the most successful fantasy writer of our time, *Harry Potter* author J.K. Rowling, was inspired by the fan's epithet for the non-fan to invent the term "muggle" for human beings without magical talents.

The term "fan" itself is telling. Quite the opposite of William Shatner's classic *Saturday Night Live* skit — which centered around the Captain Kirk actor telling Trekkies to "Get a life!"

The Heartmost Desire

— the word "fan" is short for "fanatic."

This is a book about liberating human beings from the chains on their passion.

I assure you, the word "fan" is a good description of someone engaged in pursuing a passion. They already have a life. It may be an inner life invisible to the materialist, but playboys and mountain climbers probably wouldn't think a Buddhist or Catholic monk — or scholars, philosophers, poets, or mathematicians — have much of a life either, huh?

I have news for fans of science-fiction and fantasy. If they think Holden Caulfield's lost weekend in New York City, or John Steinbeck's Joad family trekking from Oklahoma to California, or even Arthur Miller's Willy Loman dreaming of success while succumbing to despair, are any less works of imagination than stories of time-travel or visitors from outer space, then I suggest their imagination needs some work. None of these characters are real. What happens to them in their stories is a reflection of what their authors understand about life. If the author gives their characters a hard time — if what they see is nearsighted, if their choices are limited — it's because their authors want to prove something to you.

But I also have news for those snobs who consider science fiction and fantasy trivial escapism: these genres fearlessly explore those universal questions most important to human life and human happiness.

Science fiction and fantasy are the literature of "if." The "if" in these stories play precisely the same role in a narrative as the X and Y do in higher math. These "ifs" are the variables in the equations of human existence.

If the next war were not a civil war among human beings but against invaders from another planet — H.G. Wells, *The War of the Worlds,* 1898

If a small orphan girl living in the hardship of a Kansas farm could run away to a magical world — L. Frank Baum, illustrated by W.W. Denslow, *The Wonderful Wizard of Oz*, 1900

If families could be replaced by the State — Aldous Huxley, *Brave New World*, 1932

If Stalinism ruled the entire world — George Orwell, *Nineteen Eighty-Four* , 1949

I could fill up this chapter just by listing more classic works of science-fiction and fantasy, or my favorites, or the authors who created them. While I haven't hesitated to express my personal tastes elsewhere in this book, starting to reel off my favorites in my own profession would be both endless and personally dangerous. Once I start I dare not stop — what if I missed one written by a friend?

Imagination is the Sixth Sense. It's the way we interpret the mere facts of the world we live in. It sees larger landscapes than the other five senses.

Imagination is the cure to the claustrophobia that causes a gang member to think that his 'hood is the whole world, or the walls-closing-in despair that cripples the courage needed to keep going.

If by exploring forgotten worlds, or unreal worlds, or merely heretofore undeveloped worlds, we learn something useful about living in this one, that would be enough of a reason for our imaginations to make the journey. But often enough the worlds we see through imagination are unseen worlds we can discover ... or build.

It's good to imagine utopias and tell stories of the people who live in them. Those are the thought experiments — the dry runs, the proving grounds — that might help us discover the unintended consequences that turn one dreamer's perfect world into another dreamer's hell.

It's worthwhile to read stories about what aliens might be like when we meet them — even though every alien you meet in a story is just a human psyche wearing a rubber suit. But even the attempt to imagine what an alien is like might turn out to be the key to communication if we meet them ... and there is always the possibility that there are universal laws of consciousness that might mean no intelligent being we meet can be entirely alien.

Traveling through time, or into an alternate dimension, is a way of removing ourselves from our own assumptions and prejudices — if even for a few hours. When a single Einstein can revolutionize the human race's understanding of physical law by imagining what time means for an object approaching the speed of light, what can an army of Einsteins do when their imagination is set free from the prison of learned authority?

Stories are lessons in how to see the unseen, to feel what someone else feels. Without imagination there can be no empathy. Without imagination and empathy, we are all trapped in our own head, alone and afraid. We "escape artists" are the explorers taking point in clearing the brush so you can see what's outside.

The difference between what's considered a realistic narrative and what's considered a work of imagination is what the writer chooses to take for granted and what the author decides to make exceptional. In "realistic" fictions, the landscape is ordinary and the characters are exceptional. In imaginative fiction the viewpoint characters need to be everymen — as close to ordinary as possible — so we don't get lost exploring strange lands and the unusual people who live there.

It wouldn't do to have *the* Wizard of Oz take us on a tour of Never Never Land.

Or maybe it would.

Did I just come up with an escapist story idea?

Chapter 13: Science versus Omniscience

Let's start by getting one thing straight.

No real scientist would ever, ever, ever — under any circumstances — declare that a question has been answered finally and that a scientific debate is over, once and for all. Ever.

That's just not how real scientists think, or talk.

Science is a process — a set of tools to test knowledge for validity — and whenever you hear someone declare that scientific debate is over and a particular conclusion is unquestionable, not only has he given strong evidence that he never grasped the scientific method, there's a good chance he has identified himself not as a scientist but as a political operative, an ad man, a religious fanatic, a con man, and possibly a gangster in a lab coat.

The scientific method always gives its conclusions as provisional and always subject to correction by additional facts, better observations, later experiments, newer theories, more relevant paradigms, and — every once in a while — a genius turning everything we thought we knew upside down by asking a question nobody until then had thought to ask.

In his very first published short story, *"Lifeline,"* in 1939, Robert A. Heinlein — always considered one of the most scientifically literate of science-fiction writers — put these words in the mouth of a scientist: "One can judge from experiment, or one can blindly accept authority. To the scientific mind, experimental proof is all important and theory is merely a convenience in description, to be junked when it no longer fits. To the academic mind, authority is everything and facts are junked when they do not fit theory laid down by authority."

–J. Neil Schulman, *"Exposing The Warm Mongers"*
J. Neil Schulman @ Rational Review, November 27, 2009

I wrote the above as my introduction to a discussion on global warming, a week after whistle blowers released onto the Internet thousands of emails from the Climate Research Unit at the University of East Anglia. These emails revealed not only massive fraud being committed by scientists claiming proof of global warming but the deliberate silencing and marginalization of scientists who declined to agree that human-caused increases in carbon dioxide and methane threaten catastrophic global warming.

But the established United Nations' political consensus on global warming is only one of many subjects where my above words are applicable.

Today, no less than in the time of Galileo, there are those megalomaniacs who attempt to speak with Divine Omniscience to tell us what we are allowed to believe.

In a December 18, 2009 address to the United Nations Climate Change Conference in Copenhagen, Denmark, U.S. President Barack Obama declared that "This is not fiction, this is science. Unchecked, climate change will pose unacceptable risks to our security, our economies, and our planet. That much we know." The President was speaking not out of a Science that — even as he spoke — was being called into question because of reliance upon fraudulent data, but using his political office to speak ex cathedra, like the Pope, out of a grandiose entitlement to Omniscience.

No scientist claims to be a Know-It-All.

Anyone claiming to be a Know-It-All on any subject is no scientist.

Omniscience today is as much the enemy of free thinking as it was when the Inquisition convicted Galileo Galilei for heresy because he dared champion the Copernican view that the earth orbited the sun and therefore the earth was not the center of the universe. At the time the idea that the earth was the center of creation was established Church doctrine. Galileo was forced to recant, and spent the rest of his life under house arrest. It took three-and-a half centuries before Pope John Paul II admitted the Church might have been too rough on him. Excuse me for thinking that's a day late and a dollar short.

The persecution of independent scientists continues today. Today, however, as many persecutors are driven by secular ideology as religious faith.

The passionate mind longs for knowledge about what we are — as a species and as individuals — in what we know to be a tiny oasis of life in an inconceivably large but possibly dead universe. If we truly are alone on this planet — the only observers in a vast desert — we want to know it, because it tells us how special we are. If we are one of a community of intelligent species in the universe, we want to know that, too ... because it means the human race does not have to be celestially lonely.

If we came into existence by an unlikely series of meaningless accidents then we who think are the gods of the universe.

If we were created by an uncreated and eternal Designer then we have traded our notion of godhood for the comfort of not being orphans.

> Omniscience: Charles Darwin's Theory of Evolution has been proven to account for the beginnings of life and the natural selection of genetic traits for simpler life forms to evolve into more-complex life forms — including the human species.
>
> Science: No scientist has yet performed an experiment that can demonstrate how a living cell can come into existence out of non-living matter. Nor is the fossil record conclusive in showing more complex life forms arising out of less complex life forms. Evolution remains what it was when Charles Darwin's book On the Origin of Species first proposed it on November 24, 1859 as the explanation for the origins of species — an unproved theory.

The debate on the origins of species is locked in a fight-to-the-death struggle between theists and atheists on whether Intelligent Design is required to cross the chasm between a universe of non-living matter and energy and the one planet we know to contain life — our own. The debate is confused by militant atheists like Richard Dawkins who are willing to

The Heartmost Desire 79

admit the possibility that terrestrial life might have been the design of earlier extraterrestrial creators. This only relocates the first appearance of life to another address.

But the search for clues on our origins is annihilated when either side uses force and intimidation to silence their opponents.

It was an evil attack on the free human mind when in 1925 the State of Tennessee put high-school science teacher John Scopes on trial for violating its Butler Act, which made it unlawful "to teach any theory that denies the story of the Divine Creation of man as taught in the *Bible*, and to teach instead that man has descended from a lower order of animals" in any Tennessee state-funded school and university.

It is as much an evil attack on the free human mind today when teaching Intelligent Design is prohibited by law and even less savory threats are made by academies of higher learning against the academic freedom of researchers and teachers who decline to agree that Darwin's Theory of Evolution has been demonstrated to account for the existence of life and of the human species.

If you think the extermination of free thought begins and ends with global warming and Darwin, it may well be that your own prejudices are getting in the way of your seeing how universal and dogmatic Omniscience still is today.

> Omniscience: All human consciousness can be accounted for as a byproduct of neural activity in the human brain, and ceases when the brain dies. Any supposition that there is a soul or spirit that exists independent of the cerebral organ — and can exist outside it and endure beyond it — isn't science but superstition. No respectable institution of scientific research or learning should be given a dime to experiment on it. No science degrees should be awarded in these fields of study. Send

them to the Schools of Divinity or just call them cranks and let them be published in the *Weekly World News*.

Science: Conduct experiments in extra-sensory perception, precognition, communication with the dead, and out-of-body travel. Invent double-blind experiments, keep careful records, report what you find.

Omniscience: No artifacts exist from any alien spacecraft and those who claim the Army collected and hid such artifacts are just nut jobs. People who claim they've experienced alien colonoscopies are psychotics. The United States Air Force looked into it and found nothing that can't be explained away by ordinary atmospheric phenomena and previously classified technology.

Science: Interview the thousands of humans who report observations of, and contact with, UFO's and extraterrestrials, and consider that eyewitness accounts are as much raw data as anything discovered in a laboratory. Men have been sent to the electric chair on less eyewitness testimony than in many UFO cases.

Do you believe in Bigfoot, the Abominable Snowman, or the Loch Ness Monster?

Omniscience: Even though new species are being documented by scientists every day, anyone who believes they've observed heretofore uncatalogued anthropoid species or prehistoric sea creatures no older than many species of sharks are just deluding themselves.

Now you're not going to tell me you believe in prehistoric technological civilizations on this planet like Atlantis or Mu, are you, Neil?

Omniscience: Our current civilization — for which artifacts and documents of any sort can only account for several thousand of the millions of years the human species is supposed to have been in existence on this planet — is the one and only time civilization has reached an industrial technology. The repeated ice ages which have swept clean the surface of the earth every ten thousand or so years — that would be a hundred clean sweeps if the civilization we're looking for was a million years back — can't possibly account for archeologists failing to discover a prehistoric microwave oven. There's no chance we might only find the evidence we're seeking in the deepest of ocean trenches, locked below the earth's crust possibly even as far down as the earth's mantle. And it's absurd to think we'll find evidence of a previous human civilization when we finally get a chance to do some digging on Mars.

I write as a lover of science. It was my first passion. It still is.

Don't tell me what to believe in. Tell me what the facts are. Tell me what you think they mean. I'll make up my own mind.

When anyone claims the authority to say what is science and what isn't — when anyone declares a debate is over and tag themselves the winner — it makes me want to put my fist down their mind-killing pie holes.

But if any of them can get over their megalomaniacal sense of Omniscience, I'd much rather just have a lively discussion with them over a beer.

Chapter 14: Sex for Money

When I was a young lad I lived in Manhattan, where in the Fall of 1971 I met my first libertarians, at a meeting of the New York Libertarian Association, in the apartment of Gary Greenberg, who at the time was a deputy prosecutor for the City of New York. So if I'm ever called to testify before a future House Committee on UnAmerican Activities and asked to name names, my career as a subversive starts right here.

One of the libertarians I met at that first meeting was a graduate student going for a doctorate in theoretical chemistry from New York University. His name was Samuel Edward Konkin III. Inspired by a British libertarian named Chris Tame, Sam had started a Libertarian Alliance on the NYU campus, and Sam found me worth talking to at that first meeting because — prior to actually meeting any other libertarians — I had started a libertarian group at my college, part of the City University of New York.

I was the only other college student Sam met that night who on his own initiative had started a campus libertarian group. I also was starting out as a writer and Sam published a mimeographed newsletter called *New (NYU) Libertarian Notes*. So we became friends, and that was how I ended up taking the subway to Brooklyn with Sam to audit a college course on economics being given by Murray Rothbard.

Also attending those classes was an economics student named Walter Block, now Harold E. Wirth Eminent Scholar Chair in Economics and Professor of Economics at Loyola University New Orleans and Senior Fellow with the Ludwig von Mises Institute.

Walter made an immediate impression on me after the first Rothbard class I audited, when Sam, myself, Walter, and half a dozen other students accompanied Murray to a nearby pub and over pitchers of beer we continued the discussion. I should note for historical purposes that at the time the drinking age in New York was 18. I was probably the youngest guy at the table and I had a million questions for Rothbard. I was asking so many questions that Walter — using fundamental principles of the economics Rothbard was teaching — pulled me aside and informed me that Rothbard's time was a "scarce resource" and by dominating the questioning I was misallocating it!

In 1975, just a few years later, Walter's book *Defending the Undefendable* was first published. The subtitle was "*The Pimp, Prostitute, Scab, Slumlord, Libeler, Moneylender, and Other Scapegoats in the Rogue's Gallery of American Society.*"

There was no chapter in Walter's book, however, defending those who by asking too many questions misallocated the professor's scarce time. But Walter did use the value-free approach of the Austrian School of Economics to argue that if there was no force in an economic transaction, it not only should not be a crime but was a positive good.

The pimp was merely a prostitute's agent or manager — no different than a sports agent or singer's manager. If you didn't like the slum apartment the landlord was renting you, you were free to look elsewhere. You didn't have a right to keep your cheating on your wife a secret, so if you paid someone blackmail to keep your secret, that was a 100% voluntary transaction. And since everyone is entitled to their opinion, as far as Walter was concerned, writing bad things about someone shouldn't be something you could get sued for.

Walter, in his book, had a different purpose than I have in this one. I'm not out to explicate a theory of economics. I'm here to defend the passions — the loves — which freedom is necessary to enable. So you're not going to find me making arguments that people become blackmailers or loan sharks because it's their lifelong dream — nor will you find me arguing here that being a slumlord or litterer works to enhance other people's dreams.

What I am going to argue in future chapters is that just because the performance of a job or profession is illegal — or just because the possession of certain skills is regarded as dangerous or anti-social — that doesn't mean these jobs or skills can't be constructive, life-affirming, and even noble pursuits.

Let's start in this chapter with a hard case: prostitution.

I doubt very much that any little girl dreams of growing up to be a prostitute. I doubt any father is thrilled to discover that his daughter has grown up to become one.

Let me also be very clear that in referring to prostitution I am not referring to a situation where any sort of force, threat, duress, intimidation, or dependency is used to make someone perform sexual acts for money. I'm not talking about kidnapping women or children and forcing them into sexual slavery. I'm not talking of a pimp supplying one of his women drugs in exchange for the money she gets from standing on a corner and offering herself to passing motorists.

And I'll leave out gay prostitution and male escorts from this discussion because that's a whole other cultural milieu.

For the duration of this discussion I'm going to restrict myself to that subset of female prostitution where a woman, of her own free will, and with no penalty for saying no at any time, offers herself in exchange for money to perform what in Chapter 6 of this book I referred to as "Circle A" and "Circle B" sexual activity.

To begin with, let's understand what prostitution is for both the prostitute and the client. It is a professional personal service, like a physician, nurse, psychotherapist, physical therapist, speech therapist, masseur or masseuse, personal trainer, hair stylist, manicurist, piano teacher, math tutor, midwife, or tennis instructor. Many of these other professions involve personal touching and can become highly emotionally charged.

The Heartmost Desire

At first glance, prostitution doesn't actually seem all that different from being a doctor or nurse. Nurses wash their patients genitals and change the diapers of incontinent patients. A urologist might find it necessary that a penis be massaged to erection or even milked to ejaculation. A psychotherapist — like a spouse or a friend — becomes far more intimately involved with the personal problems of a patient than a prostitute ever does.

What distinguishes the prostitute from all other one-on-one professions is not that a prostitute is uniquely involved with the most intimate parts of her client's body but that the prostitute is willing to use the most intimate areas of her own body in a session with her client. Additionally, a prostitute often needs to be an actor to create a fantasy for the client. Mostly — but not always — the object is to cause the client to come to orgasm.

Earlier in this book, while discussing drugs, I wrote,

> If — at no time in your life — it has never crossed your mind that you need to go to a doctor to get a permission slip in order to buy a product that you will use on your own body, then it's my sad duty to report to you that reading this sentence, right now, is the very first time you have ever encountered the concept of freedom.

This sentence is a specific case of the general argument made by this book that each of us is a volitional being with the moral right to control our own bodies. Only if we violate someone else's rights are there moral limits of what we may do with our bodies. The counter-argument against the woman who argues that ownership of her body gives her the right to abort a fetus is that the fetus also has rights; but when there is no possible injured party involved — as there is in the case of consuming a drug or having sex for money — the morality of self-ownership is only answered by a tyrant's megalomania to rule.

A lot of the stigma attached to prostitution arises from the hostility Jewish, Christian, and Islamic scripture has for prostitutes.

But a lot of this hostility also comes from the cultural expectations both women and men have.

It's my opinion that a lot of the hostility to female prostitution is from traditional-values women who object to a woman having sex for money rather than for love, children, and the security of marriage — and maybe they don't like the competition; and a lot of the hostility to female prostitution is from feminist women who object to a woman giving orgasms to men for money rather than demanding an orgasm of her own in exchange — and maybe they don't like the competition.

That doesn't leave a lot of women to be a lobby for legal prostitution.

The other stigma attached to prostitution is because men are naturally possessive of women. If a man enjoys a woman physically he's halfway to falling in love with her. That she gets to collect payment and kick him out of her bedroom is diminishing to the male ego.

Modern men have also been trained by our egalitarian culture to be concerned with pleasing a woman sexually. A situation where the woman doesn't care about whether she comes or not is, at the least, disconcerting. And a woman faking an orgasm feels like a cheat.

Then there are men who are romantics, and ultimately find sex without love to be unsatisfactory. A prostitute needs to be a very good actress, indeed, for a man like this not to feel like a chump when he's out the door and she's using her calculator to add up the night's box office.

But where the pride and even nobility of prostitution as a profession comes in is when a man who is unattractive — flabby or painfully thin, bad teeth, bad skin, male pattern baldness, even physically handicapped, or who has peculiar fetishes —

can by the simple expedient of providing cash take to bed a woman who under ordinary circumstances wouldn't be caught dead on a date, much less in bed, with him.

Women willing to make a man like that feel good about himself even for an hour — no less than Florence Nightingale — are a gift from God.

Chapter 15: For Love or Money

This is a book about love. What, then, of money?

In the previous chapter, "Sex for Money," I looked at the most direct case possible of an act which romantics such as myself desire to be performed out of love but instead is performed for money.

But let's not forget that in my second chapter, "Romeo and Juliet," I also examined the case of sexual acts performed for something other than love — power, social standing, and again, money.

What is the moral difference, if any, between a prostitute picking up the cash left on her bedside table in the morning, and the Germanic custom of a husband paying a dower or "morning gift" to his wife on the morning after their wedding? What's the moral difference, if any, between a pimp collecting the proceeds from the woman he sends out to hook on a street corner, and the parents of a woman collecting a "bride price" from her new husband or his family? And I can't even fathom how low the social standing of a woman had to be that not only was she not worthy of being sold for her sexual value, but her parents had to pay a dowry to some guy to take her off their hands. It looks to me that prostitution is a huge step up from that.

But in almost every other human endeavor there is the possibility of doing something merely because you enjoy it, or feel it's your mission or vocation or duty, or in the alternative because doing it brings rewards.

In his sermon, *The Weight of Glory*, preached on June 8, 1942 at the Church of St. Mary the Virgin, Oxford, C.S. Lewis said,

> Indeed, if we consider the unblushing promises of reward and the staggering nature of the rewards promised in the Gospels, it would seem that Our Lord finds our desires, not too strong, but too weak. ...

We must not be troubled by unbelievers when they say that this promise of reward makes the Christian life a mercenary affair. There are different kinds of reward. There is the reward which has no natural connexion with the things you do to earn it, and is quite foreign to the desires that ought to accompany those things. Money is not the natural reward of love; that is why we call a man mercenary if he marries a woman for the sake of her money. But marriage is the proper reward for a real lover, and he is not mercenary for desiring it. A general who fights well in order to get a peerage is mercenary; a general who fights for victory is not, victory being the proper reward of battle as marriage is the proper reward of love. The proper rewards are not simply tacked on to the activity for which they are given, but are the activity itself in consummation.

Like me, C.S. Lewis was a romantic — an idealist who then becomes a cynic when faced with people who do things not for their natural rewards but for extraneous ones — such as money.

Yet this same C.S. Lewis — whom we just saw extolling virtue bringing its natural rewards — spent his life as a scholar paid by Oxford and Cambridge. The author who wrote Christian apologetics and fantasies received royalty checks from their publication.

Lewis is reported to have been a man generous with his charities; yet I have read no biography of him asserting that he never used money he was paid to teach and write to pay his rent or a mortgage, or lay a roasted goose on his Christmas table, or buy the pipe tobacco he smoked, or pay for the pints of Ruddles Ale he drank with J.R.R. Tolkien at the Eagle and Child pub.

This does not make C.S. Lewis a liar or a hypocrite.

This makes C.S. Lewis human.

If you had asked C.S. Lewis about the seeming contradiction between what he preached and what he practiced, I know what his answer would have been. He would have said that human beings were fallen, and it was only prior to our race's fall in Eden — or after our redemption — that we could act entirely out of love with its natural rewards and with no consideration for the necessity to live by the sweat of our brow.

Does not Christian charity require us, then, to consider that the prostitute who in exchange for money makes love to men who otherwise would go loveless might be performing a sacred duty — as much as a nurse — and that the money given her is merely the means that supports her in her blessed vocation?

To deny that possibility appears to me pharisaical.

I am in no position to throw the first stone because I am not without sin.

I love to write. But I write for money.

Charles Dickens' *A Christmas Carol* — which told of the miser Ebenezer Scrooge and the lessons ghosts taught him about being more charitable — was first published on December 19, 1843 and made lots of money for its author. It has made even more money for book publishers, movie producers, and other entrepreneurs who didn't write it.

The Christmas carol "*Santa Claus is Coming to Town*" was, according to its Wikipedia article, "written by J. Fred Coots and Haven Gillespie, and was first sung on Eddie Cantor's radio show in November 1934. It became an instant hit with orders for 100,000 copies of sheet music the next day and over 400,000 copies sold by Christmas."

My father was a violinist. He began playing violin when he was five years old, and played the violin until he was literally too weak to hold it up. He spent hours each day isolated in a room with his violin, a music stand, a metronome, and poker chips on the floor to keep track of the number of times he practiced a passage. Playing violin was the first passion of his life, even more than for his wife or his children. But from age 16 to age 80 my father did not live a year in which he was not paid to play the violin.

"Chick" Gandil, first baseman for the Chicago White Sox, was ring-leader of the plan to throw the 1919 World Series in exchange for money from gamblers, and was banned from Major League Baseball. Gandil nonetheless spent as much of the rest of his life as he was physically able playing baseball on any field he was allowed.

The surgical team who save a life by transplanting a kidney are all paid to perform the operation. But it's illegal for the kidney donor to be paid.

The Pope has an all-expenses life paid for by Church donations, and so does every cardinal, bishop, priest, nun, and monk — and that includes Mother Teresa who won the Nobel Peace Prize, was beatified by Pope John Paul II and given the title Blessed Teresa of Calcutta ... and who expressed a belief in the spiritual goodness of poverty. If she had been forced to live in a palace she would have been miserable; nonetheless, like the rest of the human race she needed to eat ... and some human being had to pay for the food that was put on her plate.

Deepak Chopra, M.D., makes money from lectures, books, videos, and CD's.

Jesus may have turned water into wine for the Wedding at Cana, but I'm still pretty sure the wedding band got paid.

And God paid Moses a stipend of manna for leading the Hebrews out of Egypt.

For many years the International Olympic Committee — a corporation based in Lausanne, Switzerland — forbade athletes who had been paid to play sports from participating in Olympic games, which were supposed to be restricted to "amateurs." During those years athletes completely supported by their governments were nonetheless allowed to compete.

If someone is paid by taxpayer money they're not mercenary. If they're paid by a private person they are.

What a crock of hypocrisy.

If you love doing something and can get rich by doing it — instead of having to support yourself by doing something you do only because of the money — there's a word for what you are.

Lucky.

Chapter 16: Moonshiners, Medicine Men, and Merchants of Death

This is a book about liberating passion. What do people who evade federal excise taxes on the manufacture of liquor, push drugs that haven't achieved FDA approval, and sell weapons designed only to kill other people have to do with that?

What the three examples in the title of this chapter have in common, of course, is that they are all legally and morally dubious. So it might be useful to start with a legal analysis.

We'll start where I get most of my legal knowledge — movies and TV — in this case from the movie *Legally Blonde*.

In *Legally Blonde* Harvard law student, Elle Woods, is asked by a professor if she'd prefer to defend a client charged with a crime that is malum prohibitum or malum in se. In the Latin jargon lawyers use, a malum prohibitum crime is an unlawful act only because someone passed a law against it, as opposed to doing something that is evil whether or not there's a law passed against doing it, which would be an act that's malum in se.

Elle tells her professor that she'd prefer to defend clients who are charged with a malum in se offense ... because she's not afraid of danger.

In this chapter I'll be looking only at malum prohibitum — doing things that may be perfectly fine from a moral standpoint but are crimes because it violates the law.

So I won't defend murder or theft, but I would defend killing in self-defense or using stealth to take back something which was stolen.

And in this chapter I'll be talking about people whose love is to defend freedom for freedom's sake.

How difficult, after all, would it have been for moonshiners in Appalachia — beginning in the 1930's — to pay federal excise tax, slap on a tax stamp, and by doing so open up their products to huge markets both domestically and overseas? Instead of being one of the poorest regions in the Union, legal moonshine could have made Appalachia the Napa Valley of corn liquor.

So why go to all the trouble to keep their liquor illegal with all the risks and penalties?

For the same reason my friend, Samuel Edward Konkin III, refused to complete his doctorate in theoretical chemistry and go to work for Union Carbide, Monsanto, or Dow. Sheer, freedom-loving orneriness. The moonshiners thrived on risk and the thrill of living their dream. They stood fast on their principles.

No wonder history treats them as folk heroes.

To later generations, marijuana growers and dealers represent the same spirit of liberty. Despite generations of "Just Say No" and D.A.R.E. in every public school, Cheech and Chong — The Breakfast Club — Harold and Kumar — are for generation after generation still icons of American rebellion.

Ever hear of Omega-3 fish oil? Alpha-Lipoic Acid? Vitamin D-3? Mixed-tocopherols Vitamin E? Lycopene? Green tea and white tea? All of them have clinical studies strongly indicating that they have health benefits.

None of these exist, as far as establishment medicine in the United States is concerned. They won't be covered under your health insurance — or whatever government-approved plan is passed. Doctors aren't taught about them in medical school and they're not found in hospital dispensaries. All of them — and many more "health supplements" — originated and have been made available in spite of FDA attempts to control or outright prohibit them.

Clive Amor — a violinist I wrote about in Chapter Seven of this book — was in a major car crash that compressed the ulnar nerve on his left arm and paralyzed two fingers on his left hand, without which it's impossible to play the violin. He visited every orthopedic expert modern medicine had to offer, and they could do nothing for him. Then Clive visited a chiropractor in Canada and after a single adjustment the feeling and movement returned to Clive Amor's frozen fingers. This violinist who had studied under Jascha Heifetz was able to play violin again.

Look up Chiropractic in Wikipedia:

> The American Medical Association called chiropractic an "unscientific cult" and boycotted it until losing a 1987 antitrust case.

Look up Accupuncture while you're at it. Here's the official statement from the American Medical Association — the same cartel that financed TV commercials pushing for more government control over your health care — statement on Accupuncture:

> There is little evidence to confirm the safety or efficacy of most alternative therapies. Much of the information currently known about these therapies makes it clear that many have not been shown to be efficacious. Well-designed, stringently controlled research should be done to evaluate the efficacy of alternative therapies.

What chance is there that Chiropractic or Accupuncture will be included in your options when the government gets to decide what therapies are covered and which aren't?

Want to use a nurse-midwife for natural childbirth instead of an obstetrician, and deliver in a birthing center instead of a hospital? Good luck with that getting paid for by your health insurance.

But you'll be fined if you don't buy government-approved private health insurance that doesn't cover any of these alternative therapies, hunted down by IRS agents, and sent to prison if you "evade" the fine.

Then there are the "merchants of death": gun manufacturers and dealers. People who sell guns at "gun-law loophole" gun shows. People who took the clear text of the Second Amendment listed in the Bill of Rights at its word — long before the Supreme Court of the United States got around to it — enshrining "the right of the people to keep and bear arms" as an individual right.

Well, since when have free Americans needed permission from nine robed priests to employ their own natural right of self-defense?

I don't need to get into that much here. Look up two of my other books: *Stopping Power: Why 70 Million Americans Own Guns* and *Self Control Not Gun Control*.

Why is it that someone who helped you cross the border from totalitarian East Germany to "free world" West Germany from 1961 to 1989 was always looked at as a good guy, but a "coyote" who helps someone escape from the violent narcocracy of Mexico to the "free world" in the United States of America is always looked at as a bad guy?

Why is it that a stock broker who takes a bet over the Internet on whether a stock will go up or down is a legitimate businessman, but a bookie who takes a bet over the phone on a horse race is a criminal?

Ever see the movie *Cast A Giant Shadow*? Frank Sinatra is portrayed as a hero for playing a pilot who smuggles in guns to Jews fighting the British for Independence. But would a pilot who smuggled in guns to Mexico so people could defend themselves from drug gangsters be portrayed so heroically today?

Nowhere in the Constitution of the United States is there authority for paper currency issued by a cartel of private banks to carry the signature of the Treasurer of the United States and the Secretary of the Treasury of the United States — a cartel that the Treasurer of the United States, the Secretary of the Treasury, the Congress, the Courts, and even the President are forbidden to audit.

Yet if any private bank were to issue gold and silver coins to be circulated as money in the United States, the bankers would be imprisoned, their bank shut down, their gold and silver stocks confiscated, and their customers left as helpless as Bernard Madoff's victims.

And we're supposed to believe that it's the love of money that's the root of all evil?

Chapter 17: Banned In Boston

The leader shouted, "The motherfucker's got one!" and scurried down the street, followed in close order by his compatriots.

Alongside Night, Crown Publishers, 1979

She smiled, continuing to match his pace. "I said that for five thousand blues, I'll go to the bathroom in my panties. I've been holding it in all day. You can watch me—even feel it if you want to. I wet myself, too. How about it?"

Ibid.

Soon he stood at Times Square, cursing himself methodically. You fuckhead, you prick, you numbskull! ... You were carrying a fucking revolver and still you were afraid....

Ibid.

"Oh. Okay. Why don't we go back to your room and fuck?"

Ibid.

"If this is a revolution, then let's not fuck it all up this time."

Ibid.

She noticed the erection under his pants and was furious. "If the last six thousand men who fucked me didn't make me come, what makes you think you can?"

"I won't fuck you. I'll lick you out."

The Rainbow Cadenza, Simon & Schuster, 1983

The man was also looking hard, his breathing becoming rapid and irregular. He reached down to his leather pants and released his erect penis.

Ibid.

"As I started saying before, it is crucial to

remember that the most responsive parts of the penis are the glans and the underside of the shaft. Begin by withdrawing your teeth behind your lips and take the tip of the penis in your mouth, gently massaging it with your lips."

Joan did as she was ordered, orally massaging the head of his penis until Blaine had reached erection.

Ibid.

A few seconds later, there was a high-pitched scream from across the stadium. Then a second and a third.

Joan stopped. "What was that?" she asked Filcher.

"I believe Lady Moslow has brought out the whips and chains," he said. "Go on with what you were doing."

Joan glared at Filcher and got her first reaction out of him that night—a bulge under his leathers.

Ibid.

I awakened at about 3,500 feet up and about fifteen minutes away from my bedroom window to find myself naked but not cold, flying prone with the city lights of Heaven below me, two gorgeous angels as my honor guard, and my pecker pointing down like landing gear.

Escape from Heaven, Pulpless.Com, 2002

"The entire fucking idea behind creation was to fuck things up as much as possible and make everyone else's life a living hell!"

Ibid.

"Who did you fuck that you rate the A list?" he asked.

Ibid.

"There's no mystery why every man on earth, and half the women, want to fuck her."

Ibid.

My three novels — quoted above — were published for the first time, respectively, in 1979, 1983, and 2002.

But as recently as 1966 William Burroughs' novel *Naked Lunch* had legally been prohibited for sale in Boston, Massachusetts — under pressure from the religiously conservative Watch and Ward Society — but it took the 1966 Supreme Court ruling in Memoirs v. Massachusetts to end the practice of local authorities banning books for their "prurient" content.

Without that ruling, I — and my publisher — could have been dragged into court to stand trial if some local official decided that any of the above quotes made us pornographers, and my novels obscene.

But just because I missed taking a bullet as a novelist doesn't mean I haven't had to self-censor.

When I wrote my first-draft screenplay, *"Profile in Silver,"* for CBS TV's *Twilight Zone* TV series in 1985 — a story in which a future historian time-travels back to the JFK assassination in Dallas — I was required to write a second draft of the script removing a second gunman wearing a Dallas police uniform on the Grassy Knoll. I never saw it — but it was read to me over the phone — a memo CBS executive Tony Barr wrote to the *Twilight Zone* producers that said, "The CBS Television Network is not going to rewrite history."

Nor — as President of SoftServ Publishing in 1990 — was I free from such pressures. Here's an open message I posted on GEnie — the General Electric Network for Information Exchange — which was hosting my company's distribution of eBooks:

Mon Mar 12, 1990 SOFTSERV [NeilSchulman] at 19:21 EST Sub: *Should Books Be Banned ... on GEnie?*

A few weeks back I uploaded a file called SOFTSERV.LST which was a list of titles that SoftServ has under contract, at the various stages of preparation. This was only a list of book titles; there was no description or excerpts from any of the books.

Some of the titles listed were from Loompanics Unlimited, which specializes in what they themselves describe as "unusual books."

Here is an excerpt from the introduction to the Loompanics Catalog, to give you an idea of their bookselling philosophy:

"Herein you will find controversial and unusual books on a wide variety of subjects. Most of these books cannot be found in even the largest libraries. The majority of them will never be seen in bookstores. ... So controversial are the books we offer that most magazines will not allow us to advertise. Bookstores and distributors will not carry our publications. Periodicals refuse to review our books. We know where we belong: we are the lunatic fringe of the libertarian movement. Because we do not believe in limits. We do not believe in laws, rules or regulations. We have contempt for censorship, secrecy, and dogmatism. We don't give a damn about being 'respectable.' We don't give a damn about anything except your right to find out anything you want to know. Nothing is sacred to us, not even skepticism and self-reliance."

A stronger and more unyielding defense of freedom of the press has nowhere else been seen. For their consistency of practicing what they preach, Loompanics Unlimited has been a source of endless trouble to all established institutional authority — and a source of lots of books for the 20,000 people who receive the Loompanics Unlimited Book catalog. If the contents of their books are not respectable, their sales figures are very respectable by the standards of any New York publishing house.

All of the above was why SoftServ, whose founders are likewise committed to the absolute right of people to read and write what they please, decided to become an electronic distributor for the titles Loompanics Unlimited publishes.

It has never been SoftServ's intention to specialize in any area of publication. We are a generalist. It is our intention to build up a title list in the thousands, including classics, textbooks, fiction, nonfiction, reference works, current controversies, politics, history, and so forth, and so on, et cetera, ad nauseum.

But one of GEnie's clients took one look at our list of upcoming books, saw some of the Loompanics titles on our list, and decided that SoftServ is some sort of sleazy, subversive, vanity-press operation, which a Respectable Company like General Electric shouldn't have anything to do with. This person sent a letter of complaint to William Louden, the General Manager of GEnie, and got on his case. The heat was on, and in short order I was being told by GEnie to get this list of titles the hell off their system.

Let me start by saying that I value GEnie's clients. I hope to make them SoftServ Paperless Book Club members.

But I have no bloody use for the sort of people

who think they have the right to tell other people what they can and can't read. That is freedom. If this person had written to me, rather than Mr. Louden, it is quite possible I would have told them to take their letter and put it where the sun don't shine: I have no patience with people who think their small-minded opinions are binding on others.

If I had been temperate, I might have simply quoted Jesus and asked, "What is this to you?"

Regardless of how it started, GEnie has decided that Respectability is in fact their Guiding Light. Within contractual limits, that is their right. Since the agreement by which SoftServ is distributing our titles through GEnie was fairly informal, there arose a difference in interpretation regarding SoftServ's right to market our titles without any blocking by GEnie.

As businesses must do if they are to remain in business, I found it necessary to reach an accommodation with GEnie. This accommodation will result in certain titles which SoftServ has under contract never being distributed on GEnie, and severe limits being placed on SoftServ's ability even to openly mention these titles.

Such titles will be made available on the off-GEnie computer bulletin board which SoftServ will be starting in the next few months. At least until the sheriff comes after us, at which point I may have to ask Gary Hudson to give our computers a lift to Low Earth Orbit, and hook up our modems to the nearest communications satellite.

The point to all this is that, ultimately, the fight

for a free press must be fought by those who wish the right to read banned books. We writers, publishers, and distributors are much too subject to economic, political, and legal pressure to be able to hold out, regardless of our beliefs or intentions. I found myself having to make a decision between not selling some books on GEnie, or not selling any books on GEnie.

And, I am ashamed to say, I found very few people who advised me to stand my ground for the sake of principle. Principles seem to have little social value these days.

Removing the list of Loompanics book titles from GEnie wasn't even enough to mollify G.E. management. Our one-year contract with GEnie was not renewed. It took five years, the advent of the World Wide Web, and a new company before I was able to have another go at eBook publishing again.

Of course all of my experience has been with private companies exercising their contractual rights to restrict what I write or publish. That's not actually censorship, merely editorial control.

But in countries without a First Amendment actual censorship — banning of books and arrest of authors — is quite common.

Writing a book that denies the Holocaust — or even questions historical aspects of it, such as the use of gas chambers for mass executions — can get you arrested in Canada and Europe. In 1983 Robert Faurisson was fined by a French court for his writings questioning details of the Holocaust of European Jewry. I'm Jewish. It's still censorship. Anyone who promotes censorship — Jew or gentile — is an enemy of freedom. And the more the United States becomes subject to international law and trade agreements, the less the First Amendment means.

But we don't have to leave the United States for actual government censorship. In 2004 59-year-old grandmother

Donna Dull was arrested in Pennsylvania after the film lab at WalMart reported her to police for having dropped off film with naked pictures of her three-year-old granddaughter coming out of the bathtub. She was charged with distributing child pornography and it took fifteen months before the charges were eventually dropped. She's now suing.

Under Sharia Law in effect in many Islamic countries — in Europe, and, believe it or not, sections of the United States — representations of Muhammad or Islam considered offensive to Muslims can get you censored ... or even murdered. Novelist Salman Rushdie has had a "fatwa" — in Mafia terms a contract — put out on his life ever since his novel *The Satanic Verses* was published in 1988. Dutch filmmaker "Theo" van Gogh was shot eight times, stabbed in the chest, and nearly decapitated by Dutch-Moroccan Muslim, Mohammed Bouyeri, on November 2, 2004, because van Gogh's film *Submission* criticized the treatment of women in Islam.

But Kevin Smith — according to DVD comments for his movie *Jay and Silent Bob Strike Back* — had to pay a "ten thousand dollar fine" because the Gay & Lesbian Alliance Against Defamation (GLAAD) disliked his comedy's "overwhelmingly homophobic tone."

I guess paying a little extortion is better than getting your head cut off.

I could talk endlessly about banned books — the American Library Association holds a Banned Books Week each year to celebrate books forced to be removed from school and public libraries. Classics regularly on the list include *Huckleberry Finn*, *The Lord of the Rings*, *Nineteen-eighty-four*, and *Gone With the Wind*.

Gone With the Wind also had possible censorship problems when the movie was released, because of Rhett Butler's closing line, "Frankly, my dear, I don't give a damn." The word "damn" was on a list forbidden under the Hays Code. The

Motion Picture Association board passed an amendment to the Production Code on November 1, 1939 specifically so they wouldn't have to levy a fine on the film's powerful producer, David O. Selznick.

But you know what book gets banned more than any other? I could have listed smuggling it in my previous chapter, inasmuch as smugglers of this book have been arrested and even reported executed in countries ranging from North Korea to China to Saudi Arabia. It's not *The Anarchist Cookbook* or James Joyce's *Ulysses* or *The Kama Sutra* ... and it's certainly not anything I ever wrote.

It's the *Bible*.

Chapter 18: Wash Your Mouth Out!

> There was an old hermit named Dave,
> Who kept a dead whore in his cave,
> He said with a grin,
> I know it's a sin,
> But think of the money I'll save!
>
> There was once a gent from Nantucket,
> Whose cock was so long he could suck it,
> He said with a grin,
> As he wiped off his chin,
> If my ass was a cunt I could fuck it!
>
> There was a young lady from Eeling,
> Who had a most sensual feeling,
> As she lay on her back,
> She played with her crack,
> Then came all over her ceiling!

This may well be the most important chapter in this book, because this chapter — more than all the others — is about the very essence of what you and I are, and how it is that I'm even communicating with you.

Yet I start it off by quoting three dirty limericks.

I'll connect it up for you by the chapter's end.

This chapter is a discussion of why — at least for the moment — you and I are not gods, angels, or supermen, but human beings.

Gods, angels, and supermen do not need language to communicate with each other, either spoken or written. They do not need books. Gods, angels, and supermen can communicate with each other directly by sharing the images of their thoughts, directly sharing their emotions, and if they need language at all, it's not words but music and dance. If they need to store memories or history, that's what trees are for.

Ayn Rand, in her book *Introduction to Objectivist Epistemology*, and Alfred Korzybski, in his book *Science and Sanity*, could not disagree more about Aristotle as the starting point for exploring human construction of thought.

Rand's arguments are about a pyramid starting with sensation, building into direct apprehension of things as "percepts," then rising to thoughts no longer dependent on reality called "concepts," which she believes can — possibly except for mathematics — only be expressed by words.

Korzybski starts with what he calls "negative axioms." A photograph of a thing is not the thing itself. A map is not the territory. The symbol is not the referent. A word is never the thing itself.

But even starting in such opposite directions, Rand and Korzybski agree entirely about the nature of human beings as symbolic language-using beings. To Korzybski, it's our ability to remember the past and anticipate the future — what he calls "time-binding" — that's the essence of our nature as human beings ... and it's our symbols that make it possible. To both Rand and Korzybski, to the extent that our thoughts are drawn from and tested against reality, to that extent we are functional. To both Rand and Korskybski, to the extent that our thoughts fail to reflect reality, to that extent we drive ourselves to do crazy and destructive things.

Rand and Korskybski are both enemies of the thought — perhaps "fear" is more accurate — that the use of words touch and control real things. A teenager whose rebellious words to a disciplining parent — "I hate you! I wish you were dead!" might suffer endless guilt if those were the last words spoken before the parent tragically died, hit by a train while stuck on railroad tracks, a few hours later. The grief of the parent's death might go away. The thought that somehow the words were a curse that caused the accident might never go away. Rand, Korzybski, and a psychiatrist would all argue that the teenager's guilt was misplaced because all modern, reasonable people know that angry words can't trap a parent's car in the path of oncoming trains.

The idea that words and other symbols do directly control reality — without a known path of causation, such as voice-recognition software operating a mechanism — is the basis for all sympathetic magic and much superstition, ranging from Voodoo to Kaballah.

If there are worlds touching us that we can't see — and even modern physics contemplates the idea that "perhaps only a millimeter away" there could be a parallel universe whose gravitation affects the 95% of our own universe whose matter and energy is "dark" and unperceived by us — then who's to say that living within dark matter and parallel universes aren't all the creatures of legend — imps, pixies, gremlins, demons, and guardian angels?

That's the idea Ayn Rand was scoffing at when she wrote that the universe isn't a haunted house.

I actually wrote a limerick of my own years ago in tribute to this idea:

> Thank Rand for the World where A is A,
> And not any non-A you wanted,
> For if t'were not so,
> Then as these things go,
> The whole Universe would be haunted!

So when words are forbidden, it's often because of the superstitious belief — the primal fear — that these words have power directly to affect reality.

Jewish mysticism — Kaballah — expresses the belief that the text of the Hebrew Torah is the actual "DNA" code for God's entire creation of the universe. This belief is expressed throughout mainstream Judaism where the name of God is not used but expressed through euphemisms such as "the Eternal" and "the Almighty," where Torah scribes leave out the names of God from their copying until the very last step — for fear of making a mistake and having to extinguish the divine name — and where even the English word "God" is written as "G-D." The 1979 comedy Monty Python's *Life of Brian* makes fun of New-Testament-era Hebrews stoning blasphemers for saying the name "Jehovah" in a hilarious scene where eventually — for accidentally saying it — everyone is stoning everyone else.

Christianity picks up this idea from the Hebrews and the Gospel of John accordingly starts, "In the beginning was the Word, and the Word was with God, and the Word was God."

Both the Jewish and Christian belief is the opposite of Rand and Korzybski's — and the psychiatrist's — argument that words are just symbolic and do not control reality. The Jewish and Christian mystic — no less than the Voodoo priest — believe that the word is the thing, the symbol is the referent, the map is the territory, and that God's Word is the very power of Creation, itself.

No wonder all offspring of the Hebrew religion — Judaism, Christianity, and Islam — condemn a sin called "blasphemy": the sympathetic magic contained in the words you and I speak are regarded as having the power to bless or damn.

Controlling usage is also a means of defining social classes. In the UK "Received English" defines the speech of the upper class, often as much today as when George Bernard Shaw, in his 1913 play *Pygmalion*, (made into the 1956 Broadway musical *My Fair Lady*) portrayed how lower-class speech acted as a ceiling to upward mobility. Similarly, social preferencing against American Southern usages and accent is still common in America today as an indication of lower-class speech, whether "redneck" when used by whites or "ebonic" when used by blacks.

I talked in Chapter 11 about how growing up I was a fan of *Mad Magazine*. I don't have the back issue where I can get it, but to this day I remember a Dave Berg "Lighter Side" cartoon strip from the early 60's about a next-generation where Beatnik parents have teenagers who rebel against them by being respectful, neat, serious, and pious.

Ironically, Berg came frighteningly close to describing the relationship between my daughter, Soleil, and myself. I'm from a generation where four-letter words are not only not forbidden, but often mandatory. In the Dave Berg reversal of parenting I've lived through, my daughter is constantly telling me to clean up my language.

But if I, and others of my generation, say "fuck" a lot, it's because we know those who fought for our right to say it paid dearly.

In the 1993 movie *Matinee* two teenage boys are shown sneaking a record of Lenny Bruce's stand-up monologue, "Tits and ass." It was, perhaps, the mildest of Lenny Bruce's forbidden stand-up routines. On October 4, 1961, Bruce was arrested for obscenity during a performance at San Francisco's Jazz Workshop where he used the word "cocksucker" and did a riff on the sexual innuendo of the verb "to come." Bruce was convicted of obscenity after a performance at Greenwich Village's Cafe Au Go Go, prosecuted by New York District Attorney, Frank Hogan (may this cocksucker roast in Hell!) and died many years before Republican New York Governor George Pataki pardoned him.

Dustin Hoffman performed many of Bruce's routines verbatim in the 1974 movie *Lenny* — and wasn't arrested for it.

Once arrested after a December 1962 Lenny Bruce performance at Chicago's Gate of Horn, where police stopped the show and arrested Bruce for obscenity, audience member George Carlin was locked in the back of a police wagon with Bruce merely for refusing to show ID to police.

Twelve years later George Carlin carved out freedom territory of his own when he was arrested for disturbing the peace when he performed a stand-up routine at Milwaukee,

Wisconsin's Summerfest called "Seven Words You Can Never Say on Television." The seven words were "shit, piss, fuck, cunt, cocksucker, motherfucker, and tits." In 1973 Pacifica Radio's WBAI in New York broadcast another Carlin routine containing the seven words, and a listener driving in a car with his son complained to the FCC, resulting in a 1978 Supreme-Court legal decision in FCC v. Pacifica Foundation that upheld the FCC's right to censor broadcast language.

George Carlin later expanded his list to over 200 words. Other stand-up comics, such as Richard Pryor, expanded the liberated vocabulary to the word "nigger" — although that didn't do Michael Richards much good, because unlike Pryor he was white. Freedom of speech in America today divides along racist grounds.

I portray the costs of performing politically-incorrect comedy in my 2009 short story, "The Laughskeller," in which comedian Jerry Rhymus — banned after a successful career in mainstream media after performing an over-the-top routine — now plays two shows nightly to extremist audiences at an underground Nevada club, beginning his routine to the first show, "Who wants to kill that kike-loving commie nigger motherfucker in the White House?" and to his second show, "Who wants to kill that Zionist-loving fascist fake-nigger motherfucker in the White House?"

It wasn't the first time I played with the usage of language in my fiction. In my 1983 novel, *The Rainbow Cadenza*, I portray a future in which the word "fuck" is only used to denote sexual intercourse, and the vernacular uses of the word "fuck" have been replaced with the word "rape."

Currently the FCC stands as a capricious bully, fining broadcasters and performers based entirely on non-objective criteria for what they consider either serious or provocative usages — only the former being allowed. "Shock jock" Howard Stern and his broadcast stations were fined by the FCC so frequently that Stern fled broadcasting entirely in favor of FCC-unregulated satellite radio.

There has been some loosening of standards since the 1939 controversy of Clark Gable telling Vivian Leigh, "Frankly, my dear, I don't give a damn."

The first time the word "bullshit" was heard on American network television without being bleeped was the broadcast of Paddy Chayefsky and Sydney Lumet's Oscar-winning film, *Network*.

The word "ass" wasn't allowed on *The Tonight Show* before Jimmy Carter told reporters during the 1980 presidential campaign that if Senator Ted Kennedy ran against him in the primaries he would "whip his ass."

It took broadcasts of rescue-workers on 9/11/2001 before the FCC allowed the word "fuck" to be broadcast.

Charlton Heston was so offended by the rap lyrics to Ice-T's 1992 recording "Cop Killer" that he performed them at a stockholder's meeting of the record's label, Time Warner.

If there were a Monty Python version of this event, the assembled stockholders of Time Warner would have had to stone Charlton Heston for his blasphemy.

In my imagined version of the scene, when he's hit by the first stone Heston would be miraculously transformed into the costume he wore in his Oscar winning role of *Ben Hur*.

Of course it might be more appropriate simply to recall Charlton Heston's performance with Johnny Carson on the December 12, 1972 broadcast of *The Tonight Show,* in which Charlton Heston performed the following limerick:

> There was a young lady of Norway,
> Who hung by her toes in a doorway,
> She said to her beau,
> "Just look at me, Joe!
> I think I've discovered one more way!"

Chapter 19: Don't Look Now

I was sorely tempted to start this chapter by paraphrasing my opening to Chapter 15, "This is a book about love. What, then, of Art?"

Instead, let me talk about the word "image" again. What an innocent little word that not only opens a can of worms (or a Diet of Worms?) but may be one of the two most underestimated words in the English language.

The other one is "medium," but I'll get back to that word, later.

The engima of "image" starts right near the top of the *Bible*, Genesis 1:27: "So God created man in his own image, in the image of God created he him; male and female created he them."

Everybody reads this passage to mean that men and women somehow look like God. But a reflection in a mirror shows us the original: it also means that when you look into the face of men and women you see God.

What would it do to our understanding if we read the word "image" in this passage the way professional publicists do: that man was made to look the way God wants us to see him?

Or, or, or — and I'm just spinning off ideas here — what if we read that sentence, "So God created man in his own imagination, in the imagination of God created he him; male and female created he them"?

That interpretation gives God a lot more creative freedom in what we end up being. Just so we're clear here. This isn't a chapter about God. I'm using this sentence to spark your imagination.

This is a chapter about imagery — how it moves us, and how those who would move us as puppets have an imperative to control what you may and may not see.

The cliché is that one picture is worth a thousand words.

In this book, a thousand words might be a chapter. But just the way, in the previous chapter, I discussed how what makes human beings human is our use of language, don't forget that I said direct mind-to-mind sharing of images is the primary way gods, angels, and supermen communicate.

I'm both a wordsmith and a presenter of images. I sold photography to newspapers — and spent hours in a darkroom experimenting with ways to generate artistic images — years before I got paid my first dime for writing. And, I assure you, sitting front-and-center in "video village" while directing a movie — and even more so staring at a monitor sometimes frame-by-frame when editing a movie through fourteen drafts — even the wordsmith who wrote the screenplay learns that the power of image sometimes leaves words — if not on the cutting room floor — on the backup hard drive.

Words are most powerful when they invoke feelings and images. That's how great literature works its sympathetic magic. But remember that it wasn't reading novels about Superman that ignited my infant imagination. It was moving pictures on a black-and-white television set, and primary-colored panel drawings in a comic book.

How much of the memory we have of movies is based not on taglines like "Here's looking at you, kid!" or "I'll be back!" but of the first time we saw the underbelly of an imperial destroyer in the first-released episode of *Star Wars* or Sharon Stone uncrossing then crossing her legs in *Basic Instinct*?

When image is combined with story and music — even without a single word — the synergy can be breathtaking.

Movies and television have replaced other media — books, stage plays, and radio — as the dominant popular culture, because they open up unlimited vistas — that precisely means visual imagery — beyond reach of the literary or dramatized word.

When often we hear the phrase "the book was better than

the movie" — and this is why my daughter has convinced me to read J.K. Rowling's original Harry Potter books which she considers incomparably better than the movies of which I'm already quite fond — it's that in translating literature or stage drama to the screen the strengths of visual presentation are exchanged for the history, depth of detail, and scope of canvas available to the writer or dramatist who can appeal directly to the audience's own imagination.

But when it's in its own realm — telling stories visually, and augmenting visual imagery not with words but with music or other sound — film can equal and sometimes even surpass literary and performed-word drama in its power.

One six-minute-long sequence of animation — the Valse Triste from the 1977 animated feature *Allegro Non Troppo* — combines wordless story, image, and music in a way that has stuck in my memory for over three decades, and I have never been able to watch it without tearing up. With no words it explicitly conveys the horror of war as seen through the eyes of an alley cat who has survived the destruction of the building — and the people — it used to live with.

The recent Pixar-Disney animated feature *Up* also has segments just as powerful, evoking the pity for a man — even though we know while we are watching that this is just a drawing — who has lost the love of his life.

In my own feature film, *Lady Magdalene's*, the sequence which I worked hardest on as a director — and of which I'm most proud in the finished film — is a fight and murder choreographed to Rimsky-Korsakov's *Scheherazade*. Not a word is spoken for 4,512 frames.

We see. We hear. But it is not words that tell the story.

The medium is this case is almost godlike in its directness.

All gods are invisible to men; but what distinguished the Hebrews were their insistence that the one God remain invisible, by forbidding any attempt to paint or sculpt him. Compared to the Jewish and Islamic preservations of this Hebrew tradition, Christianity is entirely pagan in its iconography.

Don't get me wrong. To this Jew, that's one of the most appealing things about Christianity. How poor the world would be without Michelangelo's painting on the Sistine Chapel of God's finger passing the spark of life to Adam, or his Statue of David. Where would Dan Brown or Ron Howard have been in their mystery lesson without Leonardo da Vinci's enigmatic mural, The Last Supper? And if Chanukah is supposed to be a festival of lights, Christmas is an orgy of them.

If George Carlin had been more visually and less verbally oriented, he might have given us the "Seven Images You Can Never See on Television." You can keep Carlin's two entries from the female anatomy — cunt and tits – but on broadcast TV you'd get in just as big trouble if you showed a fully erect penis, urination, defecation, ejaculation, or Muhammad decked out as a drag queen.

What is the flag of the United States except a visual icon, if not worshiped then saluted? In *Lady Magdalene's* I play the role of an American al Qaeda recruit introduced at a secret training camp in Death Valley, seen throwing the American flag onto the dirt and replacing it with a green banner adorned with a crescent. That scene was shot at Front Sight — a top private training facility for military, police, and civilians — and I was told later by several of the Front Sight instructors attached to our production that if they hadn't already known me as a staunch defender of the Second Amendment, I might not have walked off that set without a black eye.

Visual imagery is tightly controlled by those in power. Images lead to thoughts. Small children have been suspended from school for stick drawings considered inappropriate — you know, like drawing a gun. Publication of a cartoon in Denmark showing Muhammad in a bad light ignites fires at the Danish embassies in Lebanon, Iran, and Syria. The Taliban destroy statues of Buddha going back a thousand years. And I'll never forget — because I saw it at the 1964 New York World's Fair – that Michelangelo's sculpture, The Pieta, was attacked with a geologist's hammer by a mad scientist in 1972.

Whether it's "bourgeois" art work that doesn't serve the State, or tatoos that no decent person would ever desecrate himself with, or even wearing the wrong color shirt in a gang neighborhood, visual imagery — therefore visual imagination — provokes passion, and therefore a demand for tight controls.

Getting back, as I promised, to the word, "medium." That's like Allison DuBois on the TV series of that name, whose dreams connect her with the afterlife. The real-life Allison DuBois says she works more awake than dreaming, but my personal experiences — like the TV Allison — launch more when I'm asleep.

But I'm not a medium.

I'm an extra-large.

Dreams present images. I have dreams that show me things drawn from nothing I've seen in my own waking life. To state with government authority that there's no validity to the notion that dreams might be a medium of communication with those just-a-silly-millimeter-away universes, is more of the self-congratulatory yay-for-our-team Omniscience — rather than Science — that I wrote about in Chapter 13.

Before you join the National Science Foundation in dismissing communication with other realms as pseudoscience, have you ever considered that the plural of "medium" is "media"?

My dreams have taken me to real places and have brought me into additional realities not reachable through the five senses. The sixth sense which takes us everywhere else is the native-to-our-species ability to dream and imagine, and not everything dreamed or imagined is fantasy.

But when the National Science Foundation — an agency of the United States federal government — issues a fatwa that mediumship is pseudoscience, you must make no mistake. This is just as much an attempt at religious censorship — just as much part of a campaign to block you from having access to understanding the media which are your own dreams and imagination — as if they burned books, smashed statuary, or beheaded a filmmaker.

Whether or not you have learned how to manage these powers, you are a Medium.

Chapter 20: Fun and Games

This is a book about the pursuit of happiness. Children are happiest when they're playing. Happy adults have never outgrown their childhood love of playing. They just add better games.

1 Corinthians 13:11 reads, "When I was a child, I spake as a child, I understood as a child, I thought as a child: but when I became a man, I put away childish things."

Shekels to Drachmas, whoever wrote this passage — the Apostle Paul, Sosthenes, or Crispus — was pissed off because he didn't get his donkey saddle of rich Corinthian leather.

Or maybe he just forgot Isaiah 11:6:

> The wolf also shall dwell with the lamb, and the
> leopard shall lie down with the kid; and the calf
> and the young lion and the fatling together; and
> a little child shall lead them, singing E-I-E-I-O.!

There are all kinds of adults-only fun I've already spent time talking about in previous chapters — sex, cursing, getting high, and outrunning the Feds, to name a few.

Maybe it doesn't work this way anymore, what with all the "We Are the World" stuff kids these days get from the cradle onwards.

But when I was growing up the problems with having fun started the first time a kid brought home a friend his parents didn't want him to have. Maybe it was just that his mother didn't know this new kid's mother. Or maybe he was too old. Or wore funny clothes. Spoke the wrong way or had trouble speaking. Or had skin of the wrong shade.

Then, when kids got to the school yard, it was no wonder all the kids already knew which kids were the ones you weren't supposed to play with, and the ones you wouldn't get into too much trouble for making fun of or beating up.

That kid — the one who got made fun or or beat up — was

often enough me. I was the only Jewish kid in Massachusetts public schools filled with old New England Protestants and Irish Catholics.

I don't remember the school playground — or walking home from school — being much fun ... unless you happen to consider making your way through enemy lines your idea of a day's fun. But then again, that's a pretty good description of football, basketball, hockey, rugby, and soccer, isn't it?

I should probably get a Heisman trophy just for all the days I made it from my school to home without getting the crap kicked out of me.

Sports is one of those areas where the truth is the more violence and mayhem there is the more fun men have historically considered it to be — and nowadays a bunch of old women have set up rules to take all the fun out of it.

It's not childish things we've put away — it's games suitable for grown ups. Sports with real risk of someone getting themselves wounded or even killed. That was how it was done for all of human history — up until a few years ago.

Come on — gladiator sword-and-shield bouts? Chariot races with horses being run into each other — sometimes fatally — for a momentary advantage? Christians versus lions?

Jousting with real lances? Fights with chains and maces?

That was the "Wild World of Sports."

A century ago you still had bare-fisted boxing, and sometimes one of the boxers got clouted in the head hard enough to die. Nowadays — with the pillows prizefighters have wrapped around their fists — retired fighters just slowly deteriorate from Parkinson's Disease. But then again, ballet dancers need foot surgery and football players need pins put in their joints.

Here in modern-day Estrogenia they sent Michael Vick to the slammer because he had his dogs try to bite each other while gamblers bet on the outcome. As if people don't have dogs on their dinner plate every day in China and Vietnam. As if dog racing isn't on ESPN.

Why shouldn't Kentucky Fried Chicken be sponsoring Cock fights — with the loser ending up in the fryer? Just to see PETA becoming apoplectic would be reason enough to do it.

Let loose the hounds — it's time for the fox hunt!

Not anymore. Not even if you're the King of England.

Okay, assisted suicide is legal in Oregon and Washington State. Any reason it can't be done with a game of Russian Roulette? Vegas casinos would probably make your last days lavish if that's how you chose to end it all.

Remember the racing for pink slips in *Rebel Without A Cause*? The last driver to jump out of the clunker he's driving before it goes over a cliff wins. Sort of leaves NASCAR in its dust, doesn't it?

During the presidency of Thomas Jefferson dueling with pistols was still legal — and it's a good thing, too. Aaron Burr putting a bullet into him was the only way this country was ever going to get rid of that imperial-lusting bastard, Alexander Hamilton.

When Joe Wilson called President Obama a "liar" from the floor of Congress? Come on, be honest. Don't tell me the Obama-Wilson duel isn't one you'd have spent big pay-per-view bucks for.

It just might bring down the number of ad hominem attacks in public policy debate if shooting off your mouth could get you shot.

I'm perfectly aware that there's no good moral argument to be made for bringing violence and assorted cruelty back to sports, contests, and games. But there may be a robust argument for the proposition that when the sportsmanship of committing acts of violence left the human vista, the indiscriminate mass murders of millions of unwilling spectators took its place. When violence was limited to fields of contest and battle by civilized custom, sacking, murder of women and children, and rape of both men and women was the mark of the barbarian.

Moving along to less violent games.

We wonder why this country has become obese and out of shape. It begins with city playgrounds. Public playgrounds used to have things made out of metal and wood — Jungle Jims, tree houses and tunnels for kids to climb up, through, and around, slides with ladders that went up a dozen or two dozen steps.

I saw this change — while I was still taking my daughter to the playground — into plastic and foam things suitable for nobody over the age of two. Playgrounds for children were replaced with places parents and nannies could push around their infants in something other than a stroller. Lawyers worried about lawsuits did away with the public playground for children.

Then there's the play-acting children used to do, before playing was replaced with playing electronic games designed and programmed to control the limits of experience children can have while playing.

When children play act, they play act adult roles — and I'll use examples that show my age: G.I. Joe, Barbie, Cops and Robbers, Cowboys and Indians. When kids play act — or play with dolls and models — they don't play at being children. They're trying out being grown-ups.

In technical terms, this is called running a simulation.

Airline pilots learn to fly in flight simulators.

Buzz Aldrin and Neil Armstrong practiced landing on the moon in a simulator of the Lunar Module, Eagle.

Childhood play-acting is a kid running a simulation of — practicing — being an adult.

This is discouraged because who knows what kids might want to be when they grow up? A mercenary? A bounty hunter? Aphrodite forbid — a housewife?

So it works backwards. People who want to call 911 and hide while they're waiting for the person who broke into their house at three in the morning to rape, rob, and even kill them will give their kids toy phones, not toy guns.

But maybe killing off play-acting isn't as easy at it looks. Reese Witherspoon told Conan O'Brien on *The Tonight Show*, that when she didn't give a toy gun to her son he found something else to pretend is a gun.

There's always sticking up your thumb, pointing your index finger, curling back the other three, and saying, "Bang!" What's next to keep kids from simulating violent confrontations they see happening on Fox News — peace mittens and gags?

Don't want your kids to know anything about smoking except that there's a chance it might kill them half a century later? There go candy cigarettes. Oh, wait. Sugar is also not good for you. My bad.

There are still lots of pious homes that don't allow card games because playing cards can be used to conjure spirits and try to read the future — the same with Ouiji boards and Magic 8 Balls.

Of course any toy or game with small parts or sharp edges can't be given to your eight-year-old because a three-month-old baby might get hurt by it.

And what about shooting real guns? Yeah. that's right. Schools used to have shooting ranges — and not just for ROTC. Marksmanship competitions used to be a common American sport.

Then of course there's a ladder of games the object of which is to get to know the other sex a whole lot better. It starts with "Spin the Bottle." It starts getting interesting with "Strip Poker." And it gets downright frisky with "car keys in the potato-chip bowl."

If you eliminate sex and violence, what's the fun of growing up, anyway?

Chapter 21: The Hand Is Quicker Than The Eye

This isn't a chapter about stage magic, where the title of this chapter originated, even though — as with the escape artists of Chapter 12 — the talents I'm discussing have often enough been used "for entertainment purposes only."

The final three chapters I'm writing in this manifesto for unchaining the human heart all have in common that they're mostly about what you may or may not do with your brain. The thing is, you can't drive very far with your heart if you've left your brain behind in the garage.

The hand is quicker than the eye?

In this chapter I'm asking you to focus your gaze on my right hand, where I'm fanning a deck of cards, each of which has a different skill.

Each skill painted on one of these cards is so dangerous that if you master it the government often enough makes you an offer you can't refuse — "Work for us and follow our orders or we have a nice dungeon for you where you'll never be heard from again."

You'll find out what I'm holding in my left hand by the end of this book.

On one card you see a man in a Tuxedo swinging a shiny stopwatch on a chain, and telling you in a soothing voice that your eyelids are getting heavy.

On another card there's a man dressed in white cotton with a black belt whose hands are so fast that they might make master illusionist Chris Angel's hands seem slow by comparison.

I start dealing the cards so you can see the jacks of a trade who can make undetectable forgeries of twenty-dollar bills, driver's licenses, passports, or even centuries-old oil paintings by Rembrandt.

This next card is interesting because it shows a man sitting at a casino Blackjack table with a big stack of playing chips in front of him. Behind him in this picture it isn't a police officer or a CIA agent threatening him, but there is a scary-looking goon tapping him on the shoulder. What's that in the word balloon about "counting cards"?

Then there's a run of black-suited cards showing men opening safes with combination locks, picking locks needing keys, bumping into men in suits and palming their wallets.

There are red cards showing men with knowledge of manufacturing and deploying any sort of explosive device or weapon's system.

Finally, there's an entire suit just for scientists, mathematicians, and engineers who know everything from how to hide a complex message in your iPhone's photo of a kitten to how to refine ore into shapes of Uranium-235 that when forced together suddenly inside a suitcase-sized device can turn a shopping district into a smoldering, radioactive Hazmat-suit zone.

The cliché is that a little knowledge is a dangerous thing, but a lot of the time it's when you know a lot about something — and have really, really practiced it so that you can practically do it in your sleep — that you can use it to devastating effect.

Ever wonder what the elusive definition of "cool" really is? It comes down to a deep well of having mastered useful skills, and being so comfortable about it that you don't feel you need to show them off. So when one of them does come to light it always comes across as a surprise.

Bill Bixby played in a TV series called *The Magician* that ran only two seasons, 1973 and 1974. We're talking about a short-lived TV series that I haven't seen in a quarter of a century. I don't remember the show being all that memorable, except for one scene, where Bixby — playing a stage magician who uses his skills off the stage to help out people in trouble — is having a conversation while casually tossing one playing card after another into a hat a couple of yards away, never missing. At the end of the conversation he's asked, "How long it take you to learn to do that?" He answers something like, "About a year and a half." He pauses. "Every day. For an hour."

The reason that scene stuck with me is that I lived in the same house with that truth. My father was one of the best violinists who ever lived, and he got that way by going into a room by himself, every day, and practicing for hours. Now there have to be natural talents for all that practicing to take. Robert A. Heinlein, writing in *Time Enough for Love*, put it this way: "Never try to teach a pig to sing; it wastes your time and it annoys the pig."

Not everyone has the talent to make himself into a world-class violinist. And the talent isn't always passed down to the next generation: my father's only son didn't have it. But what I did get from growing up with such a person as my role model — my hero — was the certainty that if I found something in myself that came to me more easily than it did others, by practicing it relentlessly I could make myself excellent at it.

I have spent my life sussing out my capacities and incapacities, and if I appear slothful in some areas it's because I've made myself focus on developing to the greatest extent I can those capacities where nature has given me a head start.

I am not a man of very much natural faith, but if I do have one it's this: in each of us there is something we have a natural capacity to do which — if we're relentless about finding and developing it in ourselves, and we're not so unlucky as to have no chance at all ever to find it — this can be a gift we can offer to the world.

Each of what appears to be a dark talent in the list above — everything from hands that can kill with a blow to committing thefts, even to the ability to murder millions — has a flip side, a way this talent can be developed for beautiful and great purposes.

That's why it's so important not only that we find what it is in our selves that make us cool, but that once having found it we also make certain that we never become the slave or puppet to someone who will use us as their weapons system.

Fighting, trickery, and stealth are not necessarily wrong; but when those skills are mastered they do need to be used righteously.

I think that may be why the Harry Potter books are so immensely popular, because that's the lesson our age has desperately needed J.K. Rowling to teach us. There are always wannabe Lord Voldemorts among us — with names like Hitler, Stalin, Mao — and each of us has a Harry Potter somewhere inside waiting to be whisked away for wizard classes.

The truth is, you're going to have to find your inner Harry Potter on your own, because there's no Platform 9-3/4 to board the Hogwarts Express, and if you think about it, there's really no such thing as a Muggle.

Chapter 22: No Secrets Allowed (Except Ours)

If you live in a country where you are forbidden to keep secrets from government officials but government officials are allowed to keep secrets from you, then you are living in a tyranny.

If you live in a country where your privacy is sacrosanct but what government officials do is required to be transparent, you are not necessarily living in a free society, but at least you can watch the enemies of your freedom like a hawk.

Imagine if when the IRS asked for your income tax return you could answer, "I'm sorry, but all information about my earnings is classified. If you file a Freedom of Information Act request, I'll take it under advisement, but you should be aware that because of my backlog it will probably be a minimum of two years before I can even consider your request."

Or, if a health-department inspector came to your buffet restaurant, and you said, "I'm more than happy to sell you all the meals you want, as long as you eat them on the premises. We don't allow take out."

Here's the reality of who has privacy in this country.

A clue — it's not you.

On Sunday January 3, 2010 I drove from my home in Nevada to Los Angeles.

On the I-15, just north of Yermo, the State of California has what they call an "Agricultural Inspection Station." This is a roadblock that takes all southbound traffic on a major cross-country highway down from 70 miles-per-hour to a dead halt, causing a traffic jam.

This station was originally put up to prevent out-of-state grown fruit carrying the Middle Earth — excuse me, Mediterranean — Fruit Fly from entering into California in 1981, where it was threatening California's agriculture. This is 2010 — 29 years later — and the Medfly isn't anywhere near the problem for California agriculture that denying farmers water for their crops is. The occasional fruit fly that shows up in California is quickly eradicated by the release of sterile fruit flies.

Oh, yeah, did I mention that the State of California is having a budget crisis? The sales tax is now ten percent. What is termed "essential services" are being cut back and state employees no longer work a full work-week.

The We-Have-No-Gold State still has money to pay at least four uniformed officers, on a Sunday when presumably they receive extra pay, to stop cars for inspection of an insect that hasn't posed a threat to crops in decades, disrupts interstate traffic, and burns untold extra gallons of gasoline and diesel. Which may be the point to this slowdown since California heavily taxes every gallon of it.

Why should any traveler put up with this invasion of privacy and inconvenience to travel? Is the Medfly now working with al Qaeda?

Oh, yeah. Flying commercial.

On Christmas Day, 2009, Umar Farouk Abdul Mutallab — with visions of forty virgins dancing in his head — took Northwest Airlines Flight 253 flight to Detroit. Hell, they should have known he was suspicious when he got on a flight to Detroit since Detroit's a ghost town these days. Anyway, Umar Farouk Abdul Mutallab had the crazy idea of blowing up the plane using explosives hidden in his panties. But this incompetent mook just managed to set himself on fire, and the other passengers quickly rushed him, put out the fire, and restrained him.

You did get what I said, didn't you? It wasn't a Federal Air Marshal, or a CIA agent, or a General, or a Transportation Security Administration inspector, or Homeland Security Secretary Janet Napolitano, or even an airline stewardess who stopped this jackass. It was the passengers — the same passengers who are being made to surrender all weapons, take off their shoes, and now get radiation exposure from full-body scans (is this part of ObamaCare?) because most of a decade after 9/11 the government is still totally incapable of stopping terrorists from getting on airliners.

We sacrifice our privacy, security, and dignity for nothing. Nothing.

Archie Bunker had the right idea on how to stop this sort of thing. Just hand everyone who gets on a plane a gun. Archie Bunker was a genius compared to anyone working for the Department of Homeland Security, the Transportation Security Administration, or any of the airlines.

As I write this news and talk radio are endlessly looping speeches presidential candidate Barack Obama made in 2008 that the House-Senate conference committee writing the final health-care reform bill would be televised on C-Span instead of being held in secret. Speaker of the House Nancy Pelosi just laughed when she heard that. Since when does the President of the United States have authority over how Congress conducts its business? That would be D, Never, Final Answer, Regis.

Don't trust the dollar? Why should you? It's not backed by anything. The Red Chinese Army — which holds markers for close to a trillion dollars of American debt — could wipe out the dollar any day they choose simply by flooding the market. Then they could buy up everything in the United States at fire-sale prices.

The Federal Reserve Banking cartel — private banks exclusively entitled to issue United States currency with the signatures of the Treasurer of the United States and the Secretary of the Treasury — has total privacy. No one may conduct an independent audit of the Fed's books which the IRS may demand of you at any time without warning.

But if you try to carry your own small stash of money outside the United States to keep it safe from these Mega-Madoffs, you will be stopped, searched, and your money confiscated on the grounds that you might be a drug lord.

If a cop pulls you over for failing to make a complete stop before turning right on red, and finds a roll of cash on you — let's say it's your company's cash sales receipts for the day that you're about to deposit in your commercial bank account — the Thin Blue Line can take the cash under asset forfeiture laws — and the money can be used to buy a cappuccino maker for the station house.

You'd have the burden of proof in court to show that it wasn't made illegally.

Want to talk on an encrypted phone line that can't be tapped? Or send encrypted text messages on the Internet? Government officials are allowed to do this to keep what they do secret from you. But you try doing any of that and see how long it takes for some goon to show up at your door with a badge, a gun, and an attitude.

Here's the only tool you have to find out something the government is keeping secret: a Freedom of Information Act request. Which if they don't feel like it, they can say no.

Here's tools the government has to find out something it wants from you: arrest, imprisonment, endless interrogation, sleep deprivation, water deprivation, light deprivation, food deprivation, medical-care deprivation, bathroom deprivation until you wet or soil yourself, clothes deprivation, body cavity searches.

You used to be able to be protected from the police grabbing you by seeking asylum in a church. Not anymore.

There used to be a right to refuse to talk to police by invoking the Fifth Amendment. These days refusing to answer questions posed by any government official with a badge is grounds for them to shut down your business, seize your property under asset forfeiture, and maybe even throw you in jail for contempt of court, obstruction of justice, or hindering an investigation.

These days refusing any government official full transparency could be considered aiding and abetting terrorists, which could send you to prison for life or even get you a lethal injection as part of a terrorist conspiracy.

If you do talk to them — as Martha Stewart found out the hard way — and some ambitious prosecutor decides he can get away with charging you for lying to an official, you can end up in prison just like Martha Stewart when she denied to an investigator doing something that wasn't even a crime.

You think a reporter's sources are protected so we can have a free press?

Think again.

On December 27, 2009 — a couple of days after all officialdom failed to keep the Underwear Bomber off Flight 253 — the TSA sent an unclassified memo to all airlines informing them of new inspection policies. A travel writer for Royal Dutch Airlines, Steven Frischling, posted the memo on his blog, and the next thing he knows — while he's home with his wife and three children — TSA goons — er, Special Agents — are at his home with guns and badges, demanding he reveal his source for publishing the memo. According to Frischling,

> They're saying it's a security document but it was sent to every airport and airline. It was sent to Islamabad, to Riyadh and to Nigeria. So they're looking for information about a security document sent to 10,000-plus people internationally. You can't have a right to expect privacy after that.

The TSA agents threatened Frischling with arrest if he didn't cooperate, said they'd get him fired from his job, and confiscated his laptop computer for inspection.

Oh, try taking photos someplace the government has decided is their turf.

On a Sunday in summer 2006, when the Las Vegas FBI office

was closed, I tried to shoot video of a plaque honoring FBI agents that was posted outside the building, with open access from an empty parking lot facing the street. The parking lot wasn't chained off and there were no signs restricting public access. I was going to use that shot of the plaque honoring FBI agents in *Lady Magdalene's*.

But within seconds after I tried taking that video a security guard ran out and ordered me and my associate producer, J. Kent Hastings, to freeze. The FBI guard confiscated my video camera, kept Kent and me standing in 110 degree summer heat for over two hours, and when he returned my video camera he had confiscated my tape and memory card.

Six months later the memory card was returned by mail — they'd erased it.

Other photographers have been arrested because they were taking pictures of a bridge or a lake that's been classified a reservoir.

Any government official may ask you anything at any time, and if you don't answer you're a criminal.

But if you ask them anything you're a troublemaker and likely a terrorist.

Got that picture?

Every child looks forward to the day when he or she is old enough to be able to do what they like without having mommy or daddy looking over their shoulders. Privacy is one of the most important pleasures of growing up.

The government demands the right to search your room and make you stand in the corner until you'll tell them anything they want to know — and to spank you if you refuse.

Remember how I started this chapter:

> If you live in a country where you are forbidden to keep secrets from government officials but government officials are allowed to keep secrets from you, then you are living in a tyranny.

If you live in a country where your privacy is sacrosanct but what government officials do is required to be transparent, you are not necessarily living in a free society, but at least you can watch the enemies of your freedom like a hawk.

You need to decide how much your privacy is worth to you, how much you need your own secure space to pursue your loves, passions, and happiness — and what you're willing to do to defend it from those creepy perverts who want to be your ruler.

Then you need to decide what you're willing to do to get government officials to reveal what they're keeping secret, because otherwise you'll never know what nefarious plans they have next.

Remember, when they want to know something from you they use arrest, imprisonment, endless interrogation, sleep deprivation, water deprivation, light deprivation, food deprivation, medical-care deprivation, bathroom deprivation until you wet or soil yourself, clothes deprivation, body cavity searches.

This is a book about having fun.

Have fun!

Chapter 23: Don't Even Think About It!

"Don't even think about it!"

How many times have you heard that line in a movie or on TV? Has it been used on you? By a parent? A teacher? A police officer?

Anyone who says that to you considers himself the boss of you.

Anyone who says this to you has in that moment expressed his unmistakable intention to treat you as his property.

Anyone who says that deserves to be told — if you have the wherewithal to say it — "How would you even know? What are you, a fucking mind reader?"

Not even think about it?

Thinking is what makes us human.

Thinking is what makes us conscious.

Thinking is what makes us — in an existence so big that even trying to think about it makes me dizzy — that we're worth the trouble to raise us up.

Telling you not to even think is the worst thing one person can say to another person. It's worse than all two hundred words you can't say television put together. It's worse than "I hate you."

Yet parents do it. Older brothers and sisters do it. Priests and preachers do it. Teachers do it. Coaches do it. Cops do it. Marine Drill Instructors do it. Gangsters do it. Prison Guards do it. Judges do it. And TV game-show hosts pretending to be Judges do it.

"Don't even think about it" are the definitive words used to bully. There is always an "Or else" attached to that sentence, even if it's not said aloud.

"Don't even think about it, or else there will be no TV for a month!" "Don't even think about it, or I'll tell!" "Don't even think about it, or you'll go to Hell!" "Don't even think about it, or I'll see you in Detention!" "Don't even think about it, or you'll spend the next game on the bench!" "Don't even think about it, or I'll drop you!" "Don't even think about it, or you can clean the latrine with a toothbrush!" "Don't even think about it, or I'll whack you!" "Don't even think about it, or it's solitary for you!" "Don't even think about it, or I'll find you in contempt!" And "Don't even think about it, or I'll go to commercial!"

George Orwell — in his novel *Nineteen-eighty-four* — expressed "Don't Even Think About It!" as "thought crime." He may have made up the phrase "thought crime" but he didn't make up the idea behind it, because "Don't Even Think About It!" is the signature of every dictator and every cult leader.

If there's a standard interpretation of any Biblical passage that I despise more than any other, it's interpreting Matthew 5:7:28 — "But I say unto you, That whosoever looketh on a woman to lust after her hath committed adultery with her already in his heart" — as saying if you think something you're already guilty of it.

That interpretation is a monstrous engine for unearned guilt. That interpretation is the genesis of thought crime. I reject the notion that anyone as savvy as Jesus ever meant anything close to that. Here's one clear reason why if I don't consider the *Bible* itself full of errors, certainly many common interpretations are.

I'll go a hard step in the other direction. If a man has never looked on a woman with lust in his heart, he's either gay or a eunuch, and there's no virtue whatsoever in his not trying to fuck her. You give me a man who looks on a woman and vividly imagines her naked and straddling him, in his mind smells her musk, and shudders imagining what her skin would feel like on his — then he resists fucking her because he's made a vow to another, or she has — now you're talking about real character, Matty boy!

So it is with multiplying the guilt for an offense on a theory of amplified mens rea. If a driver chains another man to the back of his car and drags him through the street until he's dead, the driver is a monster. I do not need to add the idea of his bigotry — because the man he dragged had different skin color — to justify whatever will be done to him in return. Put him in a dark hole for life — strap him down and put him down like a dog — adding "hate crime" to the charge of First Degree Murder does nothing to make his crime any worse that the act itself did.

The legal concept of mens rea — the guilty mind — is about proving a person capable of forming a conscious intention to commit a crime, being capable of understanding the evil consequences and doing it anyway. Beyond that test for criminal culpability law must never be about what people think about doing. Law — both criminal and civil — must always be about what people have done.

For where would it end? Even saints have a thousand evil thoughts a day, and I doubt either of us has ever known a saint.

You ever wished someone was dead, maybe even plotted their murder? There's a great 1965 movie written by George Axelrod called *How To Murder Your Wife* where Jack Lemmon plays a confirmed bachelor — a syndicated cartoonist — who wakes up one morning and finds himself married to the spectacularly beautiful Verna Lisi, a wedding performed — and a marriage consummated — while he was drunk. Now, speaking for myself, I'd be patting myself on the back for a catch like Verna Lisi when I'm not even on my best game; but this idiot doesn't want to be married to her and starts plotting her murder with the help of his butler, played by Terry Thomas. And he tries out his plot with a dummy, using the cover that he always tries everything out for his comic strip.

The movie is 45 years old so I'm not worried about the spoiler here: no, he doesn't kill her, and even though she figures out he was thinking about it, she forgives him and they live happily ever after.

That's as close as you can come to committing a thought crime without going through with it — and I still say you get a complete pass.

Pointing a gun at someone is a threat, a crime in and of itself if it's done other than in self defense. But to read someone's mind and charge them with attempted murder if they lower the gun without being forced to would be a classic example of charging someone with a thought crime — a crime that never happened.

Much of conspiracy law today attempts to attribute an intent to commit a crime when ultimately the crime is never committed. A society can destroy respect for law, itself, if it punishes people for the crimes they thought of committing, but repented of before they did it.

And if someone will be punished for committing a crime even if they don't go through with it, where's the incentive to stop?

The phrase "wannabe" refers to the desire — the fantasy — to accomplish something exalted, whether it's to gain popularity and wealth, or accomplish some great task.

Conversely, there are all sorts of things people fantasize about doing which are not benevolent, everything from revenge plots to suicide.

Sexual fantasies — no matter how repellent you may find them — are harmless until and unless overtly acted upon in such a way as to cause harm to another.

A 1961 *Twilight Zone* episode written by George Clayton Johnson — "*A Penny for Your Thoughts*" — tells the story of a bank employee (a pre-*Bewitched* role for Dick York) who develops mind-reading ability, and reads the thoughts of an older bank employee whom he "hears" thinking about embezzling money from the bank. But it turns out that the older gentleman fantasizes his plot all the time, and never has any intention of doing it for real.

Even God is reported to have evil thoughts and to have drawn back from them. Jonah 3:10: "And God saw their works, that they turned from their evil way; and God repented of the evil, that he had said that he would do unto them; and he did it not."

So unless you're going to charge God with thought crime per Matthew 5:7:28, thinking something isn't reason to feel guilty when you ultimately don't do it.

Anyone who has held a loaded gun in his hand with his finger inside the trigger guard knows the difference between pulling the trigger and not pulling the trigger.

In life, the movies we play in our mind until we pull the trigger are thoughts that we may or may never turn into action.

God, himself, does not judge our thoughts unless we have already used them to make a choice to commit an action. God doesn't make the mistake Dick York's character made in a *Twilight Zone* episode.

This is both the power of the free human being and our inescapable curse, for with this freedom comes responsibility for what we do.

This is not to suggest that developing wholesome thinking is unimportant. Bad thoughts — especially when you make a habit of it — can lead to bad actions, even obsessions.

But freedom of thought is what makes us human, and possibly — someday — more than that.

I promised you that by the end of this book I'd tell you what was in my left hand.

It's this.

The left-hand path is the road of self-determination. You choose what you love. You choose what you're passionate about. You choose what will make you happy.

You may choose wrongly and have to choose again.

We call that learning. It's something only a free mind can do. It's why the Biblical image of God changing his mind makes him human, and why existence has meaning.

But the right-hand path is the path of being a puppet, a chump, a slave, a draftee, a machine. Letting someone else think for you and push you around is the path to the destruction of your soul.

Let no one do it — not President, nor Pope, nor Rabbi, nor Pastor, nor Ayatollah, nor Parent, nor Brother, nor Professor, nor Scoutmaster, nor Radio or TV Pundit, nor Drill Instructor, nor Scientist, nor even Writer.

Freedom is necessary for any of your loves or passions to take wing.

Fight for your freedom as hard as you can.

And if you're not ready to fight, you can at least think about it.

–J. Neil Schulman, January 9, 2010

The Laughskeller

A short story by J. Neil Schulman

Jerry always looked at the parking lot before each show. He scanned past license plates from New Jersey, Idaho, Arizona, Wyoming, New York, Florida, California, Vermont, Minnesota, Utah – Nevada, of course – and even some plates from BC and Alberta. There were a lot fewer pick-up trucks than anyone might have expected and a lot more Mercedes, BMW's, and Hummers. A special parking section just for Harley Davidsons. Always stretch limos with the driver smoking, eating gourmet pizza sent out from the bar, and watching satellite TV. The helipad, which tonight had a Robinson R66 and a Bell 206 BIII JetRanger – in addition to the usual Mercy Air 'copter.

Jerry had even — swear-to-God — seen an M1A1 tank parked on occasion.

He paid attention to clues like this. Jerry had to know who his audience was. When Gino first offered Jerry this gig Jerry thought he'd be playing to the Blue Collar Comedy Tour crowd, but he was quickly disabused of that notion. This wasn't your Jeff Foxworthy or Larry the Cable Guy audience. These people were serious as a heart attack. He often wondered why a lot of them even bothered coming to a comedy club much less make it a de rigueur vacation stopover. Some of them looked like their other nights out were spent watching public executions and dog fights, or playing Xtreme Komando – not paintball, but with full-auto AK-47's and body armor.

Crystal, Nevada was a nowhere town previously a tourist destination for only one reason: it had two legal brothels within a two-hour drive from Las Vegas. Heidi Fleiss had once had the idea to open a third brothel in Crystal with male prostitutes and female clients, but that dumb idea had gone nowhere fast. The closest Heidi had come to her dream establishment was a coin-op launderette in nearby Pahrump with the appropriate name Dirty Laundry.

The Laughskeller didn't open its doors until eight PM. There was no point. It was so far off the beaten track few people were going to drive there just to drink and play the slots. But even so, precisely at ten PM, the management cleared out the few locals, the regular dinner patrons from Area 51 recognizable by their no-insignia desert camo, and any stragglers from the nearby brothels.

The team of bouncers and topless girls who took the door for the eleven o'clock first show – and again at one AM for the 2 AM second show — weren't there just to collect the if-you-have-to-ask-you-can't-afford-it cover charge. They operated the magnetometers and X-ray units and checked guests' personal items. The Door Team weren't checking weapons, but cameras, recorders, phones, handhelds, electronics of any kind – even one guy's fake eye with a video camera built into it. But when it came to calling heads or tails on who got in, The Giant who commanded the Door Team was God.

There she was again. That cool blonde in the little black dress and string of pearls who looked as if she should be one of the Fox News babes, or the female lead in an old Hitchcock movie.

On her first night Jerry had tagged her in his mind as Superbabe. He would have been a lot less nervous if Superbabe was with some guy in an Armani suit and a Rolex, bait for some guy in an Armani suit and a Rolex, or even sitting with her arm around another spectacularly gorgeous woman. But this was Superbabe's fifth night here and not only was she once again sitting alone at a back table eating fugu sashimi with chopsticks but she made it clear to anyone who sent over a drink that she wasn't interested. Superbabe had snoop written all over her. But five nights in a row The Giant had taken Superbabe's money – for both shows – and passed her in.

When Gino had first offered the gig he'd asked Jerry if he

wanted to perform behind bulletproof glass. Jerry had declined, despite the previous two stand-ups ending their Laughskeller runs in the ER of Desert View Medical Center – one with a gunshot wound and the other badly lacerated from a thrown broken beer bottle. Jerry felt it was disrespectful to an audience to treat them as criminals – despite the evidence that some of them were armed-to-the-teeth maniacs. Comedians talked all the time about a joke killing the audience, but this was a metaphor. Aside from anything else, Jerry got a buzz from knowing that at any moment if a joke flopped it could really kill him.

Jerry thought of himself as the Evel Knievel of stand-up. The self-flattery was not unjustified. One of the bartenders had stolen a dry-erasable compliance sign from a construction job he worked at and put it up in Jerry's dressing room. It now read, "258 Nights Without A Comedian Being Injured On This Job Site."

Nevertheless, Jerry wore Kevlar, as did the bouncers, bartenders, parking valets, and Gino, himself. The female personnel's skimpy dress didn't allow for such body armor, but Gino being "old-school" Nevada he considered women easily replaceable anyway.

Jerry finished off the one Glengoyne 28-year-old Single Malt Scotch Whisky he allowed himself before each show, and waited just offstage for Gino to make his intro. He took a look at tonight's first-show crowd. It was, as always, a full house. Some of them wore masks.

Lots of men in tuxedos and jackboots with their elegant women wearing designer dresses and jackpradas. The usual number of leather-and-chains-clad bikers. The skinheads – though they had to meet Gino's upscale dress code. The Skull & Bones guys. The leatherboy Nazis with their black skull-and-barbwire-embroidered cowhide vests and swastika armbands. Lots of exotic tattoos and body piercings in the house. And, yes, there were the usual SS wannabes with their black uniforms seated well away from the white-hooded KKK wannabes – those two groups just never got along.

Just before Gino walked onstage, the house lights went down and the wallscreens came on with their montages of Nazi rallies, KKK marches, anti-Semitic cartoons, lynchings.

Then the stage lights came up, the medley of "Horst-Wessel-Lied," and "Nigger Necktie" blended seamlessly into "Tomorrow Belongs To Me" from *Cabaret*, and Gino walked out to welcome the audience and introduce Jerry.

Jerry didn't pay attention to what Gino was saying. He was watching Superbabe, who was lighting a Sobranie cigarette. Just what is her deal? he wondered.

Then Jerry heard Gino's wind-up, "So please put your hands together for America's most fearless comedian, Jerry Rhymus!"

Jerry walked onstage to thunderous applause.

He took the hand-held mike off the stool where Gino had left it, took a swig from a bottle of Smart Water, and waited for the applause and cheers to die down just enough that the audience could hear him.

Then he started his routine the same way he always did at the Laughskeller.

"Who wants to kill that kike-loving commie nigger motherfucker in the White House?"

The crowd went wild again.

#

The crowd from the first show was gone and the second show audience was just arriving. Jerry smoked a Monte Cristo cigar and watched a few of them pull into the parking lot. He always paid attention when a vehicle announced itself as green. A Volvo with the flex-fuel logo. A Tesla Roadster. A half-a-million-bucks CNG motor home.

Jerry went back in. The Laughskeller was cleared between the first and second show except for patrons who had paid in advance for both. Tonight that was only one person. Superbabe.

Superbabe saw Jerry walk in and gave him a shy wave. He strolled over.

"I doubt you'd remember me," she said, leaning back against the leather-padded bench.

"Since Chaminade High School is an all-boys parochial school I know you weren't one of my classmates," Jerry said, stealing a chair from another table, "and I'm pretty sure you're not one of my ex wives."

"May I buy you a drink?" she asked. "I'm told it softens having been excommunicated."

"My parents faked my baptismal certificate to get me out of public school and it's an open bar for me," Jerry said. "What are you having?"

"First of the night," Superbabe said. "Whatever you're drinking."

Jerry made a quick hand gesture to Charlie behind the bar and put up two fingers. "This cigar bother you?"

"Hardly," she said, taking out a Sobrani. Jerry struck a wooden match from the box on the table and lit it for her.

"So where don't I remember you from?"

"I used to work for *The Tonight Show*," she said. "I booked you for Jay Leno. Three times."

"Before I started doing my own stand-up," Jerry said, "I once met Sid Caesar at a huge book fair where both of us had new books out. I was introduced to Sid for about twenty seconds on day one of the convention. On day four of the convention we ran into each other on the floor and he remembered me by name. Sid had to have met hundreds of thousands of people over the course of his lifetime ... and he was able to remember me by name after one brief introduction. I envy that memory for names and faces and realize it's one of the many reasons Sid Caesar became a superstar and I didn't."

"You weren't doing all that badly," Superbabe said. "Three

movies that grossed over a hundred million and co-star on a sitcom that went four seasons. A top-five syndicated radio talk show. Three Grammy Awards for Best Spoken Comedy Album."

"You've done your homework on me," Jerry said. "I might not have remembered us meeting but I did have you pegged."

Charlie sent over a girl with their drinks. Jerry tipped her a twenty.

"You an agent now?" Jerry asked. "Is that what this is about?"

Superbabe shook her head. "And even if I were, you'd be too radioactive for me to handle."

"Yeah." Jerry took a sip of his scotch. "That's not exactly breaking news. The guy with the videophone made sure of that. Then Jesse and Al. Then the 24-hour news cycle and the supermarket tabloids. Did you know Michael Richards, Mel Gibson, Don Imus, and Alec Baldwin all phoned to give me advice?"

"They all made public apologies," Superbabe said. "You didn't. What did you expect the media would do with that?"

"I didn't expect anything from them. But I knew what they should have done. Stand up for the First Amendment. Lenny Bruce, George Carlin, Richard Pryor, and Andy Kaufman died for our sins."

Superbabe asked, "Aren't you worried that one of these nut jobs is going to take you seriously and shoot at the President?"

"The President and I both wear Kevlar," Jerry said. "If he listens to his Secret Service detail and stays out of open-top limos he should be just fine. Did you know I campaigned for him? Obama, I mean. People think I'm older than I am. I wasn't born yet when JFK died."

"A nice New York Jewish liberal and now you do this?"

Jerry grinned for the first time. "So you did know I wasn't Catholic."

"Guilty," Superbabe said.

"So why didn't you send me a note? I would have comped

you in."

"The Bell helicopter sitting outside is mine," Superbabe said. "I married for money. Twice."

"Well maybe I can marry for money next time," Jerry said. "Can you wait for me after the show?"

"I thought you'd never ask," Superbabe said.

#

It was time for the Laughskeller's second show. Jerry saw in the audience several Che Guevara wannabes, some North Korean Army uniforms, every sort of Arab and Muslim apparel, and more than a few anarchists. The video wall screens were showing their montages of anti-war demonstrations, a burning American flag, U.S. bombing runs in Afghanistan, Christians bombing an abortion clinic, homophobes attacking a Gay Pride march, Israeli tanks knocking over Palestinian homes, Hugo Chavez embracing Fidel Castro to cheering crowds waving red flags.

Then the stage lights came up, the medley of "The Internationale" and "Joe Hill" blended seamlessly into "The Star Spangled Banner" sung in a minor key, and Gino walked out to welcome the audience and introduce Jerry.

Jerry didn't pay attention to what Gino was saying. He was again watching Superbabe. He hadn't realized how isolated and lonely he'd become. He made a vow to himself not to screw it up this time and leave his outrage on stage where it belonged.

Then Jerry heard Gino's wind-up, "So please put your hands together for America's most fearless comedian, Jerry Rhymus!"

Jerry walked onstage to thunderous applause.

He took the hand-held mike off the stool where Gino had left it, took a swig from a bottle of Smart Water, and waited for the applause and cheers to die down just enough that the audience could hear him.

Then he started his second-show routine the same way he always did at the Laughskeller.

"Who wants to kill that Zionist-loving fascist fake-nigger motherfucker in the White House?"

April 12, 2009. 9:15 PM
Revised April 16, 2009. 10:47 AM
Copyright © 2009 by
The J. Neil Schulman Living Trust. All rights reserved.

Part II

I Met God

— God Without Religion, Scripture, or Faith

To Charles Darwin, Madalyn Murray O'Hair,
and Ayn Rand

*If They Still Know Anything,
They Know Whether I'm Right*

Preface by
Brad Linaweaver

Over the years many fans of J. Neil Schulman have said they want another book by him. Sometimes you get what you ask for ... but it's not always what you think you want.

Neil Schulman is one of those writers who doesn't just write the same book over and over and over. He writes a book when he has something to say.

He has been a significant force in libertarian science fiction. But he's also been an artist who has been recognized by mainstream critics for doing works of mainstream value.

The experiences that led to the book you are about to experience — whether it is the audio version or the print version — were life-changing experiences for J. Neil Schulman that resulted in two books: the novel, *Escape from Heaven* and the more personal, autobiographical, *I Met God*.

For Neil Schulman, who can pretty much express everything he has to say about an experience or a philosophy in one book, you can bet your bottom dollar Neil went through a lot when he produces two books — two works — out of a fundamental experience ... and in this case a major motion picture may also be one of the fruits from this particular tree.

J. Neil Schulman says: *"I met God."*

In addition to being the title of this book, it is also on the license plate of the vehicle he drives frequently back and forth between Nevada — which is God's country — and California — which some people believe is territory under other control.

I would say the following regarding people who hesitate to read, or listen to, an exegesis by somebody who believes he had a personal experience with God:

I am an agnostic. I have been an agnostic for many years. I used to be a Christian. I lost my faith but I have never been an atheist. I like to say that I have too much imagination to be an atheist. So I've been a believer and I am an agnostic.

Neil has been an atheist, Neil has been an agnostic, and now Neil believes in God, because he has had what he claims to be first-hand experience of God.

So, this is the challenge I put forward to Neil's fans of the past and potential new readers of Neil's works in the future.

Take what Neil has to say in this work and compare it to what you get from adherents of orthodox, traditional religions. Take what Neil has to say and compare it to what you'll find in the New Age section of your local bookstore.

What fascinates me about so many people who claim to be religious, or so many people who claim to have had mystical experiences, is how few ideas they get from that experience. One would think — if you have an experience of the Ultimate — a few ideas might stick to you. But you'd never know it from traditional religious people; you'd never know it from the traditional — if I may say so — mystic types, and the modern manifestation of the New Age types.

Neil is overflowing with ideas, and insights, that I find of great value, and I am an agnostic.

If you believe in God, it seems to me what Neil has to say may be of even greater value to you than it is to yours truly, doing this introduction.

I'm telling you, I'll be thinking for a long, long time about what J. Neil Schulman said in this interview I did with him for *I Met God*.

Foreword
By J. Neil Schulman

I was an atheist for almost half my life.

When I was an atheist the concept that God could exist was impossible to me, because the cosmology I accepted as evidently true precluded the existence of such a being.

One of the authors who most influenced me in this view was George H. Smith, author of *Atheism: The Case Against God.* Judging by 258 reviews of this book on Amazon.com, this is a popular book on the subject, and judging that seven out of ten Amazon.com readers' reviews are four or five stars, I'm not the only person who has regarded this as an important and compelling book on the subject. I knew George personally when we both lived in Southern California in the 1970's and 1980's, and I considered George a friend.

It's easy to be friends with someone you agree with. Disagreements are the test of whether a friendship is real. It's possible to be friends with someone who has profoundly different ideas if that person is generally congenial and if one has respect for their mind and character. It becomes impossible when congeniality is replaced with rudeness and one has contempt for the other. This isn't just true for friendships. How many marriages have broken up because one spouse's good regard for the other has turned to contempt?

I maintain Google alerts to send me email whenever there's online discussion of my works, my projects, or my web presence. On December 11th Google sent me an email that a discussion had been started on the website "Objectivist Living" with the title, "Is J. Neil Schulman justified (logically) in believing in God?"

In the same queue was an even earlier email from David M. Brown, a fellow libertarian novelist and long-time correspondent, suggesting I participate in the discussion.

It was a discussion stemming from a 2006 interview with me upon the release of my audiobook, *I Met God*.

I quickly discovered that George H. Smith was participating in the discussion when the second comment was his. George wrote, "Does God ever have nightmares? Yes, according to Neil's account, and they last for 'the better part of a day.'"

So much for the respect necessary to maintain a friendship. Buh bye, George.

What distinguishes my approach to God from others is that I've never abandoned my view that one should not accept the existence of anything on faith. Nor religious dogma. Nor scripture. Like anything else, I always have viewed existence of God as a fact that needs to be verified or negated. One can negate something by showing how the concept is impossible. But once a proposed existent survives the intellectual challenge that the very idea is impossible, one is still left with the problem of what constitutes sufficient reason to regard it as real.

For someone who is not put off by suspending rational analysis in favor of accepting the truth of a proposition by faith, this is not a problem.

For a rationalist it is.

I was a rationalist when I was an atheist. I'm a rationalist still. What overcame my skepticism were personal experiences that challenged my cosmology, my epistemological premises, my concept of what the nature of God is, and my view of the nature of man and his place in existence, itself.

Yet I did this without abandoning my reliance on any of the axioms or rules of logic that Ayn Rand used to dismiss the concept of God. I thought George H. Smith would have some respect for that.

I was wrong. It just annoyed him all the worse.

I've satisfied myself that I met the gauntlet thrown down at me. Beyond that, some third party not Me and not Them will have to decide whether I'm justified (logically) in believing in God … and whether my challenge to the atheists is deserving of any intellectual respect.

Here are questions that have been debated in this thread, but I think which have not been resolved to anyone's satisfaction. These are the premises upon which the question of my logic must rest.

Are there any axioms of existence or known scientific laws which preclude existence comprising multiple continua, some of which are designed, rather than the whole of existence being a single undesigned universe?

Is there any conclusive proof that human consciousness is solely a product of evolutionary biology, or could human consciousness precede evolutionary biology?

Is the human brain a generator of human consciousness, or merely a modulator of it?

Is human consciousness of an identity and nature that it can escape the termination of a human brain?

Could the "afterlife" be an actual physical destination for a human's conscious identity located in another continuum?

In the event where a phenomenal experience presents itself as paranormal or supernatural, is there anything other than an unproved assumption of impossibility that necessitates interpreting such an experience as unreal?

I repeat that I'm unable to present evidence of the reality of my paranormal experience of a person I've identified as God to anyone else.

Nonetheless, my experience has caused me to examine each of these questions and reach my own answers.

I suggest exploring each of these questions with epistemological and scientific rigor is no less of a requirement for anyone else who wishes to assert flat conclusions about the nature of existence and human consciousness.

Neil

Introduction
By J. Neil Schulman

Although this is my tenth published book, I haven't been on any bestsellers lists, so I'm going to assume this is the first book of mine you've read.

Even though I've been busy writing over the last thirty years; even though I've appeared on radio and TV more than a few times; and even though a Google search will turn up my same several thousand times, I don't qualify as a celebrity.

"So why should I believe this fat, bearded, long-haired slob?" you might be asking yourself right about now. "Why should I take this guy seriously when he tells me that, while he was still an atheist, God started whispering to him, and one February day in 1997, God merged with him for the better part of a day and let him see the world through God's own eyes?"

I'll understand if you decide to put this book back on the bookstore shelf right now. If it hadn't happened to me, I wouldn't believe somebody who said that, either.

So, in the absence of any reasonable expectation that I'm anything other than a fraud or a psychotic, why should you waste time reading any further?

Well ...

For one thing, I know how to tell a good story.

I know how to make it suspenseful and dramatic.

That's my craft, which I've been learning for the last thirty years.

I've received enough celebrity endorsements, good reviews, and checks for writing sales, to convince me that I'm a professional writer. Being a professional writer, I can promise with some confidence that whether you end up believing my story or not, whether or not you're an atheist who has me pegged as a nutcase or a believer who has me pegged as a heretic to your faith, I promise you a story you've never heard before.

Here's the part where I tease you into reading the first chapter.

I'm about to make statements that are, on the face of them, improbable and unbelievable, foreshadowing what you're going to read later in this book.

My obvious intent is to hook you so you'll keep reading.

Let's see if it works.

When I was five years old, in 1958, I decided that God wasn't real.

In 1970, at 17 years old, I had my first experience of the supernatural, when I had precognitive knowledge of my grandfather's impending death. He lived in a different city and had been robustly healthy the last time I'd seen him, about a month before.

At age 21, I was a back-seat passenger in an automobile accident while on a trip with three friends in 1974 when my friend's car spun out on any icy road, totaling it, but without any of us getting hurt. At about the exact time we were calling for a tow truck, my father turned to my mother in bed and told her about the accident in detail, even though neither I nor any of my friends told anyone other than the towing service about the accident until the next morning.

While I was attending a friend's Halloween party in 1982, at age 29, I saw a woman dancing. A voice inside my head said, "If you ask her to dance, you will marry her."

I asked her to dance and I married her in 1985.

On April 15, 1988, the night before my 35th birthday, God put his hand on my heart and said to me, "I can take you now."

Sorry. You'll have to read this book to find out why I lived through the night.

Finally, the last of these teasers.

On February 18, 1997, starting at about noon, God merged

into my mind for the rest of the day. During that experience I left a phone message for my sister that she should call me because I had a revelation that would change the world.

Part of that revelation came out in fictional form, when my third novel, *Escape from Heaven*, was published in 2002.

I'm finally going public with the rest of the revelation – or at least as much of it as I can understand – in this book – the book you're now deciding whether or not to read all the way through.

An important part of the information God gave to me is that each of us has such strong and independent free will that God feels powerless about what we will choose to make of ourselves ... and our world.

So you have the absolute, unencumbered, free will to decide to turn to the next page, or to close this book, now, quit reading it, and ignore everything I think God wants me to tell you.

What's it going to be?

–J. Neil Schulman,
July 21, 2004

Chapter 1: Kid Atheist

BRAD LINAWEAVER: Neil, you've gone through many different philosophical stages in your life, and your career reflects many different areas of thinking and experiences that you have had. What I would like to begin with in this discussion about your experience with God, the first question I want to ask you is: Do you remember your age, when you first decided as a kid that you were an atheist?

J. NEIL SCHULMAN: Yes. I remember it very explicitly. It was a very dramatic moment in my young life.

I was five years old. I was living in Forest Hills, New York — with my parents, obviously — and I was out walking on our street in front of our house with my mother. And for some reason — I don't remember what caused this but I do remember the incident — I looked up into the sky and I saw the sun coming from behind a cloud.

Now let me just stop for just a moment. The sun coming from behind a cloud seems to be some sort of universal image — almost in a Jungian sense — for God. How I, at five years old, identified or associated that image with God, I don't know. Maybe I'd seen it on television; but in any case, at five years old, I had that association in mind.

I saw the sun burst out from behind the cloud and I turned to my mother and I said, "Where is God?" and my mother said something the equivalent of "I don't know" or "Nobody knows." I don't exactly recall her response; except what it came down to was she was not going to give me any sort of definite answer that this was something that people knew. When she said "I don't know," or "Nobody knows," or some such answer, my answer to her was, "Well, then I don't believe that God exists."

That show-me attitude was characteristic of the way I'd view the problem pretty much for the next 20 to 25 years of my life.

BRAD LINAWEAVER: Were you ever taken to temple or given religious instruction when you were growing up?

J. NEIL SCHULMAN: Again yes. I specifically recall my maternal grandfather, Samuel Lindenbaum, taking me to shul with him. I do not recall it being a particularly interesting or warm experience. I mean I enjoyed being with my grandfather; I liked being out with him. Again I was very young, maybe six years old, and my mother's father and mother lived not far from us, also in Forest Hills.

Actually one of my earliest memories of synagogue is a scary one. There was this elevator in the shul and I remember we got on the elevator and the elevator went down to the basement for some reason — maybe it was going the wrong way — the doors opened up and it was a cellar — you know like a storage area — and I was very, very frightened — then the doors closed and we went up again. So I guess we'd just ended up on the wrong floor, but interestingly, one of the first associational memories I have with shul is a negative one, of being scared of the basement.

Now I had no formal education in Judaism when we lived in New York but again, we left it when I was around age seven. We moved to Massachusetts at that point. However, my impression at that age was that the neighborhood where we lived in Forest Hills was almost completely Jewish. I knew of only one Catholic family who lived across the street and I thought that that was the ratio of the world, that everybody was Jewish except there was this one Catholic family. Everyone else was Jewish. I was living entirely in a Jewish world at the beginning of my life. Then at age seven we left this neighborhood in New York City and we moved to Massachusetts where it was exactly the opposite. Suddenly everybody we knew was Christian and we were the only Jewish family.

My formal education in Judaism started with Bar Mitzvah training. That probably started somewhere around age 11 and that happened because my grandparents wanted me to be Bar Mitzvahed and it was explained to me that if I agreed to be Bar

Mitzvahed I would have to have Hebrew lessons and then at age 13 I would be Bar Mitzvahed.

I did it largely because my grandparents — on both sides— wanted me to do it. My maternal grandfather, the one I just talked about, died in 1961 — when I was eight years old — so he wasn't there anymore. But my maternal grandmother wanted me to be Bar Mitzvahed. My paternal grandmother died in 1963, when I was ten years old, so she wasn't part of it. So it was my maternal grandmother and my paternal grandfather who wanted me to be Bar Mitzvahed. Judaism was very important to them.

Around eleven I started Hebrew lessons with Louisa Munzer, who was a survivor of Auschwitz and she told me stories of the concentration camp. I found out how she had been selected for medical experiments, which left her sterile and unable to have children — this was an amazing thing for an adult to be telling a child about, by the way, stories like this.

She taught me Hebrew, a language which I did not warm to. I disliked it. It was not that easy a language to learn, it had a different alphabet — its own character set — and everything was different about it. You wrote from right to left instead of left to right. It was alien to me. I don't know what my language skills were but I did not find it easy and I did not find it pleasant. However, I did have a good accent — I was able to speak it with perfect accent — but my comprehension was very bad, my ability to read for comprehension was very bad. I could just read whatever was on the page without understanding what it was. I could sound out the words and speak it well. But it was rote, it was phonic, it was not reading for the most part with meaning.

So, I did go through a Bar Mitzvah. The last year I went to Hebrew school at the temple where I was Bar Mitzvahed, in Framingham, Massachusetts. But then as soon as I was Bar Mitzvahed, I wanted no further part of it. I had the big party, had the Bar Mitzvah, made my grandparents very, very happy and then that was pretty much it, as far as my religious education. I had almost no interest in religion for a long time after that. I'd had my fill of it.

BRAD LINAWEAVER: From the age of five to when you were Bar Mitzvahed as a young teenager and you were going through all of this training and education, did you ever express to anybody at the Hebrew school the doubts you had expressed to your mother at five about your not believing in God? Did the subject of your belief in God ever come up in your entire training on your way to the Bar Mitzvah?

J. NEIL SCHULMAN: It never came up. It was totally irrelevant.

BRAD LINAWEAVER: Can you please expand on that?

J. NEIL SCHULMAN: It was a ceremony. I could have been training for an opera in a foreign language. It was something that I was doing to please my grandparents. But what I believed was of no consequence to anybody and the subject never even came up for discussion.

Now interestingly, I do remember the sermon that the Rabbi gave the day of my Bar Mitzvah. It was a point that I found interesting. The Rabbi's sermon, that day, was interesting because he was speaking about an Eye for an Eye and a Tooth for a Tooth and I do remember that he said that the commandment was not a demand for justice or vengeance but a limitation. It was interesting to me because I'd never heard it in that context. The idea that you only get one eye and you only get one tooth. You don't get the entire mouthful of teeth and everybody else's eyes. So there were at least some moral principles there, which I guess I absorbed at some level.

BRAD LINAWEAVER: Would you say the beginning of your libertarian moral positions may have begun on that day?

J. NEIL SCHULMAN: No. First of all I lived in a household where morality was pretty much taken for granted. I was not a child who was ever interested in stealing. I mean you have kids who will steal candy or steal some trinket or something like that. It never crossed my mind. It was never even something I ever even thought of doing. Actually taking something that we didn't pay for? I would have considered it a horrible mistake. It just wasn't part of me.

Even going to school, until I was greeted with hostility and irrationality — unexpected hostility and irrationality — coming from New York, I expected adults to be, for the most part, rational in their treatment of children. That was what I had experienced in this community in New York — in Forest Hills — where I started kindergarten and first grade. When I started school in Massachusetts I started getting reactions from teachers, which seemed to me wildly out of proportion —some that I worked into *The Rainbow Cadenza*.

BRAD LINAWEAVER: How about one example?

J. NEIL SCHULMAN: The clearest example is that on my first day of second grade with my teacher, Miss Lafford — I still remember her — she gave me a piece of paper on which I was to write the numbers one to 100 in boxes all the way up — "1" on the upper-left-hand corner and "100" on the lower-right-hand corner — and I needed to fill in all those numbers. She gave it to me and said, "All right, you need to do this." I said, "Okay that's easy," and she glared at me and said, "Just do it!" Exactly like that. I was shocked. Why was she irrationally angry with me? I found that this sort of behavior was repeated to me in school, but nonetheless my expectation coming into it was rationality and evenhandedness and benevolence.

I never understood adults who treated me this way and it basically took me from really having an innocent expectation that you went to school to learn to what eventually made me very, very hostile to school and eventually to learning itself — something I had to overcome in myself by the time I was 15, 16 years old. I was a kid who loved reading and it got to the point where I couldn't pick up a book anymore.

The point that I was leading into is that morality for me at that age was simply not even a question. In other words, I wanted to please adults. My first impulse was to be good and to please adults. It wasn't until adults refused to be pleased and were hostile, and kept on throwing me all these curves, that any other impulse even arose in me. My natural state was happy and innocent and wanting to please the adults around me.

BRAD LINAWEAVER: You shifted out of that desire to please and became more cautious and suspicious and even finally had to teach yourself to want to learn again. About what age would you have been when you realized the education you were going to have in your future life would primarily be through self-education?

J. NEIL SCHULMAN: Well, it happened naturally. It happened when I discovered libraries. First in Natick, and then for eight weeks during the summer we went up to the Berkshires. My father was a violinist with the Boston Symphony Orchestra. Every summer he played at Tanglewood with the BSO and we rented a summer home near Tanglewood, right outside Lenox, Massachusetts. So the two libraries most influential on me were the Morse Institute library in Natick, the town in Massachusetts where we lived during the school year, from age seven thru around 17, and in the summers the Lenox Library, in Lenox, Massachusetts.

The significance of each of them is that the Morse Institute Library was where I discovered Heinlein, where they had most of the Heinlein juveniles. The Lenox Library was where a librarian named Judith Conklin introduced me to *The Chronicles of Narnia*. I asked her for something to read and she pointed me over to the shelves with *The Chronicles of Narnia*.

Incidentally, simply as an anecdote, this last time I was in Massachusetts I found out she's still working for the Lenox Library and she's married — she's now Judith Conklin-Peters — and I autographed a copy of *Escape from Heaven* and left it for her. I didn't see her there but she did still work there and I autographed a copy of the book and thanked her for introducing me to *The Chronicles of Narnia* in that inscription. So that story has a circle to it.

But again, as I say, it happened very naturally. I was a comic-book reader even back in Forest Hills, New York. I was reading *Superman* comic books. When I say I read *Superman* comics, I read *Superman, Lois Lane, Jimmy Olsen, Justice League, Batman, Flash* and *Green Lantern*, all of them. I read all of them, all of the DCs. But particularly, *Superman* and *Superboy* were my favorites, and when they had Lois Lane and Jimmy Olsen comics I read those. Action comics, Adventure comics, all of them, if it had DC on it I read it. So, a lot of my reading initially was comic books and that lead naturally into science fiction and fantasy.

So by the time I got to these libraries, which had Heinlein and C.S. Lewis, that was just natural to me. My main school experience was that I was a reader and was never really challenged by anything that they threw at me in those areas. Math I wasn't as good at. History I was pretty good at. Music, of course, coming from a musical family, anything they threw at me there was easy. So really the only challenge I had was math and that came to a crisis in eighth grade.

BRAD LINAWEAVER: Now, during all of this period did you find yourself thinking about God at all, and I include when you were reading The *Narnia* Books, did the thought of God ever cross your mind?

J. NEIL SCHULMAN: No, never crossed my mind. I have attended, as an adult, meetings of the C.S. Lewis Society in both New York and Southern California —and as a matter of fact, served on the Council of the Southern California C.S. Lewis Society for several terms at different times.

I have heard it said during those meetings that it is obvious that the *Narnia Chronicles* were Christian parables. Well let me say that for me wasn't obvious. I came from a family that knew almost nothing about Christianity ... and what it did know was wrong. So it never crossed my mind that Aslan was supposed to be Jesus Christ, it never crossed my mind that this had anything to do with Christianity. What's more, if I had known that — if Judith Conklin had told me that these were Christian stories — they never would have gotten into my hand off the bookshelf. Because Christianity was something totally alien to me and not something attractive.

BRAD LINAWEAVER: Did you think that Christianity might be some of the same boring experience you'd had in Hebrew school, only maybe worse?

J. NEIL SCHULMAN: No. It never even rose to that level. It was not even something I considered at that age. It just was not part of my life — even living in Massachusetts, where almost everybody I went to school with wasn't Jewish.

The only real close friend I had — who is still a friend today — was my Jewish friend, Bob Schneider. So even then, that's the friend whose family my parents socialized with. My parents didn't socialize with any of the non-Jewish parents of the school children with whom I went to school in Natick, so there was a divide even there.

BRAD LINAWEAVER: You parents did not go to temple?

J. NEIL SCHULMAN: No. My parents were entirely secular in the way they raised me. My going to Hebrew lessons and then Hebrew school and being Bar Mitzvahhed was simply for that one purpose. They never asked nor expected anything further of me once I was Bar Mitzvahhed.

BRAD LINAWEAVER: Do you remember what age it was when you next thought about God at all, since your decision at age five, when the sun appeared from behind the cloud and you asked your mom "where's God?" Do you remember the next time you thought about God?

J. NEIL SCHULMAN: In between that — and starting to

consider God — I would say that I was into odd phenomena, the supernatural, psychic phenomena — E.S.P. as we called it back then — or telepathy.

My father had told me a number of psychic-related experiences, he'd had, precognitive dreams — we were very telepathic with each other. So in other words, these sorts of things were fairly common in our family, what we would call psychic phenomena or the supernatural.

My father in his younger days had been very interested in these sorts of things, even attending séances. He told the story of going into a house he'd never been to before and standing in the entrance way and telling everybody where everything was, because he'd had a precognitive dream about being there. He told about having a dream which saved his life, where he had this dream in which his car went out of control on a certain highway in New York because the headlights went out and the car crashed, in this dream. Then the next time he was there at night he remembered the dream just before he got to that curve and slowed down, his lights did go out but because he had slowed down he was able to control the car on the exit and didn't die.

My father told a very dramatic story about when he was playing a gig at a hotel in the Catskills. He was with a woman singer — I can't remember her first name but I remember her last name, it was La Brea, like the tar pits. A stage name, I think. She was a medium as well as being a singer and my father was rehearsing with her in the rooms where the help were — the musicians being part of the staff, away from the main house.

Very dramatic things happened there. My father was telling the story: the lights went out where they were and he got scared and tried to leave and the door wouldn't open. And he tried to light matches and they wouldn't light. Then she said "You're making my spirit Indian guide angry!" and then an entire chest of drawers went across the room by itself – was thrown across the room. At that point she said "Sit down!" and my father sat down. Then things calmed down and the lights went on. My father then got out of there as fast as he could and the door opened and he got out.

So stories like that were part of my background, but I never associated any of it with God or religion or anything like that. But the possibility of the supernatural was real to me.

BRAD LINAWEAVER: Did your father talk to you about these experiences?

J. NEIL SCHULMAN: Yes, they were anecdotes. My father was always a raconteur and this was part of the repertoire of the stories he told, just like he told jokes. But he also was very interested in hypnosis and Houdini and stage magic and all these sorts of things.

My father's personality was that he was a science-fiction fan who read Amazing back when Hugo Gernsback was editing it.

BRAD LINAWEAVER: Right, the original days.

J. NEIL SCHULMAN: So in other words there were science-fiction books around the house — not Heinlein or anything like that — but I remember that *1984* and *Brave New World* were around. There was a book of Native American Nature Myths, which I read and found very interesting, as well as other things like that.

My father was a voracious reader. He loved reading eclectically and so there were a lot of books around our house when I was growing up and I sampled them and probably got a very rich and varied education from these books — far more then I was getting from school.

So to leap forward to where your question gets to: "When did I start thinking about God again?"

It probably wasn't until I got to New York again, in 1970 at around aged 17 and then met up with people in New York who had read Ayn Rand. That's when these questions started up again. This was really the first group of intellectuals I'd ever really met — the crowd in New York of libertarians.

BRAD LINAWEAVER: There was a heavy Ayn Rand/Objectivist element?

J. NEIL SCHULMAN: Right. And that really confirmed me in my atheism because I was given very strong arguments from the Objectivist viewpoint, from the Ayn Rand viewpoint. Which basically confirmed those tendencies in me. However, I was a fan of C.S. Lewis and so I was brought to the C.S. Lewis Society meetings — by Samuel Edward Konkin III, whom I met in New York — and I found out that Lewis wrote books for grownups also, not just the *Narnia Chronicles*. I started sampling those books, I don't know if I read heavily into his nonfiction before I got to California after 1975.

BRAD LINAWEAVER: At this time did you read the Perelandra books?

J. NEIL SCHULMAN: That probably also didn't happen until I got to California, but at least I became aware that there was more than *Narnia*.

BRAD LINAWEAVER: And *TheScrewtape Letters*?

J. NEIL SCHULMAN: It's possible that I read Screwtape in New York. I don't remember exactly in what order I came across them. I do remember that *Mere Christianity*, *Miracles* and *The Problem of Pain* — those books weren't until I got to California after 1975.

So, I would say that I didn't start thinking about God again until, really, I started attending the C. S. Lewis Society meetings in New York then later in California. More in California, because the New York C.S. Lewis Society was much more of a literary group than a Christian group, whereas in California the emphasis was more on the theology. I would say that I didn't start thinking about God again until I got to the Lewis Society meetings in Southern California where most of the attendees were more interested in Lewis as a theologian than as a fiction author.

BRAD LINAWEAVER: Do you remember if during this period you read *The Great Divorce*?

J. NEIL SCHULMAN: Sometime in that period in California I would have read *The Great Divorce*, yes.

BRAD LINAWEAVER: Let me ask this then, regarding Lewis. At some point, then, you realized that the *Narnia* books you had enjoyed so much as a child did have this extra Christian dimension.

J. NEIL SCHULMAN: Yes.

BRAD LINAWEAVER: You must have noticed it at this period?

J. NEIL SCHULMAN: Well, it would have been talked about endlessly at the Lewis Society meetings.

BRAD LINAWEAVER: Did that, in any way, put you off your pleasant childhood memories of the books?

J. NEIL SCHULMAN: No.

BRAD LINAWEAVER: Or did it merely enrich them ... or was it just something interesting to know?

J. NEIL SCHULMAN: It was informative. I didn't resent it at all. I mean, by that time I had pretty much been living in a secular Christian world for most of my childhood and adulthood.

For the ten years in Massachusetts, I wasn't really living in a Jewish community, so there was very minimal contact with that. I mean my relatives were Jewish, Bob Schneider and his family were very, very Jewish, so much so that Bob went off to live in Israel to live in a kibbutz for a while, and came back and told me the shaggy-dog stories they told around the campfire, and about shoveling manure.

I will say that there was a point at which I considered going to Israel myself — at around age 14 or so. But that wasn't because I had any desire to go to Israel, but simply because I hated the school I was in so much I would have considered any alternative. I mean if you had told me that going to school in Nazi Germany was possibility, it would have been somewhere on the list. It might not have been at the top of it, but I really got to the point at which I just hated the school I was at in Massachusetts.

BRAD LINAWEAVER: You were ready to try something else.

J. NEIL SCHULMAN: I was ready to try anything else. So by the time I got to California and the C.S. Lewis Society meetings I'd been living in a Christian, secular society for so long that Christianity was no longer a shock. To tell you the truth, it probably had a little flavor of forbidden fruit to me — a little sexiness because of that.

BRAD LINAWEAVER: What about the Rand arguments that reinforced your original atheism? Because it sounds to me like reaction you had at age five, to your mother, is a reaction that was worthy of Ayn Rand herself. Rand, of course was somebody who had come from a Jewish background but walked away from the Russian background, the Jewish background, the family background. She talked about the accident of birth and tried to create this highly individualist American cult, fundamentally. So she was an odd transmission belt for a Jewish libertarian, because who could be more American than Ayn Rand? Yet, what is America? It's a Christian country, and here was Ayn Rand, the ultimate atheist.

J. NEIL SCHULMAN: Look, let me try to describe myself at that age. If I thought of myself as a follower of anybody, I mean there was a period when I considered myself sort of philosophically Objectivist. But at the point when I talked to Ayn Rand, when I was doing what was supposed to be an interview with her for *The New York Daily News*, which never happened, but nonetheless we talked for hours, at that point in August of 1973 I considered myself philosophically an Objectivist.

But, there was this other strain of philosophy in me, which I considered just as important and that was Robert Heinlein. I considered myself a rationalist. I was interested in science. I was interested in space — all these sorts of pro-high-tech,

Jetson-type worlds. This was what I wanted. The past had no interest for me whatsoever. Tradition was abhorrent to me. Do something just because it was tradition? That's ridiculous — where's the sense in that? None of that had any appeal to me. Nothing drew me to the past, everything drew me to the future. I was a total and utter futurist.

BRAD LINAWEAVER: Didn't you once say, on Jack's radio show; "The trouble with Religion is it's just about the past"?

J. NEIL SCHULMAN: That's exactly right, and that was how I felt about religion. I mean, I didn't know enough about Christianity to feel that way about it then, but I certainly felt that way about Judaism. It all seemed to be about ritual and tradition and things that were not part of my thinking, not part of my world.

BRAD LINAWEAVER: So, Rand had given you this reinforcement for the atheist perspective.

J. NEIL SCHULMAN: Well, she had taken my instant childhood concept —"If nobody knows where God is, I don't think there is one"— and, in essence, given me layers of philosophical reasoning, which supported it and gave me a grown-up version of that, which was: God is incompatible with natural law. Since I was a believer in natural law, and I couldn't see how a supernatural God made any sense, her arguments were pretty well convincing to me.

BRAD LINAWEAVER: At this same period you were also getting involved with the C.S. Lewis group.

J. NEIL SCHULMAN: Particularly in books like *Miracles*, where Lewis got into questions of metaphysics like this, where he was discussing the supernatural in things like his book *The Abolition of Man* and in *Mere Christianity* and in his book *Miracles*. All these sorts of things, where he was addressing these fundamentals — the same issues that Rand was discussing — of not only epistemological issues, but also the issues of how would you conceive what the supernatural is?

If there was anything that fundamentally described my philosophy, in some fundamental sense, in those days, is the line from Hamlet, "There are more things in Heaven and Earth, Horatio, than are dreamt of in your philosophy." I knew that there was more than just materialism because I had experienced it.

BRAD LINAWEAVER: Which is your psychic experience?

J. NEIL SCHULMAN: Yes.

BRAD LINAWEAVER: But now talk about Neil Schulman, the author again for a moment. In your novel The *Rainbow Cadenza*, the encounters between a character who follows Rand — I guess you could say — and a character who is inspired by Lewis, those exchanges that must have been very personally important to your intellectual development. Was that what was going on in you at that time — both sides of the debate? The argument from the C.S. Lewis side that there might be something beyond the immediate material realm of the senses versus the Randian argument that this is all we've got, this thing we have here in front of us basically? Was that your own mind working in the debate — in that exchange — between those characters in *The Rainbow Cadenza*?

J. NEIL SCHULMAN: That is exactly what was going on. Now *Rainbow Cadenza* was published in 1983 but I finished it Christmas Day, 1981. And the conception of it had started five years before. Almost as soon as I finished *Alongside Night*, I started working on what originally had been outlined as The Carnal Commandment and later became *The Rainbow Cadenza*.

By the time I actually got to the writing of the book, the bulk of which was written in 1981 — the latter third of the year was probably when all but the first few chapters were written. By that time, I'd read a lot of Lewis, a lot of his nonfiction. So the arguments were swirling back and forth, almost like one of those movies where you have a devil on one shoulder and an angel on the other shoulder. Well in this case it wasn't a devil and an angel — it was two opposing philosophies.

BRAD LINAWEAVER: I was going to ask you who's who, who's the devil and who's the angel?

J. NEIL SCHULMAN: Well, obviously we have to allow Lewis to be the angel, simply for traditional purposes. So I have a Randian devil and a Lewisian angel debating with each other over my soul. But nonetheless, I was thinking of it not in terms of anything other than: who's right? In other words it was an epistemological question, which Lewis raised in me. That is: are there ways of knowing other than the five senses which Rand talked about as the primary source — the only source — of human knowledge?

BRAD LINAWEAVER: "Can emotions be tools of cognition?"

J. NEIL SCHULMAN: Well "feelings," because I do see an important semantic distinction between "feelings" and "emotions." The word "emotion" implies that it is a reaction to something that's going on around you. The word "feeling" is not so defined that it doesn't allow for feelings being a source of other information in the psychic sense — almost more like intuition, or something like that.

I was, of course, conflicted because I'd had these experiences and believed that they were real. I was convinced that they were real, as a matter of fact. But, nonetheless, I was an atheist and if there was going to be a supernatural then it had to be one that was as scientifically possible as the natural world that I knew about.

Chapter 2: First Doubts

BRAD LINAWEAVER: A crucial question now arises. Is it possible you went into the writing of *The Rainbow Cadenza* — your second novel — an atheist but came out an agnostic?

J. NEIL SCHULMAN: I don't know if I'd crossed over to being an agnostic, but I do recall somewhere near the end of writing that book, sometime in late 1981, having some sort of bad night, where I was up and really going through something emotionally on this issue. I was really, really scared in some sense. I'm not sure exactly of what, but I was being confronted somehow.

I would say that perhaps that was where I first had the experience that C.S. Lewis had talked about in *Surprised by Joy* of feeling that maybe there was something on the other end of this conversation communicating with me, that it wasn't just a debate going on in my own mind. Not that in, any philosophical sense, I considered myself an agnostic. That didn't happen until later. But I would say that emotionally, I started having the sense that there was somebody else in the conversation with me, that it wasn't simply books I had read.

BRAD LINAWEAVER: Were you living the experience that C.S. Lewis wrote about that the young atheist must be very careful about the books he reads?

J. NEIL SCHULMAN: Well, I was long gone once I'd read *The Chronicles of Narnia*. I was not going to get through that without considering those arguments. Coming from a background of so little faith, I didn't have a resentment of Christianity or anything like that. I wasn't raised in a Catholic school with nuns teaching me, or anything like that. I didn't have any religious indoctrination. So I was willing to give these ideas a fair shot. But nonetheless, I was simply trying to figure out if there was a supernatural what was it? Again, I was expecting that anything supernatural —anything above

Nature — was going to have laws that it followed, the same as the nature which we understood.

BRAD LINAWEAVER: Now why did you make that assumption?

J. NEIL SCHULMAN: Because I was a rationalist.

BRAD LINAWEAVER: Natural law?

J. NEIL SCHULMAN: Yes, as far as I was concerned natural law would apply even to the supernatural. That whatever there was that was above the plane of existence which we experienced would have its own natural laws as well.

BRAD LINAWEAVER: Let me make sure I understand this; what you are saying is that in your system, or what you were beginning to divine to perhaps be the nature of the universe, it is a mistake to assume — and let's use the term supernatural for now because it's the concept I can get my brain around — that it is an error to think that the supernatural is simply a suspension or violation of natural law.

Your position is if the supernatural or other realm exists that natural law applies to it as well, but it is a mistake to view the existence of that other realm as a violation of natural law, if natural law applies to that realm as well.

Is that a proper paraphrase?

J. NEIL SCHULMAN: Almost, but I do have to make some distinctions.

I saw it as quite possible that there could be laws which would be true to our plane of existence as local phenomena such as the laws of chemistry, the laws of physics, the laws of how space/time worked, gravitation, speed of light. All these sorts of things were local phenomena. But there had to be some overriding natural laws which would apply in all modes of existence, all the universe, all possible universes. So in other words, I saw that there had to be some sort of universal natural laws, laws of logic or something intrinsic to the nature of reality, which would guide the formation of the physical laws with the universes.

Okay, so I saw that even the meta-law, which created the natural law of our universe, would have its own rules, its own principles, its own necessary logic. So I saw that the supernature would have supernatural laws. In the sense of laws which would necessitate certain things, exclude other things. That there were things that would be impossible in any existence of any sort.

BRAD LINAWEAVER: So, is it fair to say that the philosophical position you were developing at that time in many ways transcends the normal debates between say, the Aristotelians and the Korzybskians? That a large part of the General Semantics' case against Aristotle is a too-narrow application of what Aristotle might be? Or to phrase it differently, if you're very much part of classical philosophy with your commitment to natural law but somehow you're able to be modern as well, in terms of how you deal with the details of the machinery, there's where you're more like Korzybski. But your overarching theory is more like Aristotle in terms of natural law. How about that?

J. NEIL SCHULMAN: Yes. I think that says it.

BRAD LINAWEAVER: This is very interesting. You're the first person I've ever encountered who accepted some kind of supernatural universe when the issue of God was still very distant from you and you were still on your way from an atheist perspective to an agnostic perspective on the issue of God, while already having accepted a more multi-layered universe than most people would ever consider when they call themselves an atheist or an agnostic.

So having said all that, do you remember what it was that finally brought you to the intellectual position of agnosticism about God?

J. NEIL SCHULMAN: Well, before I answer that question I have to say where I got this idea of an overriding supernature. I got it from Lewis and Heinlein. And it wasn't mostly from Lewis's nonfiction arguments, but simply from how he portrayed things in *Narnia*. In *Narnia* you have different worlds with their own laws. For example, magic works in *Narnia*. But when the Queen of Charn – who has magic in her own world – comes to ours, she doesn't have the power. It seemed obvious to me that you could have different worlds with different natural laws – different physical laws – because Lewis portrayed that in *Narnia*.

I've joked before that the difference between *The Chronicles of Narnia* and *The Lord of the Rings* is that *The Lord of the Rings* is fantasy and *The Chronicles of Narnia* is science fiction. Because Lewis treats it like science fiction. When you have in *Narnia* the Woods Between The Worlds - where, in essence, there is really nothing going on, but that every time you go into one of these pools and enter into another universe, you get a different set of natural laws – well how, in that sense, is *Narnia* not science fiction, because you are going into a different universe in which magic is possible?

So in that sense, being a child who grew up on Superman comics – and Superman was always sort of like pseudo-science fiction – then getting into science fiction explicitly, Lewis fit in there perfectly.

Lewis didn't sell *Narnia* to children in the way that L. Frank Baum sold *The Wizard of Oz*, in the sense that anything could happen. There were definite things that could and couldn't happen in that universe. There were laws that worked there and things worked a certain way. The magic in *Narnia* operated according to obvious natural laws there as much as the way that physics and chemistry worked in our world.

Now in Heinlein we go into things like *"The Unpleasant Profession of Jonathan Hoag"* and *"They."* Heinlein in his *Unknown* type stories–

BRAD LINAWEAVER: – for John W. Campbell's fantasy magazine, *Unknown* –

J. NEIL SCHULMAN: – he was dealing with the same sort

of things. Things like *Magic, Inc.*, in which again, if magic existed, there were going to be rules and there were going to be ways it worked and there were going to be ways it didn't work. And so from both of them, I was getting a sense that even though there could be things which were apparently supernatural, particularly in Heinlein's story "Lost Legacy," where you had all these ancient psychic powers which were innate in us but simply had been forgotten, it was obvious to me that if psychic phenomena and the supernatural – and even ghosts and afterlife existed – there were rules. There were ways that things worked and it may be that we didn't know how they worked but that didn't mean that it was chaotic. It didn't mean that anything could happen. It simply meant that we didn't understand the rules yet.

BRAD LINAWEAVER: Now, at that time when you were reading all this material you wouldn't know what you would learn later, as you learn more about the actual writers that you admire so much, because Heinlein and Lewis are two of your favorite writers?

J. NEIL SCHULMAN: Yes.

BRAD LINAWEAVER: But it's interesting to realize later on that these two authors were doing a form of logical fantasy that was quite unusual. John W. Campbell was getting logical fantasy from Heinlein for *Unknown* the same way he was getting some of the most logical science fiction ever written by anybody for Astounding. But, isn't it interesting that C.S. Lewis who you first read as a kid – not knowing the *Narnia* books were Christian parables and so forth – isn't it interesting that C.S. Lewis's *Narnia* books are logical fantasy by the same set of standards Campbell required for *Unknown* and that Heinlein met perfectly? And yet Heinlein had very strong anti-Christian biases and here you are coming from your secular Jewish background, isn't it reasonable to assume that the last writer in the world you would find whose is a master of the kind of logical fantasy that pragmatist John Campbell, materialist pragmatist John Campbell, published in *Unknown*, that such a person should be the best-known Christian apologist of the twentieth century, C.S. Lewis? Aren't the odds against that? Isn't Lewis a rather bizarre character?

J. NEIL SCHULMAN: Yes, except for one thing, that Lewis was a fan. Lewis read American science fiction. He read Astounding, he read *Unknown*. I'm sure he snuck off the campuses of Cambridge and Oxford to the magazine stands and hid them under his coat and snuck them back to his rooms to read them. But he kept up with all that stuff. We know that because he makes references to it in his literary commentary.

BRAD LINAWEAVER: And also he actually appeared in an interview in *The Magazine of Fantasy and Science Fiction*. He even did some short stories for the *American Magazine of Fantasy and Science Fiction*.

J. NEIL SCHULMAN: And he even comments, I think, on some Heinlein stories in some of those discussions.

BRAD LINAWEAVER: That is correct and you can read some of that in Lewis's *Of Other Worlds*. But I'm talking about the young J. Neil Schulman who doesn't know a lot of this –

J. NEIL SCHULMAN: Right.

BRAD LINAWEAVER: – coming from your secular Jewish background. Of all the people for you to find as a master of logical fantasy – if you had been asked to make a bet at the time – the last person you'd bet on is one of the best-known Christian apologists of all time. It's not the guy you'd expect to be the logical fantasy writer – you see what I'm saying?

J. NEIL SCHULMAN: Yes. However, at that age, thinking of Lewis as primarily a Christian writer never would have occurred to me.

BRAD LINAWEAVER: No, but you find that out later and this is very important. We're back to *Rainbow Cadenza*. I believe a huge watershed in the development of your thought – and preparing you for the experiences that you later had, which is the primary thrust of this book – I believe is in that exchange between the Lewis fan and the Rand fan in *Rainbow Cadenza* that I studied very closely to do my afterword. I realized that I had been given the best assignment of all the "rainbow" of afterwords because something in me told me way back then, that there was something, in that exchange between those two minds from such opposite worlds, that was crucial to thinking going on in you, and that something was changing in your philosophy toward the universe. That was the impression that I had at the time that I wrote that afterword.

So you were an atheist coming to agnosticism?

J. NEIL SCHULMAN: Right. And, by the way, let's look at my cultural milieu then. I was surrounded by other atheists. There were no believers around me you know. I was hanging around with a libertarian crowd of whom atheism was simply taken for granted.

BRAD LINAWEAVER: You didn't know anyone like me at that time who was an intellectual agnostic?

J. NEIL SCHULMAN: Heinlein called himself an agnostic.

BRAD LINAWEAVER: But I mean in your immediate group?

J. NEIL SCHULMAN: The distinction between agnosticism and atheism at that point wouldn't have been a very sharp distinction for me.

BRAD LINAWEAVER: And you had never met somebody with my form of agnosticism?

J. NEIL SCHULMAN: No

BRAD LINAWEAVER: My deeply intellectual committed agnosticism?

J. NEIL SCHULMAN: No. Agnosticism to me merely was a different word to describe, as far as I was concerned, that "I need more proof that there is a god."

BRAD LINAWEAVER: By the way, I sounded very pompous when I just said "deeply intellectual agnosticism" what I was trying to say was "a well-thought-out agnostic system." Most people say they're agnostics because they don't want to be bothered. I actually do have a developed agnostic system, as you know.

J. NEIL SCHULMAN: Right. And of course that was how Heinlein described himself, also, because when I interviewed Heinlein in July, 1973, I described myself to him as an atheist and he described himself to me as an agnostic, but both of us used the same paradigm to describe ourselves and that is that there is insufficient proof that there is a God. He used the word "agnosticism" to describe that and I used the word "atheism" to describe that. So as far as I was concerned it was a distinction with no difference.

BRAD LINAWEAVER: It's the old Scot's jury verdict that instead of saying "not guilty" said "not proven."

J. NEIL SCHULMAN: But the one source for me, at that time, of people who believed in God, were the people at the C.S. Lewis Society and some of the Mythopoeic Society. Those were the only people I knew who believed in God.

BRAD LINAWEAVER: Now that was the New York group?

J. NEIL SCHULMAN: No, in California. Now, I knew observant Jews in New York. They were part of our circle at the NYU Science Fiction Society meetings, which I attended. But it never crossed my mind whether their being observant really had to do with whether they believed in God or not.

BRAD LINAWEAVER: Oh please amplify that remarkable sentence. Elaborate.

J. NEIL SCHULMAN: Because, in my experience, being a Jew had very little to do with whether or not you believed in God. It had to do with following traditions. It's almost like Judaism, you know, it's the debate whether it's a religion or a race. It's neither. It's a tradition. It's a series of ritualized performances, in the same way that my Bar Mitzvah, to me, was like rehearsing for a stage show or something like that. It was, in essence, learning a performance.

BRAD LINAWEAVER: Like rehearsing for the ultimate play or something like that.

J. NEIL SCHULMAN: Like rehearsing for a play.

BRAD LINAWEAVER: And the grandparents are the audience.

J. NEIL SCHULMAN: Right. So to me Judaism wasn't a religion. Judaism wasn't a race. Judaism was in essence a tradition which was passed down from generation to generation to generation of observing and enacting certain behaviors.

BRAD LINAWEAVER: Oh, what a beautiful way to put it! You're going to allow me to do this now, Neil. I'm going to give you a Gene Scott quote you will like.

J. NEIL SCHULMAN: All right, you're entitled.

BRAD LINAWEAVER: Gene Scott when he said, on the first book of his I ever read and the blurb right on the back cover was a quote from Scott, and Scott said "Traditions make void the Word of God," and my Roman Catholic aunt was horrified by that and wouldn't even read a book that had that on it. I thought the Roman Catholics would be the ones most offended by such a sentiment. But now I'm beginning to realize that actually the observant Jews might be more offended by Gene Scott's statement than even the Roman Catholics – is that a fair assessment?

J. NEIL SCHULMAN: I think the Jews I know who would discuss this, particularly Dennis Prager, wouldn't be offended by Gene Scott's comment so much as they would want to argue and explain.

Dennis Prager has described himself as a behaviorist – not in the B.F. Skinner sense of operant conditioning or something like that – but in the sense that — in his view — God does not judge our thoughts. Which is a great distinction from Christianity where Jesus, in the Sermon on the Mount, in essence invents thought-crime. "You've been told if you commit adultery it's a sin. I tell you if you lust in your heart that's an equivalent sin" is, in essence, Jesus inventing thought-crime.

From the Jewish conception there is no thought-crime. There is only behavior. There's only what you do, not what you think. If you observe what is expected to happen, I imagine – from the Jewish perspective – is that the actions that you take will form your character.

Now Heinlein himself reiterates this in *Stranger in a Strange Land* when he has Valentine Michael Smith explain that the action you take at cusp is your identity. Okay. That's a very Jewish thought. The action you take at crisis is your identity. What you choose to do at the important moments – where you can go off into the different alternate universes which are the future –

BRAD LINAWEAVER: Yes.

J. NEIL SCHULMAN: – the choices you make are who you are forever, that, that is what defines you. And that's a very Jewish thought in the sense that behavior – how you act – is more important than what you think.

BRAD LINAWEAVER: A more traditional Christian point of view might be summed up as "character is destiny," as a different concept than being concerned with behavior, because the thing is there's different Christian traditions. Some Christian traditions are very concerned with the law, and then are very concerned with behavior. But Grace Christianity is of course much less concerned with behavior and much more concerned with intent.

But I understand one thing about the thought-crime point that you've made – from what I understand about Jesus Christ saying that in The Sermon on the Mount. What I understand Jesus Christ to be saying is no one can stop these sinful thoughts therefore you will be sinners no matter how many rules you keep. Therefore you need another way to salvation. That keeping 600 rules — not ten but 600 rules — the way to salvation is the thing I'm going to give you. You can't get to Heaven on your own by keeping rules because you're going

The Heartmost Desire 191

to sin no matter what. It's "thought-crime" as a way to escape from the yoke and burden of trying to be perfect, as opposed to, say, thought-crime in *1984*, where if you think the wrong thoughts you're in for it.

So it's almost a libertarian version of thought-crime if you say you can't help but sin. You see what I'm saying? The whole Christian tradition took those thought-crimes and created control, control, control, and others took to free up those things.

J. NEIL SCHULMAN: But you see I see where that's coming from. That's coming from the idea that we're fallen, which is a big deal in Christianity. That we're fallen, we're suckers who don't have an even break.

BRAD LINAWEAVER: That's totally correct. That's what it says.

J. NEIL SCHULMAN: Okay, you may have free will, but forget it – you've already lost.

BRAD LINAWEAVER: Until you accept this deal, you got it.

J. NEIL SCHULMAN: But the Jew doesn't believe in Original Sin.

BRAD LINAWEAVER: Right that's a Christian invention or contribution.

J. NEIL SCHULMAN: It's not part of Jewish thinking. If I was taught anything about Christianity, in my childhood, it's that Jews don't believe in Original Sin and Christians do.

BRAD LINAWEAVER: Right. That's right

J. NEIL SCHULMAN: Now you could argue about whether or not Jews believe in free will or predestination.

BRAD LINAWEAVER: I think there's two sides to that argument too.

J. NEIL SCHULMAN: But nonetheless, destiny is not something like predestiny. In essence, if anything, every action you take is a creation of destiny. Every choice you make is a creation of destiny. You are creating destiny with every free-will choice you make. That would be the way that I would conceive it and I think that's a Jewish viewpoint. So when Dennis Prager talks about behavior as being what's important, he is looking at it from outside of the consequence of choice.

BRAD LINAWEAVER: You've given me an epiphany. Let me ask you this question. Could it be that something that the ancient pagans and the ancient Hebrews had in common was no part of this original-sin belief and Christianity brought the original-sin concept in? Is it not a reasonable assumption, though obviously it requires more research, the ancient pagans and the Jews who fought like crazy over many things, neither would have a clue what Original Sin was? The pagan didn't have Original Sin either. That's what I'm asking.

J. NEIL SCHULMAN: Let me make a further distinction between the Jew and the pagan here. The pagan – you're correct – didn't have any concept of Original Sin in that sense. The Jew would believe in the Fall of Nature and the Fall of Man but not think of it as a generational curse.

BRAD LINAWEAVER: Ah, here's the distinction I wasn't getting. They go along with the Christian view up to the point where the Christians took the Jewish concept and added this to it.

J. NEIL SCHULMAN: You might think of it as, remember and this is again where I read Genesis and I seem to get things out of it that other people reading it don't focus on. It's not just the Fall of Man it's also the Fall of Nature.

BRAD LINAWEAVER: Yes that's right.

J. NEIL SCHULMAN:
Now that tells me something okay, that tells me the physical universe around you is different.

BRAD LINAWEAVER: Oh you're not alone in this view, by the way. Lewis is totally with you on this.

J. NEIL SCHULMAN: Okay. The physical universe around you is different and that means that you have greater obstacles than you would've had. As far as I was concerned – in reading

Genesis and looking at it and trying to analyze it and make sense out of it - it was telling me that, not living in Eden, we had a steeper hill to climb but it was still a hill which we could climb. It was just going to be harder. Maybe, if you want to talk about it almost like in a physical sense, instead of living on a planet with one-sixth earth's gravity, we are now living with six times the gravity than living on Earth. In other words, we're living on a planet where things are harder because of what had happened.

Well, harder does not mean that you've necessarily lost. It merely means that you need to put in more effort and rise to a higher standard to overcome. Okay? You could still do it; it was just going to be harder.

BRAD LINAWEAVER: Sisyphus rolling the rock in hell right up to lip of the cliff and than it always rolls back down on him? Is that an original-sin type of notion? Basically you're saying you could get that rock over the hill.

J. NEIL SCHULMAN: Yes.

BRAD LINAWEAVER: I want to get back to one thing. You were having your experience with the C.S. Lewis Society Christians and you were having your experience with the Rand/Objectivist-tinged libertarians. And you were dealing with these two groups of people, both of whom had a set of convictions. With the passage of time, it turns out you've got something very different going on in your head. Something very different is going on in your head than a traditional Christian view, a traditional Jewish view or a traditional atheist view – where the Objectivists are classical atheists.

What I want to ask is, with this back-and-forth, did you sense both that – A – both sides had some legitimate arguments but – B – both sides had an inadequate or incomplete case? There was something missing. That's what I got from your stuff in *Rainbow Cadenza*, in that section I studied for my afterword. I got the feeling that you had the feeling that something was missing. I'm still trying to get that crossover point where you go from atheist on God to agnostic on God. I'm still trying find where that happened.

J. NEIL SCHULMAN: I'm not sure I can characterize it in a continuum that way, but let me tell you how I experienced it. There was a long period, while this was going on, I felt that I was carrying multiple philosophies in my head.

It's like in my story *"The Musician,"* where my character, Jacob Schneider, has two possible realities and he doesn't know which one is true. And so he is going along, taking only those necessary actions to fulfill that which is immediately before him. Not knowing whether what is going on is, in fact, a conspiracy against him, or, in fact, whether he is going through some sort of psychological episode which is presenting to him something which isn't real.

And this is very much a sort of story which is very, very important to me, the story of psychological tension where you don't know what reality is. It's a very Philip K. Dick-ian type of thing. Which is one of the reasons why I've read and admired and enjoyed Philip K. Dick so much.

BRAD LINAWEAVER: Same here.

J. NEIL SCHULMAN: I think that he must have had something akin to my experience, at some point, to put him in this state of mind.

BRAD LINAWEAVER: I agree.

J. NEIL SCHULMAN: And Robert Anton Wilson, when he talks about his Large Rabbit experience – which I'm sure, he's talking about fancifully but nonetheless – he's trying to encapsulate that he had some sort of experience. Again, he refers to it as Chapel Perilous or something like that which shakes your world, and you don't know. You're being presented with multiple possible realities and you're trying to figure out which one is the real reality.

Heinlein, in his story *"They,"* has a character who is being treated as if he's a psychotic but nonetheless he believes that there is an actual conspiracy and world-changing going on around him, and of course at the end of the story the twist is that turns out to be true.

BRAD LINAWEAVER: I find that the most solipsistic vision in the history of literature.

J. NEIL SCHULMAN: But it's not solipsistic because in solipsism you're creating your own nightmare. This is a nightmare which is being created by others.

BRAD LINAWEAVER: I'll rephrase, emotional solipsism projected into a universe where all of the worst suspicions of the main character turn out to be true.

J. NEIL SCHULMAN: That's right.

BRAD LINAWEAVER: That's more accurate.

J. NEIL SCHULMAN: Right.

BRAD LINAWEAVER: Paranoid. It's the greatest paranoid short story of all time?

J. NEIL SCHULMAN: Yes. But what all these visions have is the tension of living inside a work of suspense fiction. Where you are living in a situation like a character in a plot where you are living in suspense — the definition of suspense being doubt of outcome of intent, where you do not know from where you are what the truth is. It's living in a mystery story.

Okay. And I found myself living in a metaphysical mystery story in which there was more than one explanation of what was going on and I was carrying them all in my head simultaneously, taking those action only which were immediately before me, while trying to get more data and trying to figure out which of the things being presented to me was true.

Now I would say that that, carrying more than one paradigm in my mind and running them as simultaneous programs as if I were a computer with compartmentalization of programs running in different sections, that I would call my agnostic period.

BRAD LINAWEAVER: But that is the answer to my question. That is where you were. To that extent you were agnostic.

That's a more unusual form of agnosticism than mine and I know that mine is not run-of-the-mill common.

J. NEIL SCHULMAN: Right. When I was an atheist I was running one paradigm. When I became an agnostic I was running multiple paradigms. And when I got to the point where I was a convinced theist, I was back to one paradigm again.

BRAD LINAWEAVER:

And that is where I think we should take this up in the next section, because we talked about how you got from atheist to agnostic. In the next section I want to talk about your journey from agnostic to your experience.

J. NEIL SCHULMAN: Excellent!

Chapter 3: Contact

BRAD LINAWEAVER: Neil, when we left off we had just gotten to the point where you moved from atheism to agnosticism and you gave a position on agnosticism having to do with considering the possibility of more than one paradigm being true, kind of a multiple reality-tunnel approach, perhaps.

I am reading from your book *Self Control Not Gun Control*, where you write "How about a computer metaphor? We are Software in a PC, even if we have a modem to other PC's or that Great Main Frame in the Sky. Oh, Lord, DeBug Me, Deliver me out of RAM and Save me to Disk, Repairing all my corrupted Sectors, Amen."

I would like to address the issue that when you moved from atheism to agnosticism I get the impression you did not stay in agnosticism very long, because in your essay, *"Why I Am Not A Jew And What I Am Instead,"* you did say "I believe in God, but I would believe – and have believed -in goodness per se even in the absence of my belief in God."

I see that as a reference back to your natural law beliefs that you had I think as far back as you were able to formulate beliefs of any kind. So my question here is: was it a pretty short step from your form of agnosticism to a belief in the God of natural law?

J. NEIL SCHULMAN: Let me first try to put the limits on the timeline here, because that might be useful in helping to answer the question. As you were zeroing in yesterday, something happened to me during the writing of *The Rainbow Cadenza*. I had some sort of event happen to me, probably in the last month of writing, that puts it somewhere in November to December of 1981, and I would say that my atheism was pretty well done at that point because I was seriously running at least a second or third paradigm, at that point. The materialistic view that Rand had given me was in suspension along with other views at that point so I would say I was agnostic by that point. Obviously, by the time I'm writing that statement "I believe in God" – it's dated March 24, 1992 – my agnosticism is pretty much over.

I also talk about having the experience with God, I don't think we've gotten to it yet in the first part, where I had an experience in 1988 around my birthday in which, I had been praying daily The Lord's Prayer by 1988 probably for about a year. The 1988 experience I have told you about but I'm going to be putting on the record here and this is as good a place to do it.

But first let me just say that the transition starts to happen during the writing of *Rainbow Cadenza* when I start playing off the arguments, in my mind, between C.S. Lewis and Ayn Rand, which is characterized in the characters of Joan Darris and the underground "Mere Christian" priest Hill Bromley in *The Rainbow Cadenza*.

BRAD LINAWEAVER: Right, we talked about that in a previous section.

J. NEIL SCHULMAN: Joan Darris is an Objectivist, in our argumentation. Hill Bromley is arguing from the standpoint of what I was reading from C.S. Lewis and he is a priest of the "Mere Christian" Church, taken directly from the title of one of C.S. Lewis' most famous books *Mere Christianity*. There is no "Mere Christian" Church. Lewis would have scoffed at the idea that there could be a "Mere Christian" Church because as far as he was concerned denominations had meaning — you just had to choose one.

So, by the end of 1981 when I'm finishing the writing of *Rainbow Cadenza* I'm going through this transition period. It then starts accelerating so that by 1987, I've decided to make the experiment. We can call that period from 1982 to 1986 — at least five years — we can call that my for-sure agnostic period.

In 1987 I decide to make a leap of faith — an experiment — and that is to pray.

During this agnostic period I was running these multiple paradigms and I had the feeling that C.S. Lewis talked about, of being pursued. He talks about this, as I said, in the first section of his autobiography *Surprised by Joy*. And I had the feeling that there was an active intelligence in me answering my arguments. Whenever I was thinking over the Ayn Rand/Objectivist arguments against the existence of God, I kept on coming back with images and answers and information, which confounded those arguments, which annihilated them. So much so, at the point of 1987, I decided that I was going to start praying and see if anything happened.

Lewis talks about jumping across the chasm. Interestingly, this imagery of the chasm is also used in business. *Crossing the Chasm* is the title of a book, which has to do with entrepreneuring a new product and going from the early adopters to the mainstream market. So in essence what I was doing was, I saw it as a scientific experiment because the idea was either I was going to find out that there was a real intelligence on the other end by praying, and that this was not simply some psychological event. Of course I was familiar with the idea of bicameral minds and subconscious, and I'd read a lot of Jung during this period. I'd always been interested in psychology, reading Freud's *A General Introduction to Psychoanalysis* by the time I was fourteen.

BRAD LINAWEAVER: Oh, I have to ask you a question there. Jung has always been preferred over Freud by those who believe in God, because the archetypes and other aspects of Jung — synchronicity, all these things — tie in with the more religious viewpoint. Whereas Freud has always been a darling — or used to be — of the atheist-materialist until the feminists got so mad at him. Back when you were an atheist, where did your emotions tend to pull you, toward Freud or toward Jung? Or did you not see a conflict?

J. NEIL SCHULMAN: Well, I wasn't thinking of it in those

terms. I was thinking of it in artistic terms. I started reading Jung because symbols and imagery were an important part of the artistic motif of *The Rainbow Cadenza* itself. So I was reading Jung as well as a lot of different writers. I mean I did an encyclopedia's worth of research on the various fields of *Rainbow Cadenza*. That is a very heavily research-driven book. Probably in the same way that you had to read every book about the Nazis there was to do Moon of Ice.

BRAD LINAWEAVER: You really taught me things about music and about lasegraphy I never would have known without reading *The Rainbow Cadenza*.

J. NEIL SCHULMAN: I was trying to derive fundamental principles. I don't want to digress too much here, but there was a fundamental principle that I learned during the writing of *The Rainbow Cadenza*, which I think of as the theory of everything when it comes to art. And that is the theory of dialectic. The idea that all art in one way or another comes from a collision of opposites, which creates tension and then a resolution, which really leads to release of tension. In drama, it is plot — doubt of outcome leading to resolution of outcome or doubt of intent in suspense leading to resolution of intent. In music, it is dissonance leading to consonance, or a harmonic expectation being fulfilled, such as the third note of a triad being expected and then becoming a full chord. You know things, which are set up to create expectations in drama, in music and all these forms of art, which are dynamic, which move. And I even started thinking of ways, in dancing for another example, contraction and release of the muscles.

BRAD LINAWEAVER: You've always agreed with Aristotle's theory of catharsis?

J. NEIL SCHULMAN: Right, but what I was looking for was a universal common denominator to all of them and then having found it in the tension-and-release dialectic, I then applied it to an art form which was just starting out and was not yet using it and that was the Laserium visual light art form. And so what I was able to do was take these principles and draw examples from these various different existing art forms and then apply them, in the novel, to an art form that, in essence, did not yet exist.

But it told me something also basic about all art and that in essence, that's when I started to think of us as a creation, an existence we were living in, as a work of art. Because I saw the same principles existed in our lives,. The very principle of creation, of procreation, for example, involved a male – or masculine – principle and a female – or feminine – principle uniting to create a synthesis, which is a unique human being.

BRAD LINAWEAVER: Neil you're not saying kids do better with having a mother and a father are you?

J. NEIL SCHULMAN: Yes, I think I would say that. And as a matter of fact, of course, I was way ahead of the curve in discussing that in *Rainbow Cadenza*, where you do have gay marriages.

But, I'm going into digression after digression after digression here and I do want to develop these points in some coherent fashion.

The very exploration of art in *The Rainbow Cadenza* started giving me new paradigms having to do with existence itself. I started seeing God, in the sense that Hill Bromley was talking about God, as being an artist. And this paradigm, that's when it started running alongside in my head, these other paradigms, these purely mechanistic science paradigms. And, of course, there were the quantum paradigms, also, which I was getting from reading things like *Illuminatus!* and the *The Schrodinger's Cat* books by Robert Anton Wilson. And of course Sam Konkin was a theoretical chemist and so I was given some, at least a Sunday supplement version of quantum mechanics and statistical mechanics. Not that I had any mathematical understanding of them, but at least that was one more of the paradigms that was starting to run in my head as I started thinking about quantum uncertainty as possibly having to do something with free will and freeing us from the mechanistic clockwork universe that seemed to be so much a part of the secularists.

BRAD LINAWEAVER: Crucial question, it'll keep us on track. Are you saying that when you first started seriously thinking about God during this highly creative agnostic period, you first started thinking about God in esthetic terms?

J. NEIL SCHULMAN: Yes. Yes. God as an artist, as a creator, was where it's first coming up. And again it comes because in writing a novel you have to be honest to your characters. I never liked writing straw-man arguments for my characters, I always wanted to have the people I disagreed with having as strong arguments as they could come up with.

BRAD LINAWEAVER: You know I agree with you on that Neil.

J. NEIL SCHULMAN: Why yes, Brad. So much so, that I have the villain of *The Rainbow Cadenza*, Burke Filcher, making arguments that I disagree with one-hundred per cent, but making them so compellingly that to this day I have readers think that those are my actual positions.

So this transition that I was going forward with, again a lot having to do with tension and release and realizing that Creation itself utilized these artistic principles, made me start at least running the paradigm of the created universe alongside the uncreated universe. Again, the contradiction in my mind was how could you have a created universe if existence exists? That existence exists was where Rand was starting out, how could you have a created universe if existence has always existed, how can something come out of nothing? That was one of the main problems that I was trying to resolve in my mind. If there has to be something which is uncreated, how could you have a created universe? Okay, so that was the unresolved problem in my mind.

BRAD LINAWEAVER: You did not like the idea of Creation ex nihilo.

J. NEIL SCHULMAN: Right, and to this day I reject the concept of creation ex nihilo.

BRAD LINAWEAVER: But you, of course, have discovered that is not a basis for atheism, though most people think it is, but you've discovered that?

J. NEIL SCHULMAN: But it took me a while to get to that point and I would say that the transition during the agnostic period was when these questions were open and unresolved in my mind, when there was all this tension of these various different paradigms bumping against each other and coming out of me and being objectified in the characters in *The Rainbow Cadenza*.

So, by the time I get to 1987 I'm willing to make the experiment and pray. Interestingly, I chose The Lord's Prayer.

BRAD LINAWEAVER: Why?

J. NEIL SCHULMAN: Jesus seemed cool to me, that's the only way I can put it. Hanging around all these Christians at the C.S. Lewis Society, Jesus just seemed cool to me.

BRAD LINAWEAVER: By that point had you read C.S. Lewis' famous remark, but I don't remember which work it's in, that Jesus Christ in the Gospel accounts in The New Testament, is equivalent to God writing Himself into His own novel. Had you encountered that Lewis remark by this point?

J. NEIL SCHULMAN: I would say that by 1987, I had probably read the bulk of C.S. Lewis' nonfiction theological writings.

BRAD LINAWEAVER: It is very possible that Lewis' observation helped contribute to your choice of The Lord's Prayer?

J. NEIL SCHULMAN: Yes, and so that was the prayer and I started doing it.

Now here's where I need to lead up to this by giving psychological background on one aspect of myself because it plays a part in the transition that happens in 1988. There's two things I have to mention then, one of them is I was phobic about death. So much so that it made me a physical coward.

BRAD LINAWEAVER: When did you first discover that about yourself? Let's go further back in time if necessary.

J. NEIL SCHULMAN: There is an old Yiddish expression which I heard growing up — "Ken dort gehargit verren" — which means you could get killed doing that. And that was pretty much my watchword for a long period of my youth. The idea of deliberately going into a situation where you could get killed was not something I wanted to do. Particularly, you know, because I had no emotional certainty of an afterlife. I was phobic about death. I was phobic about pain, but particularly death. So much so that I had to have nighttime rituals to get to sleep, to blank out almost the obsessive thinking that would happen to me in the stillness and quietness. I would start thinking about my own mortality and freak.

BRAD LINAWEAVER: About what age did this first begin?

J. NEIL SCHULMAN: It was always there. As far back as I could remember there's always been this phobia about death.

Now something else weird. Remember that I mentioned that I had always had psychic beliefs. I'd had psychic experiences including some precognitive events of my own.

I remember a day in 1970 that I was expecting, all day, a telephone call to come in saying that my grandfather, my father's father, was dead. That call came around two in the afternoon. I'd been expecting it. This was when we were in the process of moving from Massachusetts to New York.

Our house was for sale. The real estate agents were calling. I was going in with my father to Boston that day for testing at a school which was a tutorial academy with branches in both Boston and New York. I was going to test in Boston and complete high school at this tutorial academy in New York City.

When the phone rang that morning, it was clear in my mind

they were calling to say Grandpa Schulman is dead. It wasn't. It was a real estate agent calling to make an appointment.

I went into Boston with my father, I did the testing. After I was finished the testing they were doing grading on it — the marking on the achievement test to find out what my levels were.

The phone rang. The person who ran the branch of that school in Boston, Alexander Smith Academy, got on the phone and I again thought they're calling to tell me that my grandfather's dead. Why should I think that this random phone call, ringing at this academy, had anything even to do with me?

He handed me the phone. It was for me and it was my mother, calling to say that my grandfather had died about an hour before. So my first thing about it happened before he even died because that had happened around 8:30 or 9:00 o'clock that morning. And this was around 2:00 in the afternoon, and my grandfather had died around noon or something like that.

BRAD LINAWEAVER: Important question. Why wouldn't the view that you'd had when you were fairly young, that the universe might have more going on in it than we immediately perceive with the five senses, which is what precog experiences suggest — extrasensory perception experiences suggest — which is real-time brain-to-brain communication, precog, you get the feeling you have an edge on the future, all these type of experiences. Why wouldn't any of these experiences, and the fact that you had a number of them over the years, make you less phobic about death for the very simple reason that these experiences, if you don't just rule them out the way Isaac Asimov would as just statistical and accidental and they don't mean anything (the old Carl Sagan approach), if you're drawing the other conclusion, that the universe in weirder than we think, why wouldn't that make you less phobic about death?

J. NEIL SCHULMAN: Because it was at a too deep an irrational level, it was not subject to reason. I could distract myself from it I could not defeat what was going on inside of me. It was a neurosis of some sort.

BRAD LINAWEAVER: And you have no idea where it came from you have just had it for so long?

J. NEIL SCHULMAN: Well at that point I had no idea where it came from.

So, here is where I was leading up to my psychic thing. It would have to be sometime in the area of around 1987, when I learned that Robert Heinlein — whom, of course, I'd first met in September, 1973 after doing the interview with him in July, 1973 and had become friends with – when I learned in 1987 that Heinlein was dying of emphysema, which by the way was what killed my maternal grandfather, at the point where I knew that Heinlein was dying of emphysema I did something very, very strange in my own mind. I tried to psychically link my energy to his to keep him alive.

Now that sounds crazy. Why would I have even thought that I could do something like that? And here we come to a year of praying, sometimes more than once a day. Almost clinging to God in a sense "Don't let me die," "Don't let me die," "Don't let Heinlein die," "Don't let Heinlein die." I mean this really crazy neurotic mental cycles.

BRAD LINAWEAVER: And this is still when, if somebody asked you pointblank, at that moment, you'd still say you're an agnostic but you're running a prayer experiment, perhaps. Because in one of your interviews with Jack, you say years after you have convinced yourself or had the experience of God, years after that experience you told Jack, in one or you interviews, that you think the best way to think of God is God is an experimental scientist.

J. NEIL SCHULMAN: Yes.

BRAD LINAWEAVER: So, God is running the experiments?

J. NEIL SCHULMAN: Yes.

BRAD LINAWEAVER: And here you were at your end, you

were running an experiment on God, the way that you could argue God runs experiments on us?

J. NEIL SCHULMAN: Yes.

BRAD LINAWEAVER: Both ends of the microscope.

J. NEIL SCHULMAN: Yes.

So, we get to April, 1988 and somewhere in that period, I'm not sure exactly when, I had my last telephone conversation with Heinlein. It was one in which he was talking about Jean Kirkpatrick for president. He must have known he didn't have much time left but somewhere in the month preceding that I'd had my last telephone conversation with Heinlein, he spoke about that. He also probably shook my anarchism pretty heavily at that point by simply at a certain point he made some sort of offhand comment, "Well, Neil you know that's crazy." I think it was when I was telling him the reason why I didn't vote or something like that because Heinlein, of course, believed in voting. I was coming up with the standard argument that we in The AnarchoVillage — our little libertarian group in Long Beach, California — were always talking about why we were nonvoters, quoting Jack Parr, "Don't vote. It just encourages them.

Heinlein did something he'd never done before; he basically dissed me on this point. That had an impact on me emotionally, but nonetheless I loved the man.

BRAD LINAWEAVER: Do you remember what your response to him was?

J. NEIL SCHULMAN: I don't think I even gave him a response.

BRAD LINAWEAVER: You just thought about it.

J. NEIL SCHULMAN: I started thinking about it.

BRAD LINWEAVER: He did that to make you think about it?

J. NEIL SCHULMAN: Yes. But also, interestingly, he immediately pulled back as if he had said it unintentionally.

BRAD LINAWEAVER: Ah, because he was so polite?

J. NEIL SCHULMAN: I'm not sure it was politeness, I almost had a sense it was something else.

BRAD LINAWEAVER: But he was a very polite man.

J. NEIL SCHULMAN: I think it was more than being polite. I think it was almost like that he saw what was going on with me and knew that I was going to end up there where he was anyway.

BRAD LINAWEAVER: But it may have been your first helping hand to the recognition that the brilliant observation you have made, you made this in your own words I'll just through this in here but you say it awfully well: if we say we have the right to defend ourselves with weapons like guns, we recognize — as Emma Goldman always said — that the vote is a weapon also, and why only allow your enemies to wield that weapon?

J. NEIL SCHULMAN: And of course I was taking that directly from the anarchist writers who compared ballots with bullets. So in other words, at the point, a few years later than that, that I started literally endorsing carrying guns around with bullets in them, the arguments that the anarchists made to me came back in the exact opposite direction that they wanted to. If bullets and ballots are the same thing — as you're always saying — then why can't I use a ballot defensively like I use a bullet defensively?

BRAD LINAWEAVER: You turn this argument on its head and I have never seen it done better. For all I know it's an original argument with you. But whether it is or not, your expression of it is very effective and I have not seen the argument from anybody but you.

J. NEIL SCHULMAN: Okay. We come to April 1988.

BRAD LINAWEAVER: The year of Heinlein's death.

J. NEIL SCHULMAN: Right. That's May.

This is a month before that and I was living bicoastal at that point.

My *Twilight Zone* episode had been aired March 7, 1986, and I started getting pulled back out to the West Coast for work reasons because movie and television production was West Coast. But nonetheless, before that, I had gotten married in July, 1985, and was living in Jersey City, New Jersey, and I needed to return to the West Coast. And that happened at various different stages.

But by that point, in April, 1988, I had already established a second apartment back in Long Beach — not back in the AnarchoVillage but just a few blocks away from it — with a roommate, John Strang.

It was a two-bedroom apartment, and we each had our own bedroom with our own privacy, shared a common living room and kitchen, and when my wife at that time came out to the West Coast, we would stay in my room and had the use of the apartment. That's where I was starting to run SoftServ, the publishing company out of, the electronic publishing company. So in essence I had two homes again at that point, I was bicoastal.

I need to bring up the physiological component because the physiological component is going to play an important part later on.

I was a very heavy coffee drinker. I seem to have some sort of allergy to coffee which I've never fully figured out. I thought for a long time that it had to do with the acid of the coffee, or the caffeine, and it doesn't seem to be either of those, because acid by itself or caffeine by itself does not do what coffee does to me. It sends me into irregular heartbeat and hyperventilation. It seems to be almost an allergic reaction. I think that it might have something directly to do, that there is some substance in coffee — and Sam Konkin, the theoretical chemist pointed out to me that there are so many substances in coffee that if you put them in a gas chromatograph you can't even figure out everything that's in there. They've never even been able to do a full analysis of what's in coffee. So there's something in there which I think may directly affect the brain in the regulation of breathing and heartbeat. It goes directly to the autonomic functions in some sense.

BRAD LINAWEAVER: And it's not just the caffeine?

J. NEIL SCHULMAN: It's not just the caffeine. It's not the acid. It is something else in coffee.

BRAD LINAWEAVER: And that's why they used to call it the devil's brew when it was first introduced into Europe.

J. NEIL SCHULMAN: Well, they may be right.

But nonetheless, for the week before my birthday in 1988 — and it even took me a few days to realize that it was coffee that started it — but I had a week where I was uncontrollably and unexpectedly going into hyperventilation.

There was not such a great tension going on that these were panic attacks, although I had just taken out a lease on this apartment so I could work on the West Coast again and my guild was on strike again, was throwing us out on strike sometime in that period. I don't remember the exact time of the strike. I do remember that it was a very long strike.

BRAD LINAWEAVER: That would be The Writer's Guild?

J. NEIL SCHULMAN: The Writer's Guild, yes. But nonetheless I don't recall that this was a particularly stressful time but this week preceding my birthday in 1988 – my birthday is April 16 – I kept on going into fits of unexpected hyperventilation and they were causing panic attacks, so much so that I was having to carry around a paper bag with me to breathe into it, to try to get myself out of it. I didn't know what was going on. I stopped drinking coffee after the first day, or something like that, when I realized it was linked. But nonetheless, even after stopping the coffee, it was not stopping and it was going on day after day after day. So by around the fifth or the sixth day I was a wreck.

And I'd started having a very strange thing happening. I'll use a technical psychological term here. I became extremely emotionally labile. Emotional lability means that you do not have any self-control over your emotional response.

What was happening to me is that I became so emotionally sensitive to everything around me that if I watched a TV commercial with a little mini-drama, in that commercial to sell some product, it became like watching *Hamlet* or *MacBeth*. In other words, I was just responding to everything way out of proportion. I was feeling everything. In terms of sound you would think of it as 120 decibels or something like that.

BRAD LINAWEAVER: Total empathy?

J. NEIL SCHULMAN: Total empathy.

Now, I had thought of myself as somebody who, if he identified with any character out of *Star Trek*, it was Spock. I was out of control. Suddenly my emotions were out of control. It was *"Amok Time"* — or something like that — without the mating ritual.

It got to the point where on the night before my birthday I lay down in bed and this feeling of uncertainty — and remember this combined with this death phobia — I was afraid I was going to die from this, that something was happening in me that was killing me. I didn't know what it was.

I lay down in bed – and bed for me was a futon on the floor in this bedroom – and I felt a hand on my heart inside my chest. I can't describe it any other way. I felt a physical presence of a hand, as if it was holding my heart. Not squeezing it but holding it so I could feel it. In my head I heard this voice and it said to me, "I can take you now."

Suddenly my worst fear, death was coming, you know, God is going to take me. I'm in the middle of a *Twilight Zone* episode. Hand on my heart. I'm scared to death – literally. And a voice — The Voice, which I knew was God's voice — was saying, "I can take you now." And I was scared.

Something unusual happened at that point. The Voice, which had just said "I can take you now," started laughing at me.

And I said, "Why are you laughing at me?"

And The Voice — God, I might as well just say God, because that's how I identified it — God said to me then "Because I can't believe that you're scared."

I said, "Why would you be surprised that I'm scared? I've always been scared of death. You're surprised that I'm scared?"

It was totally inexplicable to me that while this is going on, God's first reaction is to be astonished, and laugh, that I am scared of death. Who am I that God would be surprised that I'm scared of death? I'm not a war hero, who's been an Audie Murphy who's charged machine-gun nests, or anything like that. Why on Earth would God be surprised by that? This was one of the things going on while I am, in essence, scared out of my mind.

After He stopped laughing at me, God said "You have to make a choice. I can take you now. You will die now or I can let you live but here's the thing. No more promises. No more deals. You have in your mind somewhere that you can make a deal with me and I'm going to make everything come out all right and you're going to be safe from everything and you're not going to die and the people around you, who you keep on praying for constantly, are not going to die. And if you stay – if I don't take you now – all bets are off. You stay, unconditionally, with no promises, and whatever happens, you have to let happen."

And I was more scared of death than of fate. And so I said "I'll stay."

And I felt The Hand leave my heart. I had accepted the contract.

I thought, at that point, I wonder if this is simply some sort of psychological event, some fantasy my body is having to tell me that I'm having a heart attack?

BRAD LINAWEAVER: While this was going on, weren't you thinking about Heinlein's situation as well as your own?

J. NEIL SCHULMAN: Well, I was thinking in terms of everybody. Not just Heinlein, but I was praying for my parents, and my wife, and all my friends, you know, "Don't let any of them die, don't let me die, don't let anybody die."

BRAD LINAWEAVER: I just remember conversations I had

with you at the time. Heinlein seemed to be very prominent in your mind.

J. NEIL SCHULMAN: Very prominent, but at that particular moment I don't know, okay? But again, it was this clinging to God, praying so tight that nobody dies, that no harm comes to everybody. You know this panicked clinging, which was what He was breaking. In essence He was telling me, "Don't pray so much! Because I'd been praying every day, constantly. Not just the Lord's Prayer, but also the prayers for everybody to be okay – and not in the Christian sense of praying for their soul – but praying for them physically not to die, not to get hit by a truck.

So, God ended that at that moment.

Nonetheless, again, being the rationalist, I'm thinking maybe this is my science-fiction writer's brain telling me that I'm having a heart attack. So at this point I woke up my roommate and I said, "Call the paramedics, I think I'm having a heart attack."

The paramedics arrived and they put those sensors on me to do the electrocardiogram, which they do instantly, and they looked at me like I was crazy. They said, "Your heart is perfectly fine. What are you talking about? There's nothing going on." One of them asked me an interesting question. He said, "Are you going through a divorce right now?"

"No," I said, "everything's fine. My wife is coming out tomorrow to celebrate my birthday. Everything's great. But I thought I was having a heart attack."

"No, you're not having a heart attack. Forget it, you're fine!"

They didn't even want to take me down to the hospital for observation. My heart must have been rock steady at that point.

They left. My roommate went back to sleep. And my panic was over.

Whatever had happened – now that I knew that I was not dying — what had been going on for a week, with this recurring hyperventilation, this emotional lability, it stopped at that instant.

It was over. The event was over.

BRAD LINAWEAVER: Now, important question. So what would have been your first contact with God — when it was over you thought it might very well be God but you weren't one-hundred-percent certain that it was God?

J. NEIL SCHULMAN: I was pretty certain that it was God.

BRAD LINAWEAVER: Ninety percent or one-hundred percent?

J. NEIL SCHULMAN: Ninety-eight percent.

BRAD LINAWEAVER: But there was still two percent of doubt?

J. NEIL SCHULMAN: Right.

BRAD LINAWEAVER: So you thought very likely it was God but you weren't totally convinced, just almost.

J. NEIL SCHULMAN: Right. There was always that two percent of doubt because I might be crazy. I knew that the human body was capable of doing odd things, and the human brain was capable of doing odd things. I thought that maybe I was suffering from some toxic poisoning from coffee or something like that. Maybe this was some sort of hallucinated experience.

BRAD LINAWEAVER: Now another question. What would be your first encounter with God? Because a lot of people who have known you over the years, when they see your license plate *"I MET GOD,"* or when they see the title of this book, are going to be thinking about your second encounter — which we we're not getting to for a while yet — which you call the Mind Meld with God, which is the most intense meeting with God. But, in fact, this is the first meeting with God?

J. NEIL SCHULMAN: This is the first direct encounter, or actually the first one which I identify as a direct encounter, because I have had experiences –

BRAD LINAWEAVER: But this is not the Mind Meld. That was a later experience?

J. NEIL SCHULMAN: That is correct. This is a frightening

and entirely confronting and unpleasant experience.

BRAD LINAWEAVER: And, it's the most unusual thing about what would be your first encounter of God. The first time you move from agnosticism to pretty damn close to the theistic position, that you now believe there is a God. You're awful close to it now, that the first thing, in effect, you get out of your first encounter with God is?

J. NEIL SCHULMAN: God telling me to stop praying.

BRAD LINAWEAVER: Right! You don't normally hear that from somebody who prays, prays, prays — God finally communicates and says, "Stop all that praying!"

J. NEIL SCHULMAN: Yes. Bizarre. And also, just as bizarre, God laughing at me because he can't believe that I'm afraid.

BRAD LINAWEAVER: Right, so there's two things. The sense of humor, which a large part of your argument about God, you've argued. A large part of your novel, *Escape from Heaven*, and many times on Jack's show when you're explaining your real beliefs, your view that God has a sense of humor, is a very, very important part of everything you've been building out of these experiences. This was the first time you had the idea that God had a sense of humor, his laughing at your fear?

J. NEIL SCHULMAN: Yes. You know a really rough sense of humor.

But two events happen. One of them is Heinlein dies. I let go and a few weeks after that he's dead. Okay? I'm told that I can't keep him alive any more and a few weeks later he's dead. And it's almost like what was going on with me was not, in fact, a caffeine reaction, or a coffee reaction or something like that. But in essence this link, which I have set up psychically with Heinlein, is killing me, and unless I let go I'm going to die.

BRAD LINAWEAVER: Die along with Heinlein or in place of Heinlein?

J. NEIL SCHULMAN: Along with, I'll go with him.

BRAD LINAWEAVER: Were there were links to others, too?

It sounds like there were a couple of links.

J. NEIL SCHULMAN: Yes, but the others weren't dying. I've linked up with a number of people and one of them is dying and it's going to drag me along with it. On the metaphysical level if we want to look at it in these terms, that's what was happening.

BRAD LINAWEAVER: This psychic link with a dying person, dangerous move.

J. NEIL SCHULMAN: Right. And then he dies, May 8th, was that the date?

Now. Something else happens, very significant. I have a dream.

In my dream I am in a courtroom and to my side is my counsel and my counsel is a woman and my counsel is God.

Not, in some same sense, the God who had his masculine hand on my heart a few weeks before that. But God as a female and God is my lawyer.

And there is a panel, a panel of judges up on the judge's bench, and I'm at the defendant's table. Although it's more of a hearing, an inquiry, than a trial, I'm not on trial for having done something wrong. But it is a court of inquiry. And the question before the court, I am told by God, my lawyer who is female, is, "Why was I afraid?"

BRAD LINAWEAVER: The same question repeated?

J. NEIL SCHULMAN: Right. What was it, why was I afraid? God is obviously surprised that I could be afraid and apparently it's something that needs to be resolved.

Here is something very interesting, I am told by God, my lawyer who is female, "The judges need your permission to unlock the records. They are sealed. None of us are allowed to look at them without your permission. Will you give us permission to look so that we can find out why you are afraid of death?"

I said "Yes, permission granted."

BRAD LINAWEAVER: But God is asking for permission to look at sealed records in effect.

J. NEIL SCHULMAN: Not only God but all these judges in this courtroom.

BRAD LINAWEAVER: But what's impressive is, God won't look at these records without permission. Do I have this right?

J. NEIL SCHULMAN: That is correct. And I said, "Yes you can look." And only a few seconds go by — it's not like court is adjourned, we'll be back later — a few seconds go by and they have the answer immediately after I give permission.

I am told, "We have just searched the records and what we found out was that in your immediate incarnation before this you were murdered as an infant and died not understanding what was going on, that the imprint of this carried over into your current life as fear, as an irrational fear of death."

Now, I woke up from this dream and the phobia that had dogged me my entire life up to that moment was gone.

BRAD LINAWEAVER: The phobia was gone?

J. NEIL SCHULMAN: The phobia — something, which had dogged me my entire life – was gone. Okay?

Now what sort of dream is it that you have, that changes your life, that changes something fundamental about you? This was remarkable to me, I have a dream and then suddenly, this thing which I have never been able to go to bed without distracting myself so I wouldn't think about death, suddenly this is gone?

BRAD LINAWEAVER: The dream reinforced the first meeting with God. You could actually argue that this dream is either an epilog to or a second encounter with God, but it's logically tied to that first encounter. It is all of a piece with the hand on the heart and that you've got to let go what you are afraid of, all of that is a piece of the same experience, the same event. Therefore, at the end of what might be called this first encounter with God, you've had a major psychological change and you as somebody who used to be an atheist, and then have gone through this agnostic period, are wondering why the thing that would get you over the hump of such a dire problem, why you of all people ould be imagining that it's God? Since you've never felt for most of your life a need for God.

J. NEIL SCHULMAN: Right

BRAD LINAWEAVER: And yet God shows up in this situation and suddenly a huge life problem of yours is resolved. It's like, what is it eight years later when you have the Mind Meld? There's a good chunk of a decade that separates this event from the next encounter with God. Which means you're not just having — like these people who claim they have born again experiences and God's in their heart and they're in communication with God all the time — you go through a long period of time from this moment to the next time you have an encounter with God.

J. NEIL SCHULMAN: Yes. But something significant happened in between.

Chapter 4: No Religion, Too

BRAD LINAWEAVER: Okay, let's hear that.

J. NEIL SCHULMAN: And it happens in 1995 when I went to a summer event of the C.S. Lewis Society. It happens when I meet C.S. Lewis's stepson, Douglas Gresham. He's come to the United States and is talking at this event that I, as a member of the C.S. Lewis Society, am attending.

After my agnostic period pretty well ends in 1988, and I pretty well consider myself a theist from that point on, I start shopping around to see: am I supposed to become a Christian?

Remember, I don't have anybody Jewish really vying for my attention at that point.

Again, I've met Dennis Prager and I knew he was a practicing Jew. But I was left out of it. In other words, again, the performance aspect, the behaviorist aspect, of Judaism — the rituals, the tradition all that — these were still not things which were appealing to me. My God encounter wasn't drawing me in that direction, and Christianity was.

And it reaches the point where I meet with Douglas Gresham. He's giving this talk, and I really, really warm to the guy immediately. I mean, all my prejudices were in favor of him. I'd read a lot of Lewis and here's his stepson — in essence, one of the only two sons he ever had, the other one being his brother David, who wasn't there.

Douglas Gresham was a very fundamentalist Christian, and on this day, where I attended a C.S. Lewis event at this monastery where Douglas Gresham was the speaker, I had a long conversation with him, and I was right up to the point of thinking maybe I should convert to Christianity at this point. Maybe I should go through the whole thing and be baptized and take Communion. Maybe that's what all of this as been leading to.

I contemplated it and bounced. I tried to take the leap into Christianity and I bounced off it as if it was a solid wall. The results of that are memorialized in the last poem in the *Self Control Not Gun Control* volume called "*A Non-Christian's Prayer to Christ.*"

BRAD LINAWEAVER: I agree, it's in there, more than any of your other poems.

J. NEIL SCHULMAN: The poem is dated June 29, 1995, and so this event happened June 28, 1995.

And the results of it were that I discovered in Christianity something that bothered me about individualism for the first time. That was the idea that if I were saved because I accepted Jesus the way that Christianity was being taught to me – that it demanded that as a precondition to being a Christian you had to accept Jesus as your personal Savior – it was going to be leaving behind everybody I loved. It was going to leave behind my mother and father, it was going to leave behind all of my friends, it was going to leave behind my sister – none of whom were Christians who had accepted Jesus into their heart as their personal Savior.

It seemed evil to me. It seemed wrong to me that I couldn't do anything about that. I mean, I'm supposed to be so selfish as to save myself and leave everybody I love behind? What's that? How could I do that? I can't do that. I know that I'm never going to be converting all of them to Christianity. That means that I'm going to have to accept eternal life by myself.

That's not a gift. That's a punishment. And what god would set things up in such a way as to punish you for following him?

At that point I decided, as much as Christianity had been attracting me through C.S. Lewis and all that, if that was what Christianity actually said — if that was what the nut of it was — I wanted no part of it.

BRAD LINAWEAVER: I've shown your poem to "conventional" Protestants. I've shown your poem to "conventional" Catholics, quite a number of them. Since 1995 when this came out – we're now in the year 2004 – so for almost a decade I've shown this poem to quite a number of "conventional" Christians. The reaction of most of them is exactly what you would expect.

J. NEIL SCHULMAN: Well, what is the reaction that I would expect? Tell me.

BRAD LINAWEAVER: The majority are deeply bothered by your poem because it's making them consider the very point you just raised. Therefore they have to reject what your poem is saying because that's where their minds start. They shut down their brains. To use a phrase from Ayn Rand's *Atlas Shrugged*, when you stop thinking it's a "blank out." In Objectivism, if you challenge an irreducible primary — this is some of the content of their faith — it's an irreducible primary.

However, from my perspective as a lapsed Episcopalian, what I've discovered that's really interesting is those Christians who understand C.S. Lewis the best, when I showed them this poem, their reaction is not negative.

Therefore, I use your poem as one more way of reaching a conclusion I've been moving toward for a large part of my life, which is that C.S. Lewis is so out of step with the rest of Christianity, it's astonishing that most of Christianity — that uses him to try to make people into converts — do not understand the deep message of C.S. Lewis.

I don't believe the "Mere Christian Church" idea in *The Rainbow Cadenza* is a foolish idea at all. Even though Lewis would think that it's foolish, and maintain there's something to be said for the denominations, that's not essential to his message. His message is far more radical. I believe, in earlier eras, C.S. Lewis would have been condemned by all the Christian churches you've ever heard of as a Gnostic heretic, and I believe that C.S. Lewis's Christianity is totally radical, when you consider what he's actually saying in the seventh book of the *Narnia* series, which was your first positive impression of a Christian mind — when you didn't even know it was a Christian mind — and that is that the soldier who is worshiping what everybody else thinks is a demon or an evil god —

J. NEIL SCHULMAN: His name is Emeth.

BRAD LINAWEAVER: Right. Because he thinks that he's worshiping the God of goodness, he is in effect and in reality worshiping the God of goodness, because his intent is such. Because he thinks he's worshiping goodness, he is worshiping goodness.

J. NEIL SCHULMAN: What Aslan says is that no worship that is vile could be directed toward me and no worship which is good could be directed to the demon, that the prayers reach their true heart's desire.

BRAD LINAWEAVER: This point I'm making, this is a very important point. Very few Christians or Jews, or anybody else, are going to pay attention but it's very important. If I ever do become a Christian again, I will be of the C.S. Lewis stripe. When you're dead — in the C.S. Lewis version — you are not finished and your chance to still hear the message of Jesus, and still be saved, continues after death.

Oddly enough, the Roman Catholic Church — which should take that position with their doctrine of Purgatory, something you would think would permeate Roman Catholic teaching — does not.

And oddly enough, many Protestants believe that when you die your chances are all used up. You can see that in all the fundamentalists and all the evangelicals.

Here we have C.S. Lewis who is an Ulster Protestant, a High Church Protestant, who I think has thought this thing through further than the Roman Catholic Church which has a structural legalistic afterlife bureaucracy that might be indistinguishable from Hell, or the militant fundamentalist Protestants who just can't wait to send you to Hell if you make the least mistake.

What's fascinating to me is the Lewis version of Christianity is not normal Christianity at all.

J. NEIL SCHULMAN: And it goes back further than the seventh book of *The Narnian Chronicles*, *The Last Battle*. It goes back to *The Great Divorce* where you have a bus of people from Hell who get to visit Heaven and get new chances.

BRAD LINAWEAVER: And they stay in Hell because they turn it down.

J. NEIL SCHULMAN: But one makes it through.

BRAD LINAWEAVER: I know. But why are most people in Hell? Because, in effect, Lewis is arguing, they choose to be in Hell.

Now, I've heard all kinds of orthodox Catholics and orthodox Protestants, of different denominations, recite those words in various forms. You hear it on the surface and I swear, underneath the surface, they don't mean it. They say the words but they don't believe it. I've heard "conventional" Christians, Catholics and Protestants, who, when I read Lewis' comment that the sins of the spirit are worse than the sins of flesh, they nod, they agree, they say the words right back ... and they continue living lives that are absolute monuments to not believing one word they just said. They live as though they don't believe it, as though they believe the sins of the flesh are worse than the sins of the spirit. That's how they live. Then they say, "Oh, yes, of course Lewis is right — the sins of the spirit are worse than the sins of the flesh." And they go right back acting like the sins of the flesh are worse.

J. NEIL SCHULMAN: And you're right. Lewis did not believe that. He literally believed that the sins of the spirit are worse. What's more, he believed that we retain our free will even after death. That we still have the ability to turn around. It may be harder then. It's like we talked about how the Jewish conception of original sin is that it's harder but not impossible.

BRAD LINAWEAVER:And every fundamentalist Christian,

every evangelical Christian, and all too many Catholics, actually, have used the line from Jesus Christ, from the New Testament, "No one comes to the Father but through me" but they finish the sentence as follows: "Nobody comes to the Father except through me in this lifetime, in the choices you make in this incarnation, right up to the moment of your death, in this particular fraction of space-time."

But that's not what it says. It says, "No one comes to the Father but through me." It doesn't say how many chances you have. It doesn't say when your opportunities end. It does not say!

J. NEIL SCHULMAN: Also, let me tell you something else it does not say. "No one comes to the Father except through me" does not mean that you have to say a particular recitation of words, do a Jewish sort of performance, such as "Yes, I declare that Jesus Christ is my personal Savior and I except Him into my heart!"

BRAD LINAWEAVER: Yada yada yada!

J. NEIL SCHULMAN: It's not demanding the performance. It's not demanding the behavior. It's merely stating a fact like, "If you want to get to Los Angeles you have to take the I-10 Freeway. There's no way to get to Los Angeles unless you get on the I-10."

BRAD LINAWEAVER: You're a guy who walked away from all that Jewish ritual and here's your Christian alternative: Christian ritual. But the fascinating thing — and why I think that Jesus Christ is such an interesting figure to you — is you're actually paying attention to some of the actual content that's coming out of what he is supposed to have said, according to those gospel accounts.

And the last thing is, you are not having any of the conventional Jewish responses. You don't have one molecule of that in you. And instead of getting rewarded by Christians for liking Jesus, your reward is, "Oh, but you've got to be just like us!"

You're right back in Hebrew school.

J. NEIL SCHULMAN: Right.

BRAD LINAWEAVER: Do you think it's possible that most conventionally religious people, Muslims, Christians, Jews and others — and we'll throw in the Buddhists and the Shintoists and the Hindus — would not allow God to have a direct contact with them — would not allow a revelation from God to take place — if it interrupted one of their prayers?

J. NEIL SCHULMAN: I think your question is entirely on point. I think that religion for most people — I'm not going to say for all people, because there are always the exceptions within the system — but for the vast majority of people religion is not fundamentally about seeking God at all.

Chapter 5: *Escape from Heaven*

BRAD LINAWEAVER: So, Neil. I don't believe you have ever had any major experience in your life that you didn't find a way of working into your fiction writing — either a novel or a short story or a script — at some point or other. Therefore I guess none of us should be surprised, with the experiences you were going through, that your latest novel is *Escape from Heaven*. So, why don't you tell us about the genesis of *Escape from Heaven*, as an artist, as well as with your experiences?

J. NEIL SCHULMAN: Well, where I have to start off with are the experiences, because we're doing this book so I can finally — in one comprehensive way — document the reality of my experience and tell people why it might worth paying attention to. That I have, in fact, learned some things from the experiences that are worth my sharing with other people.

Escape from Heaven started, again, with a dream. We've talked about the important dream I had in 1988, following my incident where I had God's hand on my heart, and then the follow-up dream where I was told that in my previous incarnation I had been murdered as a baby and that the trauma of that had gone with me into the current life and that's why I was phobic of death. And that dream ended that phobia.

So, I had already had the experience of at least one dream significantly changing something essential in my life.

Let's go through a few things that have happened to me in the mean time.

Thanksgiving of 1991, I'm going to be divorced. Expectations of raising my daughter in a marriage, suddenly that's shattered.

Shortly after that, I start getting a reputation on Second Amendment issues, first being published in some publications of the California Rifle and Pistol Association, then doing an interview with Professor Roy Copperud on the linguistic analysis of the Second Amendment, which got me a wide reputation.

Then, on January 1, 1992, the first of my Los Angeles Times Op Ed articles appears, and really puts me on the map in the Second-Amendment community. It puts me on the map so much that it leads to three more *L.A. Times* Op Eds, and eventually my book *Stopping Power: Why 70 Million Americans Own Guns*.

So that's what's going on overtly in my life during that period. That's when I meet Dennis Prager. As a consequence of my *L.A. Times* Op Eds, he invites me on his show. The relationship with him starts with my being invited over to his house for a Friday night Shabbat dinner, and I brought my parents along. I met his wife Fran and I met Fran's daughter, Anya, and she became a fan of my writing and we ended up in a lot of interesting conversations.

BRAD LINAWEAVER: And I met some of them through you.

J. NEIL SCHULMAN: Right. Anya was very, very bright. I haven't seen her in a few years.

And I liked Dennis a whole lot. I had not been a fan of talk radio at that point, I didn't know about Rush Limbaugh. So my going on Dennis Prager really started me paying attention to talk radio. And so these are some of the things that are going on in my life.

Now, we go back to, I believe it was February, 1991. I have my first dream in which I go to Heaven. And I'll describe the dream to you.

I find myself in Heaven and I'm going along and I pass an outside café where John F. Kennedy is having coffee with Jackie. Now at that time Jackie was still alive and JFK, of course had been dead since November 22, 1963. And, of course, JFK meant something to me because I had written the "Profile in Silver" episode. So, he was in my consciousness.

But I found it significant, even during the dream, that he's back together with Jackie. Because, after all, Jackie had remarried Onassis and lived many years after 1963 and I had no idea that she would be dead within a couple of years after that. So that again could almost be considered slightly precognitive. Because there was no reason to think that Jackie Kennedy didn't have another 20 years in her, unless you were in the inner circle, which I wasn't. I certainly knew nothing.

So I have this dream and Heaven falls under attack, while I'm there. And I remember flying out of Heaven, flying like Superman.

BRAD LINAWEAVER: Under attack by what or whom?

J. NEIL SCHULMAN: I don't recall but I do know that it was sort of like a civil war. It was war going on in Heaven.

BRAD LINAWEAVER: Well, was it the fallen angels, the demons trying to take it back?

J. NEIL SCHULMAN: I don't know. Heaven falls under a military attack. I need to escape and I jump through a portal, a time portal or something like that. And remember, I'd written time travel before in "Profile in Silver." So, I mean, there are elements of "Profile in Silver" there, with JFK being there.

And I jump through, and I'm trying to get back to my own time. Because Heaven is in the distant future — this part I know — that Heaven is in the future.

I'm trying to get back to my own time and I overshoot and find myself on a corn field or a wheat field of a farm in the 1940's, in Midwestern America — in Iowa or Kansas or something like that. I'm back there trying to figure out if I'm stranded there or if I can I get back to my own time.

So this is the sequence of the dream I had. Now this was a significant enough dream for me that I wrote it down at the time. I made notes of it. And I started playing around with it.

Now I've been asked in previous interviews on the radio where I came up with the name Duj Pepperman. I did not come up with that name for *Escape from Heaven*.

I didn't know why I came up with that name. It was just by sound and who knows where that came from in terms of psychology, why I did that. I didn't know. Duj Pepperman arose in another novel, which I was outlining.

It was going to be set in a world in which nobody slept, in which everybody was awake 24 hours a day. The consequence of that is that it is a world which is psychological entirely different from our world. For one thing, because nobody sleeps, nobody has a concept of dreams. Nobody has a concept of fantasy or imagination or anything like that. It is as prosaic, practical a society as you could possibly have.

It is also a society which doesn't have bedrooms, because you don't need to sleep. And really, if you think about it, having your own house is so you have a place to go to be safe while you are sleeping, while you are vulnerable.

So in other words, that world which I'm outlining, in this novel which I never wrote, is a world in which you really don't have private houses, you really don't have bedrooms. There are places where you can keep your stuff, but more or less you are active 24-hours-a-day and so it's not like you need to go home and rest. There is no need for rest.

BRAD LINAWEAVER: No need for sustained privacy.

J. NEIL SCHULMAN: Right. And so it is a much more communal society, in the sense that there are bath houses for cleaning up and public facilities and rooms which you rent for a few hours at a time or something like that. The entire social structure is different because of that. Duj Pepperman was going to be the freak who was thought to be a medical defective, somebody with a disease.

BRAD LINAWEAVER: Because he slept.

J. NEIL SCHULMAN: Because he sleeps and he dreams. He is trying to tell this society of non-dreamers about his dreams, and they consider it to be a defect of some sort.

BRAD LINAWEAVER: I hope you write that sometime.

J. NEIL SCHULMAN: It's one of those ideas, which, again I've had since the 1980's and haven't written yet.

BRAD LINAWEAVER: At least a short story.

J. NEIL SCHULMAN: Well, I used part of it in *Escape from Heaven*, because, as you recall, I describe the angels in those psychological terms. I took that idea and transplanted it into *Escape from Heaven* in my description of the angels. I made them the non-dreamers who never had to sleep, the ones without the imaginations. And I give the description about how they write beautiful, elegant verse and encyclopedias, but they have no sense of fantasy. An angel could not be a Walt Disney. An angel could not be an Albert Einstein. These require the ability to imagine. What angels lack in *Escape from Heaven* — because I took this model here — is God's creative power, the power of fantasy, the power of philosophical "what if."

BRAD LINAWEAVER: And we have this as humans largely through the gate of dreams?

J. NEIL SCHULMAN: Right. This is where I started the entire thing — which I developed really in discussion with Jack Landman on CyberCity — about how dreams are a medium.

That dreams are, in essence, part of the same imagination mechanism that I was using as an artist.

That, in fact, dreams are the universal art.

That dreams are a universal medium, and a medium in the same sense that we talk about newspapers as a medium, television as a medium, movies as a medium.

That dreams are, in fact, a medium, and there are critical rules that you could apply to dramas in the same way that you have critical rules for these other media.

BRAD LINAWEAVER: By the way, I'm pretty sure that's original.

J. NEIL SCHULMAN: Thank you. But more than that, what it started leading to was the idea that we have always talked about: what is the sixth sense?

BRAD LINAWEAVER: Normally people say E.S.P.

J. NEIL SCHULMAN: Right. But it came to me what the sixth sense really is, is imagination.

Now this is so significant because it was the power of imagination which led me to the experiment of praying in the first place.

Let's realize that "imagination" starts with the word "image," which is a very significant word when you start getting into theology, when God says he created men in His image.

We have image, form, all of these things have to do with Creation, this entire Logos idea which I use in my "Logorights" article having to do with the spirit which enters into the book. That it's all pattern, its all array, form, all of these essential, crucial concepts all come down to us in dreams. Dreams are the medium in which we learn imagination.

BRAD LINAWEAVER: When you say, "God created Man in His own Image," one of the points you're making is that unlike the angels, but like God, we can dream. A very good point, but secondarily –

J. NEIL SCHULMAN: And I use that in *Escape from Heaven* as saying that angels cannot become gods until they've gone through the stage of being human beings so they can learn to dream.

BRAD LINAWEAVER: And could it also be that this is part of the rage Satan — or Lucifer — felt against God and his opposition to God creating these lowly material creatures – us — and giving us all these advantages over what he viewed to be higher spiritual beings? The devil's rebellion against God, which is admittedly first really articulated well by the Puritan Milton in *Paradise Lost*, seems to be logically derivable from an awful lot of religious text preceding it.

J. NEIL SCHULMAN: Right, except — Yes, I agree. But the point is that I'm being a revisionist mythologist here and I'm coming up with my own version, and in my case I'm not going with Milton's mythology of Satan with the pride of sin and "It is better to rule in Hell than to serve in Heaven" and all that. I'm not doing any of that.

In my novel, in my approach, I'm giving Satan her own motivation and that is: she has an actual artistic criticism of Creation. She thinks that God screwed up.

And notice I make Satan a "she."

BRAD LINAWEAVER: Right. The Adam and Eve thing.

J. NEIL SCHULMAN: And again, the paradigm I'm developing here is that in the existence before the creation of Earth you have angels, and you could argue whether they are created by God or spin-offs of God. I use the phrase spin-offs, the same way that they talk about spin-offs of TV shows. That God, in essence, spins off parts of himself into individual souls.

And again, it's not Creation out of nothingness. It's creation out of that which existed. It starts out where everything that exists is God. So the main part of Creation is not merely creating the universe to encapsulate these new souls, but the spin-offs from God. So we all originate as God stuff. As God mind.

BRAD LINAWEAVER: Instead of star stuff from the suns, God stuff spiritually speaking.

J. NEIL SCHULMAN: Right. But the point is that we're not trying to be absorbed back into this big blob. The whole point is that God did this so that we would be separate, so we would be individuated. So we would be something that he can relate to other than Himself. In other words the way I phrase it most eloquently in Escape from Heave is that in the Creation specifically, the spinning off of Minds and Souls and Wills other than His own, God trades or sacrifices — it's a trade because he gets something back — His Omnipresence, His Omnipotence — because these other Souls have powers of their own which matter — and His Omniscience, because they now know things which He doesn't know — it's a trade because what He gets in exchange is the possibility of love.

BRAD LINAWEAVER: This is another area where you are not like a New Age Mystic, though just as many critics will accuse you of various Gnostic Heresies, other critics will accuse you of being some kind of New Age Mystic. Yet the New Age Mystics, almost without exception, are always trying to merge in "The Great Primordial Cosmic One" or "The God Soup," I call it. They want everybody back in the original "God Soup." And you're making the opposite argument. You saying that the last thing God wants is a merging into this pantheistic ultimate "Oneness". That God wants differentiation and basically God wants individuals?

J. NEIL SCHULMAN: Yes.

BRAD LINAWEAVER: That is your central tenet?

J. NEIL SCHULMAN: Right.

BRAD LINAWEAVER: And you certainly express it well in many different ways dramatically in *Escape from Heaven*.

J. NEIL SCHULMAN: And I give His motivation, I say that it's not a sacrifice because God is trading his aloneness for love.

BRAD LINAWEAVER: Right.

J. NEIL SCHULMAN: And that's a powerful imperative for God to create in the first place. Because in doing so God is inventing love.

BRAD LINAWEAVER: And he takes the hate as the price tag.

J. NEIL SCHULMAN: Right. The consequence of Free Will is that there is going to be a down side. There is going to be dissonance as well as the consonance. But what does he get out of it? He gets a higher artistic tension, a higher emotional tension, and a higher thrill than ever before. I identify God as creating because he's a thrill seeker, in the literal sense. He's seeking new thrills.

BRAD LINAWEAVER: I think that's original, too.

J. NEIL SCHULMAN: That Creation is God, as an artist, being driven by esthetics.

BRAD LINAWEAVER: What I think is fascinating about *Escape from Heaven* is you've got Duj Pepperman, who is an extremely interesting character. And by the way you have never ever had your, at least for me as a reader, I have never identified with any Neil Schulman character faster than you made me identify with Duj Pepperman. Chapter One, I love that guy, you had me totally identifying with him. I think it's also, you've done something no writer has ever done, to my knowledge, which is make this loveable identifiable radio talk show host character and every radio talk show host in America's got to have you on and say; "hey making your hero a radio talk show host seems like a good idea to us."

J. NEIL SCHULMAN: Yes.

BRAD LINAWEAVER: That all works.

J. NEIL SCHULMAN: If only it had gotten me on Dennis Prager and Rush Limbaugh.

BRAD LINAWEAVER: But it got you on a lot of radio shows.

J. NEIL SCHULMAN: It got me on some radio shows.

BRAD LINAWEAVER: And the thing is the whole opening gag, for want of a better phrase, which is just as powerful a hook as I've ever read, you know, "I'm God and your biggest fan, I can't believe I got through." The fact that trying to get through to one of these talk radio hosts, God would have trouble too…

J. NEIL SCHULMAN: And by the way, I need to interrupt you at this point, because that particular line "this is God calling, I'm your biggest fan," that itself was given to me directly by God, explicitly, on February 18, 1997. He said, "I've got a gag for you; you have to use this in your book."

BRAD LINAWEAVER: I'm glad you used it.

J. NEIL SCHULMAN: You remember how I talked about being a fan of God, wanting basically be God's fan being able to just hang out with Him?

BRAD LINAWEAVER: Right.

J. NEIL SCHULMAN: You know, get that all–access backstage pass? Okay, but also it struck me that God is our biggest fan because — having given us free will — God is no longer a direct manipulator of us. We could argue about the Old Testament times, but as it is today, God prays that we will do something but He has no way of making us do it because of the free will. God is powerless when it comes to us because He has given us the power over our own lives and all He can do is be our fan and applaud when we do it and go "Awww!" when we don't.

BRAD LINAWEAVER: In other words now the show is up to us and what you're going to suggest is maybe God is bored with the regular traditional religious play and likes it better when we go off on our own and try to do something new. Avante garde theater at least means you don't know the ending of those particular individuals Free Will choices?

J. NEIL SCHULMAN: Yes, my concept of God is an addict of reality TV.

BRAD LINAWEAVER: I said avante garde theater but if you're going say that because the whole universe becomes reality TV. Anyway the only reason I don't agree with that is –

J. NEIL SCHULMAN: –because reality TV is too contrived.

BRAD LINAWEAVER: I think there's nothing more fake than reality TV.

J. NEIL SCHULMAN: God is really a fan of reality TV.

BRAD LINAWEAVER: There is some really good writing going on in the actual real universe, I'm not quite sure how to square that with the free-will concept but I just know that the universe is better written than reality TV.

J. NEIL SCHULMAN: Let's just say that God is a better producer of reality TV than Mark Burnett.

BRAD LINAWEAVER: That is a true statement!

J. NEIL SCHULMAN: Now, having said that we then come up with the multiplicity of souls, first as angels, and the differentia is angels are all intellect and no imagination. And in coming down to Earth, God creates Earth as a kindergarten. Because the angels, being eternal and not having gone through the experience that God did of creating, they don't know what their place in existence is. They don't know their purpose. They can't find meaning, and when you're eternal, not having purpose or meaning is profoundly destructive and chaotic. What I'm really talking about is the spiritual progress here of going from angel, the idea is you come to Eden –

BRAD LINAWEAVER: Earth? To the Edenic earth?

J. NEIL SCHULMAN: Well, yes you come to this and the whole point is that it is a physical existence that encapsulates, where the physical body, in essence, imposes rules and limitations, which didn't previously exist, on the angel and that the angelic spirit takes on the human body and is now subject to gravity, is now subject to force, to be able to push. It is now within a body, which has physiology and a specific anatomy and sees through eyes restricted to certain waves of light and hears sound and touch, all these physical things. The whole point is to become physical rather than merely spiritual, that the journey is exactly the opposite of what everybody seems to be saying in the New Age movement, that we're trying to become more spiritual. No! They come here specifically to be physical. Pure spiritual wasn't working. There was nothing to push against. There was nothing to form a personality.

BRAD LINAWEAVER: Is it that pleasures grow out of the limitations?

J. NEIL SCHULMAN: Yes, because there can be no release if there is no tension. And physicality, physical materialism, provides the tension to allow a unification and a direction, to be able to grow in a particular direction, to be able to align yourself, to be able to center yourself.

BRAD LINAWEAVER: Yes, I've got that. Was that in your head when you wrote *Escape from Heaven*, the novel, or did writing the novel *Escape from Heaven* help coalesce this in your head?

J. NEIL SCHULMAN: It helped coalesce it in my head. A lot of this came out of the writing of *Escape from Heaven*, itself. The writing of *Escape from Heaven* was a revelation to me.

BRAD LINAWEAVER: So, writing the novel as a piece of fiction, or as a work of fiction, helped you understand some of these actual new beliefs that were colliding in you in the same sense that you know that Rand's *Atlas Shrugged* is a novel but her beliefs, and her understanding of what she thinks, is also worked out in the course of writing the novel. Is that how we should view *Escape from Heaven*?

J. NEIL SCHULMAN: Yes, but you need to be aware of the timetable, the timeline of the actual writing of the book itself. Because I have the dream in 1991.

By 1992 I have written an outline of the book and have written excerpts, various different scenes, as samples of what the writing of the book itself is going to be and that's around 60 pages worth of material.

I submitted it to John Douglas, who had been my editor at Avon Books, and he had bought the paperback rights to my first two novels. So naturally, I submitted it to John there. Then John moved over to Harper Prism, when Harper Collins started its science fiction and fantasy line — one of the major media publishers — and I submitted it to him there again.

But the outline I wrote for *Escape from Heaven* back in 1992 was very, very different than what the book finally became and the differences were significant enough that it's worth me noting them.

BRAD LINAWEAVER: Okay, by the way, was the outline back then for a full-length novel also?

J. NEIL SCHULMAN: Yes. But I had not written a full-length novel. I had written around 60 pages, which consisted of a plot outline and samples of various different scenes, a lot of them being dialog, including particularly, a dialog between Duj Pepperman, whom I have now transplanted into this novel from that other thing. I've taken him whole, and I've put him into being brought to Heaven, where God is calling upon him.

Now the situation that I created in that novel, I could almost write a second novel from that original outline, it's so different from what I ended up writing. Because in that version, Lucifer is making a fundamental challenge against God, and by the way — in that novel — Lucifer is male, Lucifer is not a female, Lucifer is not Eve, none of that is in the first outline.

BRAD LINAWEAVER: And there's no Adam either.

J. NEIL SCHULMAN: Right, exactly.

BRAD LINAWEAVER: And no Jesus?

J. NEIL SCHULMAN: You know I don't even remember whether Jesus is a major part of it, I think it's mostly God, and Lucifer, Lucifer being a male.

Here's the distinction that I made in that novel. I have all sorts of time loops and time paradoxes going on. It's much more of a science-fiction feeling book, than the novel as it turned out to be.

Understand the difference.

Nineteen-ninety-two is when I'm writing this. That is five years before my "Mind Meld." I've had the frightening encounter with God. I've had the dream with God as a woman as my lawyer. But I haven't had my "Mind Meld," which doesn't happen until February 18, 1997. This is back in 1992.

And so I'm not as far along, and remember that the actual writing of the novel itself, as it finally got published, happened almost all of it, except for maybe the first few chapters, in the three-and-a-half or so weeks following 9/11 – September 11, 2001.

BRAD LINAWEAVER: Now, I remember the intensity, because I came back a week after the attack, because my flight had been delayed in Atlanta. When I returned I remembered very vividly you during the creative process of writing the novel.

J. NEIL SCHULMAN: Right. And, again, it was the most intensive experience I'd ever had in my life, and certainly I had had nothing that intense. Remember, I mentioned in one of the earlier discussions, that something happened to me during the last month of writing *Rainbow Cadenza*? It's coming back to me now.

BRAD LINAWEAVER: Yes, refresh my memory.

J. NEIL SCHULMAN: Well, I just refreshed my memory. Because again, that happened in 1981. I just remembered it was the writing of the argument between Joan Darris and Hill Bromley, on precisely the theological argument, was when I think that I first apprehended that God was inside my head talking to me.

BRAD LINAWEAVER: But don't forget that in an earlier section of these interviews that we are doing, I talked to you about the fact that I first sensed a huge sea change in you when I read that in *Rainbow Cadenza*, which I had to read that section over and over in order to do my afterword.

J. NEIL SCHULMAN: But there is a significant difference that I have to note now.

BRAD LINAWEAVER: Okay.

J. NEIL SCHULMAN: It scared the Hell out of me.

BRAD LINAWEAVER: Because?

J. NEIL SCHULMAN: Because God was inside me and was, in essence, feeding me this stuff, and I wasn't ready for it.

And I found myself one night sitting in a chair and shaking violently because of what had just happened to me.

BRAD LINAWEAVER: In other words you could never be a happy atheist again?

J. NEIL SCHULMAN: Right. In other words, I didn't know what was happening to me. I was not prepared for it. It was not a pleasant experience. But God was in essence collaborating with me and it was shaking me, physically. And of course, 1981, that's even before I'd had the hand-on-my-heart experience. That's the first time, now that I think about it, that I have God really touching me.

So we have that in November or December of 1981. Then we have the hand on my heart in April, 1988, and the dream where I learn what causes my fear of death a few weeks after that.

The dream of Heaven, which leads to *Escape from Heaven* in

its first version, in 1991, and then the "Mind Meld," in February 1997. Those are the sequences here.

We're getting these jumps. It's not just one experience. It's a series of evolving experiences, with me being better and better prepared to deal with them, without being confronted.

By the time we get to 1997, which we haven't gotten to yet, it's an entirely thrilling and pleasurable experience, as opposed to these frightening experiences that I've had before. The first contacts with God shake me up. This one I'm in ecstasy.

BRAD LINAWEAVER: It goes from pain to pleasure, I had to say that.

J. NEIL SCHULMAN: Yes, it goes from pain to pleasure.

Now, we're back when I'm writing my first outline of , the outline which is so different it could actually be a different novel.

And in many ways it has more of the sense, in terms of style of something like *Dogma*, than it does *Escape from Heaven*. *Escape from Heaven* does not have the sharpness, the sort of anti-religious sharpness. I have Duj Pepperman, in dialog in the first outline of *Escape from Heaven*, really lipping off in a major way to God. He's being very, very accusatory, and God comes across as a lot more cynical and defensive in the first version of *Escape from Heaven* that I'm doing back in 1992, the one that I submitted.

Here are some of the differences. Okay, first of all, Lucifer in that one is male, but Lucifer is not one character. I have Lucifer making the charge against God that God is not a Trinity, that there is a fourth personality — one that we haven't heard about — and the fourth one has gone insane.

BRAD LINAWEAVER: Oh, I like that!

J. NEIL SCHULMAN: Then I have God arguing back and saying, "Well, here's the problem. Lucifer doesn't realize that it's he who's insane."

What has happened, you have had a time loop in which you have two of them, one who calls himself Lucifer, the other one who calls himself Satan, and they are at war with each other.

BRAD LINAWEAVER: I like that. You should write this sometime. It's not necessarily contradictory to the *Escape from Heaven* world and it could be done as kind of a subcreation or even as an alternate –

J. NEIL SCHULMAN: It's a totally different novel. It is fundamentally different because all of the characters are different except for maybe Duj who's pretty much the same, except that Duj is not so accepting of God. Duj is really a militant atheist in the first version.

BRAD LINAWEAVER: Does he change?

J. NEIL SCHULMAN: Well, yes. But he changes because in essence he is given the responsibility of trying to find out the truth — which paradigm is correct? Again, it goes back to this tension, which I'm always talking about, which I had as an agnostic, of here you are presented with multiple paradigms, different people are telling you different things — which one is true? And you're the one who has to figure it out, and everything depends on you choosing right.

BRAD LINAWEAVER: You know what happened to you esthetically? Because I have an idea about this.

J. NEIL SCHULMAN: Go ahead.

BRAD LINAWEAVER: The earlier book would have been an easier sale to a commercial publisher and the older Neil Schulman fans would have preferred it precisely because it was before the experiences you had that did not so much soften you as awaken you to a different universe. In other words instead of being on the attack — which was what they wanted — you're writing a book that's more of a revelation, of, "Look what I found out."

Actually, on a purely literary level, this book you've written *Escape from Heaven*, is more interesting, because a revelation or "look what I found out" is more interesting than just one more programmatic attack.

But the fan base that we've all built as libertarian science fiction writers, and Prometheus Award winners, our fan base is happiest when we're on the attack, not when we're putting forward something that we've learned from just being around awhile, and if not gaining in wisdom at least expanding our database. You've got a lot more thought in *Escape from Heaven* than the first book would have had.

J. NEIL SCHULMAN: Right, because I'd had another mind collaborating with me, which wasn't fully there in 1992.

In other words, the first version I really wrote as a human being. I had some ideas which had been given to me, but it wasn't inspired the same way that what became the final novel was inspired. Most of the inspiration happened during the actual writing in September, 2001.

Chapter 6: Mind Meld

BRAD LINAWEAVER: Neil, the license plate on your vehicle says, "*I MET GOD.*" Is it fair to say that that license plate is not so much referring to the encounters we have discussed up to this point, as the event you're about to describe which almost could be more accurately described from your point of view experience as you merged with God?

J. NEIL SCHULMAN: Yes. Now, we've gone through some pretty dramatic events in my life up to this point.

We've talked about, how at five years old, it's almost like I'm having an encounter with God. I even need to say that looking back, I have a sense of God, early in my life. Not as in any intellectual sense but simply as almost like a taste of benevolence which I have been exposed to. That disappears for a long period of time and starts coming back with my childhood and adult exposure to C.S. Lewis.

Once I am told that Aslan is Jesus, well, that's when Jesus starts becoming very very interesting to me.

BRAD LINAWEAVER: Is that right, the day you were told that?

J. NEIL SCHULMAN: Yes. At the point when I know that one of my favorite characters as a child is supposed to be Jesus, that is the point at which Jesus becomes interesting to me.

BRAD LINAWEAVER: But if as a child you had been told it was Jesus then you never would have read the *Narnia* books at all?

J. NEIL SCHULMAN: That is correct.

Now moving forward, I have a number of different experiences, which are leading up to this thing, and a lot of them are confrontative and not pleasant.

The experience at the end of writing *The Rainbow Cadenza* when I have a feeling that God is possibly within me. I don't even know that it's God at that point but there is something going on and it's shaking me to the core and is making me very, very afraid. At that point I don't even know that its God, I don't recognize it yet.

Nor on those occasions before that, when I had a voice telling me something. For example, precognitive voices telling me things. The event at a Halloween party when I see the woman who later becomes my wife, and I hear a voice saying, as I am looking at her dancing at this party, "If you ask her to dance then you will marry her."

Okay, so I'm having things like that but then it's getting stronger and the voice is becoming more identifiable.

I need to say that all of the times that I am hearing this voice, it's my own voice. It sounds like me talking to myself. It's not like I'm hearing Charlton Heston and it's one of the reasons why later on when we are discussing some of the techniques of the writing of *Escape from Heaven*, why I identify God as a twin of Duj Pepperman. It's because the experience is as if you are experiencing an image of yourself.

Then we have the incident in April of 1988, the hand on my heart, and then a few weeks later the dream where I'm finding out why this pathological fear exists and afterwards has gone away.

We have the dream in 1991 in which I am visiting Heaven for the first time.

And there are two other dreams later on that I'll be talking about in discussions I recorded with Jack Landman on CyberCity.

But then we get to February 18, 1997, and the character of what happens then is so fundamentally different, and so much more intense — of a different character — of everything that has led up to this that it's a singularity in my life. It is so much of a singularity that, even at the time, I marked it as having the effect on my life of being a birthday. That this was a date — February 18th — was going to be an anniversary in my life, very much as important to me as any birthday or anniversary or anything else.

You can almost, if you want to apply the Christian term — and I'm not sure how much of the Christian term applies or not — calling it the day I was "born again." I have used that terminology in conversations, that this was the day I was "born again."

Now, what happened to me on that date. Let me go back –

BRAD LINAWEAVER: Yes, please say everything that happened that day before the event.

J. NEIL SCHULMAN: Right, I have to go back before the event, before that.

Going back five months before that, I started a diet. I had put on weight, probably as a consequence of the unhappiness of going through a divorce. I put on weight and I started a severe diet, and it was a diet which had worked for me before in my life very, very effectively. A diet of reduced calories, usually under 900 calories a day, but also restricting carbohydrates as well to under maybe 30 or 40 grams a day. In addition to which I was walking, exercising.

So the combination of restricted calories, restricted carbohydrates, and exercise put me into the state which the Atkins Diet and the Atkins diet books and Dr. Atkins talk about, which is you go into a state of ketosis.

BRAD LINAWEAVER: And describe what that is...

J. NEIL SCHULMAN: Ketosis is the releasing of ketones into the blood. Ketones are a particular substance, which is released by the process of reducing intake, and having your body in essence be metabolizing from its own resources, in other words metabolizing fats and ketones are released. Now if you ask me why that happens, go talk to a biochemist or a dietician or somebody like that and they'll explain the chemistry to you. I'm simply relating to you that what happens is ketones start appearing in the blood and this is necessary for the burning of fat to happen, a necessary consequence, it's part of it.

Now, an extended period of ketosis, when you add it to

something that happened maybe a month before February 18, 1997, perhaps starting in January, I think I got a mild virus flu cold or something like that but below the level where it was more than sniffles. But I was feeling a little bit of congestion and when that happens you breathe more shallowly, breathe more rapidly. So I was breathing more shallowly. Now in breathing more shallowly, the consequence of that is that you're taking in less oxygen.

Now. You and I have had a discussion previously — and I'm going to put it on the record right at this point — of a few days before we started these tapings, of my going back and reading the beginning of the Four Gospels — Matthew, Mark, Luke and John. Matthew, Mark and Luke agree on the following sequence: that after Jesus is baptized by John the Baptist and John the Baptist hears the voice of God saying "this is my Son whom I well love" — all three of these gospels say that Jesus went into the desert for forty days to be tempted by Satan.

BRAD LINAWEAVER: Yes.

J. NEIL SCHULMAN: Now. Jesus is a physical human being and what is going to happen to Him in the desert is the same thing that I have done to myself by going on this diet and exercise program. He is going to go into ketosis because he is going to be fasting. We don't know how many extra pounds of fat Jesus had at that point. We don't have a physical description of Him, He may have had 30 or 40 or 50 pounds extra fat on Him from high living which are burned off during those 40 days and he becomes the lean, mean Messiah machine in the desert. Okay, but he is going to be in the desert He's going to into ketosis He's going to be dehydrated and that is something that happened to me during this period I became dehydrated.

Within a couple days before February 18, 1997, which was a Tuesday, I have been in the hospital emergency room because I feel myself fainting. I feel my heartbeat is irregular. I feel in serious danger. And so I go into the Emergency Room and what do they do? They say you're dehydrated and they rehydrate me by putting an intravenous saline drip into me to get me back up to rehydration.

This happened twice, at least once before the 18th and I'm not sure exactly which day but it probably would have been the Saturday before. I think it happens within a day or two after the event, on around the 19th or something like that.

So two times during this period, I am in such ketosis of blood poisoning from the excess of ketones in my blood caused from five months of severe diet and exercise and just before and just after that I am dehydrated in ketosis and breathing shallowly. Now breathing shallowly, we have Moses going up to talk to God and he goes to high altitude to do it, less oxygen. So there's a physiological thing going on there too with less oxygen. With Jesus out in the desert as Matthew, Mark and Luke describe it for 40 days — He's going through ketosis and dehydration.

BRAD LINAWEAVER: I've never made that connection before.

J. NEIL SCHULMAN: But in essence the precondition for what appears to happen to me appears to have a physiological component to it and it is described in the *Bible* and I unwittingly, simply by trying to take off weight, have put myself in the same situation as if I'd gone out to the desert to fight the devil.

BRAD LINAWEAVER: As are all the famous mystics throughout history, who have done fasting as a ritual.

J. NEIL SCHULMAN: As a ritual, right. Fasting puts you into ketosis. Apparently the ketones have some toxic effect on the brain, which enables something to happen.

This is not a drug experience. We're not talking about taking an artificially engineered substance, or even a natural plant substance, into the body, to produce some sort of effect. We're not talking about my taking Peyote or Marijuana or LSD or anything like this. This is something, which is in the body's mechanism, itself, which can be triggered by a specific technique, and that technique is denial of food. And something happens in the brain.

Now, the other thing that was happening in my life at this particular time is the civil verdict in the O.J. Simpson trial, where O.J. Simpson is found civilly liable. And I had been watching the criminal trial avidly, and had written couple of articles about it, and paid somewhat amount of attention, but not as much attention to the civil trial.

A week before the February 18th thing, I see something which creates cognitive dissonance in me, something odd. And that is at the end of the civil trial, I see Ron Shipp, who is supposed to be one of O.J.'s friends, hugging the man who has sued and just won a lawsuit against his friend, O.J. Simpson. I see Ron Shipp hugging Fred Goldman at the conclusion of that trial.

BRAD LINAWEAVER: And that strikes you as very odd?

J. NEIL SCHULMAN: It strikes me as very, very odd. Yes! He testified against him but now he's hugging who is in essence O.J. Simpson's worst enemy and he's supposed to be a friend?

It created cognitive dissonance in me to the extent that I woke up and said, I have been looking for somebody who could have possibly framed O.J. Simpson, and here we have Ron Shipp, who is an intimate friend of O.J. –

BRAD LINAWEAVER: Or supposed to be.

J. NEIL SCHULMAN: Well, intimate in the sense that he has access to the property, okay? He's done security work for O.J. at various different times. He is an experienced police officer who describes himself on the stand as having detective skills. Even though he wasn't a detective grade, he nonetheless had L.A.P.D. training, and had worked detective details, had been a training officer at L.A.P.D. Academy. And he fulfills all the psychological conditions of somebody I would have looked at to be a fan boy who then turns on the object of his worship.

Okay. At that point I started doing the research which

eventually, a few years later — actually a few months later in the web version but then a few years later, in 1999, in the published book version — becomes my book *The Frame of the Century?*.

So that is what is the center of my focus during that week, while these physiological things are going on with me, is that I am starting, for the first time, to become an active researcher in the O.J. Simpson case, triggered by my observing, in essence, the last legal aspect of it, which is the liable verdict in the civil case.

So that's where my focus is.

Now, on the Monday before, when I go to the Karl Hess Club, suddenly it occurs to me I have done things over the previous few days. I have, in essence, sent out information to various different people. I have met during that previous week with detectives at the L.A.P.D. and presented my theory to them. I have presented it to O.J.'s attorneys. And that night it occurs to me, if this has gotten to Ron Shipp, if this information that I am presenting a theory that Ron Shipp was involved in these murders and framing O.J., I could be in physical danger.

BRAD LINAWEAVER: I remember you from that period and I remember I've never seen you more paranoid.

J. NEIL SCHULMAN: Right, because I suddenly thought, "what have I done to myself? I've exposed myself, I've exposed my family here, and I need to take immediate action to batten down the hatches before because if I am vulnerable I wouldn't know about it." In essence I go to high alert.

That night I went to my bank, I withdrew cash, got into my car and started wondering where should I put myself for the next few days, while I'm making further contacts? Who can I go to who I wouldn't necessarily be traced to, if I were to go there as a safe house? Should I drive to Jean, Nevada, and stay in one of those $18 a night hotel rooms, which I could easily afford to do? Is there some friend who could be useful to me?

What I essentially decided to do that night was drive out to Randy Herrst's house and ask him for help. I drove out late at night to Randy's. He came down with me, and we basically sat in my car, and I laid out all of this to him. And I said, "Look, am I just being paranoid or is there a real possibility that I'm in danger here?"

He said, "Neil, the point is that you have no way of knowing, and so, yes, you were right to take protective steps. Now let's figure out what we're going to do, to resolve this quickly, in such a way that you don't have to go into hiding if somebody really is pissed off with you and is going to take some action."

Okay. Now what we resolved to do was go to an attorney whom we both knew, through Second Amendment work, who had been involved in filing some of these suits against the Los Angeles Police Department about concealed carry licenses for handguns, and seek his advice here.

So, we made an appointment that morning to go to this attorney in Beverly Hills, and sit with him, and ask him what should be our next step?

So around 10 o'clock in the morning of February 18th I've been up all night talking with Randy and strategizing this. So now in addition to the physiological condition of ketosis and dehydration, which I've been experiencing, I've now gone without a night's sleep.

And we go have the meeting with this attorney in Beverly Hills. He says, "Well, look, I know another attorney who has a direct contact with Gil Garcetti at the Los Angeles County District Attorney's office. Let's present your material to him."

And so we make an appointment for me to go back to his office later that day and meet with him again.

Now, having had this first meeting with Randy and this attorney, in the morning of February 18th, I need to get some sleep. Randy thinks it's a good idea if I not go to sleep unprotected. That I not go to sleep and simply be alone.

BRAD LINAWEAVER: You mean have somebody on guard?

J. NEIL SCHULMAN: Have somebody on guard. This is Randy's suggestion. Randy is acting in essence as my bodyguard at this point. But Randy also has gone a night without sleep and he needs to go home and sleep as well, before this meeting, and so we called up another friend of ours, Dafydd ab Hugh, and I said, "Dafydd can you come over to my place?" and I explained the situation in brief. I said, "There's some potential for danger. I don't know exactly how to calculate it. It may be a small potential. It may be a large potential. But we don't know. Could you just come over to my place and just sort of watch my back while I get some sleep?"

And Dafydd said, "Yes," and he came over.

Dafydd gets there around 11:30 or 11:45 in the morning. And Randy says, "Okay, I'm going to go home and get some sleep and I'll meet you later today, and we'll go over to the attorney's office again."

So Dafydd is out in the living room, and I say, "Okay, I'm going to lie down." And I go into my bedroom, and I close the door to lie down and get some sleep before the meeting.

And I lay down on my bed, and about ten seconds later — almost immediately — something has happened and I sit up in bed.

The first impression I'm having is that I have just traveled a long way, and I've just arrived.

And I'm looking around and I'm thinking, "Where am I? What's going on?"

Remember, all of this is from my internal perspective.

Okay. I am sitting up and saying, "Huh! Now I'm here. I've just arrived." But I wonder what's going on.

And suddenly I sit up, stand up, and I remember that I am God.

The only way to describe it is not, this is unlike these previous things that have happened to me where when God has His hand on my heart I know that it is God's hand or I am in a dream and God is next to me as a woman or any of these other contacts where it's a voice. This is none of those. I am God at this point. I wake up and I remember that I am God. I stand up and the first impression I have standing up is that I feel too tall.

BRAD LINAWEAVER: Hmm, that's odd.

J. NEIL SCHULMAN: Why am I so tall? This is bizarre, I'm looking at myself — I'm looking at my body — I'm so tall and this body is so out of shape. How is it that this body is so out of shape? What happens then is that I walk out of the room and I see Dafydd sitting in the living room.

BRAD LINAWEAVER: What is Dafydd doing?

J. NEIL SCHULMAN: He sitting there reading or maybe watching TV or something like that, and I'm just looking out there, and he's saying, "Is everything okay?"

I say, "Yes, everything seems to be okay." I said, "I guess I'll go back into the bedroom."

BRAD LINAWEAVER: You have not slept yet?

J. NEIL SCHULMAN: I have not slept yet. But I have chatted a little bit with Dafydd and suddenly it's starting to come to me that I'm looking around and –

This was at an apartment that I was renting on Overland Avenue in Culver City. This was a two-bedroom apartment and it was very cluttered because every career that I've ever had accumulates stuff, and I'd been doing a radio show in 1992 and so I had all the recording studio stuff I had set up to do a radio show in there. And I had all the things from my previous electronic publishing venture, SoftServ, all those business records and filing cabinets. I had been writing about the Second Amendment and so I had stacks of newspapers with articles that I'd written, and the place is pretty well cluttered. The place is as much a storage closet as it is an apartment. It's an office, a storage closet, and a living residence, and I had always been very frustrated at how cluttered this was, and felt really like it was a cage that I was trapped in it. That I didn't have enough space.

Suddenly I'm looking around at this little two bedroom apartment with all this stuff in it, and I have a different view of it then I've ever had before. I'm not seeing as a cage anymore. I'm seeing it as a nest, which I have built for myself as a protection.

I'm realizing as this is coming along, as my mind is sifting through all the new stuff, that J. Neil Schulman is a fictional persona, which I have created my entire life, because up until that moment I was hiding from myself the fact that I was God.

This is what is going through my mind while this is happening.

Now. One can say that I'm going through a psychotic episode at this point. Certainly the physiological conditions for a psychotic episode — ketosis, dehydration, lack of sleep — all of these various things can add up and say that I'm having a break with reality.

But the problem is that I'm not experiencing it as a break with reality. I'm experiencing it as the most clarity and intense ability to perceive, and to think, that I've ever had in my life. Far greater. It's not that I am diminished in any sense. I am enhanced.

Okay? And I am looking at Dafydd, and I'm experiencing something in looking at him that I have never had before, a cognitive enhancement. Because what I am able to do — and it's hard to describe this even today because the words don't really match any other experience that either I have had or you have had — presumably.

I'm looking at Dafydd and suddenly it's like there is a twist going on in the way that I am looking at him and I am seeing him in four dimensions. I'm seeing the core of his soul and I'm seeing him as a four-dimensional event, with a beginning and something going off into the future. I'm not seeing a death but I'm seeing a different segment, as if I'm looking at him through a different time angle or something like that.

Suddenly my angle of looking at him is shifted and I'm not seeing him in the normal way from the surface, as one segment. I'm seeing a four-dimensional event. And what I'm really seeing is, I'm seeing into his heart. I'm seeing his desires.

BRAD LINAWEAVER: You mean his soul.

J. NEIL SCHULMAN: I'm seeing the core of his desire and I'm seeing that the core of his desire is to make it as a serious writer. Above everything else, that's what he wants, is to really be a serious writer.

I don't say any of that to him. I realize that I am revealed to myself. The game of hiding from myself is over and now obviously I'm here. And now the mission begins.

This is what's going through my mind at that point and I begin asking myself certain questions about what's going to happen.

Am I going to have to go through a crucifixion? No that won't be necessary this time.

What will happen? A circle will form around me.

What's going to happen in terms of the O.J. thing — is my investigation correct? Yes, your intuition there was correct.

All of this libertarian stuff, which I had been writing about — yes that's all correct. The principles of natural law and free will and that sort of thing. Yes that is correct.

Guns. I'd been doing all this stuff with guns. Well, yes, we eventually die, but protecting the good requires that good people protect themselves from the evil people.

And all these sorts of things are going through my mind. It's not even like I'm being told things or something like that. It's like a continuous revelation going on as I'm remembering who I am and who I've been.

Chapter 7: Revelations

BRAD LINAWEAVER: Do you remember the 1988 event, the hand on the heart event and the dream with the female God figure, do you remember them now from the God point of view and remember Neil as a different party during those events?

J. NEIL SCHULMAN: Yes. In other words, Neil Schulman has been a separate personality who's been invented to hide from me as God who I really am. And I'm seeing that it is a separate being but one who is invented. It's my cover story to prevent me from knowing myself so I can acclimatize myself to the situation.

There's also something else and this also relates to one of the reasons why I take the existence of Jesus seriously, is that somewhere in the back of my mind is some sort of memory of having done this before. I don't remember the time or the place but I know I have been here doing this before. Now I don't know whether it's as Jesus or somebody else but I recall: I have done this before I have done this journey where I enter into the body and reveal myself to myself before.

BRAD LINAWEAVER: But it's vague?

J. NEIL SCHULMAN: Yes. I don't have full memory of what's going on but there are certain things that I'm able to do.

Now, I tell Dafydd, "You know what? I'm okay here. I'm not going back to bed. Why don't you go home?"

BRAD LINAWEAVER: Even though you've not slept?

J. NEIL SCHULMAN: Even though I've not slept. I don't need to sleep at this point, okay. I have a higher level of energy than I have ever had in my entire life. The idea that I would need to sleep is irrelevant. I'm not feeling tired. I'm feeling at the highest energy level I've ever been.

BRAD LINAWEAVER: You've been awake how many days?

J. NEIL SCHULMAN: I've probably been awake, at this point,

for probably 30 hours. But I'm in another space. I tell Dafydd, "You can go home. You're okay to go."

I turn on the TV and I'm watching the news. And I find that the people on TV, I have the same ability to look at them as I did with Dafydd. The fact that they're on TV doesn't restrict me, I could look at them and I have this same four-dimensional view of their souls and looking and seeing who and what they are, that I had with Dafydd in person.

Now, I'm going to do something a little out of sequence here. Dennis Prager, years later, talking about how we know God is God, on one of his radio programs, says that what distinguishes God from everything else is that only God has the power to look inside the soul.

Now, from Dennis's standpoint, the fact that I'm able to look into people's souls while this is going on, Dennis — even though he would probably disagree with the conclusion — by his logic, I am really God during that period. Because I had that power of God that only God has.

And here's something else, people constantly ask me "How do you know that it wasn't a demon pretending to be God?"

BRAD LINAWEAVER: Actually, I was going to ask you that, but you already asked yourself.

J. NEIL SCHULMAN: Right. And the answer is: because I know who I am. I know myself, and I know my own identity, and my own identity while this is going on is: I am God. There's no question about it. It's not somebody fooling me, or something like that. You know who you are. You know you're Brad Linaweaver, I know I'm Neil Schulman. While this was going on I knew I was God. That's who I was.

BRAD LINAWEAVER: So it's not you were on the receiving end of the entity. You are the entity. And when people ask that question, they could more legitimately ask in 1988 — the hand-on-your-heart experience — they could ask, "Was that a demon?" Or they might ask the woman in the dream you thought was God, they might ask, "Was that a demon?" But the reason this is not the right question to ask about this event, which you call the Mind Meld, is precisely because you are not at this point on the receiving end. You are the entity yourself, there's the difference. Is that right?

J. NEIL SCHULMAN: Yes, that's correct.

Now, I am observing people all day long. Every single person I'm seeing I am in essence having this God's eye view, this cognitive penetration beyond the skin, being able to go beyond the shell. I'm starting to see people almost like fish swimming in an ocean and the fish imagery is very important because that, of course, is something, which is very central to the imagery in Christianity. But in essence, because I am seeing people not just as the physical flesh anymore, but I am seeing them as this four-dimensional event — with the present thick right here and then becoming thin at the two ends as it sort of like goes around this curve — from this odd angle that I'm at looking at them. People look to me almost like, it's almost like this emanation around them is like fish swimming. That's the impression I'm getting when I'm wrapping around and able to look at their past and their future.

A couple of people I saw on TV, three of them I remember seeing on TV; one of them was President Clinton, one of them was Dick Gephart, and a third one on a talk show was Gordon Liddy

And I'm going to go in a different order. Dick Gephart I simply got the impression of, here is a man who is not being honest with himself. I got a sense of somebody who is not really fundamentally being honest with himself. That he's hiding something important from himself. It's like he's putting on a mask to prevent him from knowing who he is.

Gordon Liddy I'm seeing on a talk show and he's trying to make jokes and they're falling flat on the audience and I realize that he's talking over their heads, that he's far too intelligent for the audience he's trying to tell these jokes to. What I'm getting off of him is the severe sense of regret of an ex-military officer and an ex FBI man –

BRAD LINAWEAVER: –reduced to this.

J. NEIL SCHULMAN: — reduced to this. The thought which comes across most strongly looking at him, and sensing this, is, "What I would give for one more mission where I could make a real difference." Now I later found out that he wrote a novel with somebody in that situation as the premise of it. But I didn't know that then, so I take that as almost like a validation of what I was seeing.

BRAD LINAWEAVER: What about Clinton?

J. NEIL SCHULMAN: Clinton? I had been extremely hostile toward Clinton before this, because of all his support for anti-Second-Amendment gun control. And I got such a burst of warmth in looking at him because this is what I saw.

I saw him alone in his bedroom — walking into his bedroom at night — and a Secret Service man saying to him "Good night, Mr. President." And he goes in there and he feels that he is at the center of the world with this gap of loneliness around him, alone in this bedroom, as he walks in for the first time. With the entire world around him and he feels the weight of it and he's thinking, "How did I ever get here where I have all this responsibility? I thought I was just playing this cute game of running for office and I would get all this benefits and be able to do all these neat things. Here, I find here, with this weight on me and I'm all alone and there's really nobody who I can ask and share this with. That this is such a responsibility and there's no way I can share it with anybody."

And I got the most immense sense of responsibility and loneliness of a man who saw himself as a con man and now he says, "What have I gotten myself into?" and he feels the responsibility of what he's gotten himself into. That was what I perceived from him.

BRAD LINAWEAVER: And you never had anything remotely like that as a thought or a feeling about Clinton before?

J. NEIL SCHULMAN: Correct. Before I simply hated him.

Okay. Now, later that day, Randy and I went to the meeting with the lawyer in Beverly Hills and there was really nothing dramatic that happened there. But it was just the same sort of internal thing going on, while externally I was still being the J. Neil Schulman. I was not telling anybody what was going on inside me.

BRAD LINAWEAVER: You never told Dafydd?

J. NEIL SCHULMAN: I never told Dafydd. I never told Randy. I wasn't telling anybody.

BRAD LINAWEAVER: Until later?

J. NEIL SCHULMAN: Until much, much later. Because it was like J. Neil Schulman was going to be my secret identity. In other words I wasn't going to reveal myself, but this was what was going on inside. And so we went to this meeting and this other lawyer was there, who knew Gil Garcetti and had that meeting then.

Later that evening I went home, and probably around maybe eight o'clock that night, suddenly I had the feeling of withdrawal. That suddenly there was a separation again, and suddenly — as shockingly to me as it had begun — it was over again, and I was just Neil Schulman again. That was as surprising to me as when it started. Because it was shocking to me when the identity change happened and then again it was just as shocking to me when, only few hours later, it ended again. Because I thought that this was the new situation. I had no idea that it was going to stop.

Now, during that day, a number of different thoughts came to me and it's hard for me to even keep an inventory about them.

But for example, when I thought about race and blacks — African Americans — the thought came to me immediately, "Magnificent destiny. These people have a magnificent destiny."

I didn't know exactly what in the future, or how far in the future, but I knew that even speaking in terms of race — which is, by the way, alien to me, since I'm a thorough individualist — that there was something about the African Americans, that at some time in the future they were going to do something which was going to be glorious. And all the suffering that they've gone through was going to have meaning.

BRAD LINAWEAVER: Did you think about any other "races" during this period?

J. NEIL SCHULMAN: No. It was basically just catch as catch can. There was no organization to it. First of all I felt no pressure for time because I didn't know that the experience was going to come to an end. I thought it was an ongoing sort of thing.

I also had, during this period, thoughts about churches, and one of the things that came to was the idea that churches are so dull and boring and ritualistic and they're not fun. They should be a place that everybody wants to go because they're so enjoyable, rather than dry and dusty and ritualistic and authoritarian. And the specific thought, during this period, that came out, was that it would be the sort of place that a child would say to his parents, "I have my homework done. Can we go to church, now?"

BRAD LINAWEAVER: Yeah. I got that. Excellent.

J. NEIL SCHULMAN: And that all the top acts would be dying to play in church.

So it was just little things, all the way through.

And, of course, during this period, God was aware that I was writing the novel on *Escape from Heaven*, and He gave me the joke, "I'm your biggest fan."

And very little of the novel had been written at that point. It was probably either a chapter, or less than a chapter, at that point.

BRAD LINAWEAVER: But you're saying that God gave you your best gag?

J. NEIL SCHULMAN: Gave me my best gag, right.

BRAD LINAWEAVER: One serious question about this period of the experience. Did you at any point, even for a few seconds, in the God mind, think about the Arabs and Jews?

J. NEIL SCHULMAN: No.

BRAD LINAWEAVER: Interesting. I wonder why that is?

J. NEIL SCHULMAN: Because I was focusing on things around me, things that were coming into my view. First of all, it was a busy day with everything that was going on, and so it was like everything was speeded up and that there was an awful lot going on. But it wasn't organized in any sense. It felt like the beginning to me of a much longer process.

Now, later that night, one of the first things I did, after this happened, was I went to the computer and I wrote the poem which is titled "A Revelation," which appears on the frontispiece both of *The Frame of the Century?* and then I later put it as the frontispiece of *Escape from Heaven*. That poem was my first attempt, now that it was over — even though it had only ended a few seconds or few minutes before — to memorialize it.

BRAD LINAWEAVER: The next question of import I'm going to put to you, in fact it's the only important question I have left for the rest of this book, is attitudes, opinions feelings, that are in any way different after -

J. NEIL SCHULMAN: Oh, yes! Something crucial that I did leave out, you just reminded me! And this is absolutely crucial, because this is the core of the "revelation." How could I have left this out? Thank you Brad, thank you!

The core thing that came to me during this experience, while it was going on, was that I got a sense of how God's mind works, because I was inside of it. And what I saw, first of all, was that I had always thought of God looking out universally and seeing everything going on at the same time and just sucking everything in, and then He just does a little something here and a little something there, and it's like this all encompassing warm cloud.

That was not what I was getting. What I was getting was a direct focus. That God focused on one particular task at a time, just like we do. Now, He was seeing it in four dimensions, because I was seeing it in four dimensions, okay? I was seeing an event cycle when I looked at a person, this four-dimensional, beginning and an end, sideways sort of view, in the God-mind perceiving this. But it was focusing on one thing at a time. God acted specifically. He focused on a task then He would do whatever He needed to do there and then He would go on to something else. It wasn't like He was doing everything at the same time. And that was one of the things that changed my concept of God, that He was an actor.

Something else, and the main thing that was conveyed to me during this experience was how utterly powerless God felt about what was going on here, about the planet. That the free will that operated in every single person was real, and that the choices that everybody makes have real consequences, so much so that God, He could invite, He could try to persuade, He could try to sweet talk, all of these sorts of things, but ultimately He was powerless to impel what was going to happen from our choices. He could try to convince us, just like a parent talking to a child. But ultimately He had to let what was going to happen, happen by itself and He was thrilled when we made the right choice — I could feel the joy when He observed something happening where somebody made the right choice at the point where the moral choice needed to be made — and it was like this lonely disappointment when somebody didn't. That was the core of this, this feeling of and again during this entire period... People are always talking about the cliché "God is Love, okay?"

BRAD LINAWEAVER: I thought that was only part of it...

J. NEIL SCHULMAN: Right but everybody says, "God is Love." What I was experiencing during this was a benevolent outlook that I had not felt since I was a small child.

BRAD LINAWEAVER: But is that necessarily the same as love?

J. NEIL SCHULMAN: Well, I'm not even going to try to parse the word right now. Words are inadequate to describe what was going on. That's something that I cannot emphasize enough. That the verbal forms that we use are entirely inadequate to describe what I was experiencing, but I have to try and the label doesn't matter here. Let me just try to get it out, okay? That's what I'm here for right now is to try to document this. To try to go from the experience of what was going on to get it into words to communicate to other people.

This warmth, this benevolence, this jolly sense of humor, this feeling of caring, you could trivialize it with some cynical statement about warm and fuzzy or something like that...

BRAD LINAWEAVER: No I like benevolence because that's actually a more descriptive term than love, but does the benevolent warm feeling apply to all humanity or only certain select groups and select individuals?

J. NEIL SCHULMAN: It was not an angry, critical God. He wasn't looking out and being angry at everything that's going on. It's not this stern looking around and, "Boy, this is terrible!" Its not like George Burns in the *Oh God!* movies saying, "You're polluting my oceans! See if you can make a mackerel!" It was none of that. Okay...

BRAD LINAWEAVER: That's why I'm asking...

J. NEIL SCHULMAN: It was none of that. It was looking around and it was the feeling of either thrill when He saw what we were doing right, and just this forlorn despair when He saw somebody who at the point when they had to make a correct choice failed to make it.

BRAD LINAWEAVER: Well, hold that thought for about three seconds while I ask this question.

God being full of joy when we make a right decision and God being sad or frustrated when we make a wrong decision, the way a parent might feel about a child?

J. NEIL SCHULMAN: Yes.

BRAD LINAWEAVER: Then what I want to ask — I am stuck with words so you've got to give me a chance to express the question in words, because I don't know how to ask the question in any other way then with words. Is it fair to say that the impression you have from, and of, the God mind, is regarding human conflicts, God does not take sides?

J. NEIL SCHULMAN: That far too abstract and intellectualized and removed for me to respond to, from the standpoint of the experience that I was having.

BRAD LINAWEAVER: Then let me phrase it...

J. NEIL SCHULMAN: But let me...

BRAD LINAWEAVER: I was going to try again, but all right.

J. NEIL SCHULMAN: Try again, but let me complete this one more thought that's coming out here. Okay? Again, you're drawing me out, and it's starting to bubble up.

The first thing that I experienced early on in the experience was the sense of benevolence about my life up to that point. In other words, I'm a very hypercritical person. I was always looking at my failures, the things that I considered wrong about myself. They all seemed unimportant while this was going on. It was like, "Well, that is so unimportant, these flaws that you've experienced, as compared to the important things." In other words, I got such a sense of approval. I was experiencing a self-approval. But I don't think that I have ever had such a feeling of self-acceptance, at that moment. So it was acceptance of myself, acceptance of everybody around me, feeling that it wasn't going to be a tragedy. The mission as it was going to unfold was not going to have to be this violent tragedy that you see in *The Passion of the Christ*, where you're nailed up on a cross. That this time, it was going to be different. The mission was going to be more fun this time and not like the last time. Okay, now I think I've probably characterized the essentials of it as much as I can.

BRAD LINAWEAVER: Is the "God" idea that God has an idea of what is good and evil, in terms of choices, but does not view human beings as good or evil on the basis of the choice, but views the choice as good or evil? I hope I phrased that very precisely.

J. NEIL SCHULMAN: This is what I was experiencing precisely. What I was looking out and looking for when I looked into somebody was: what was their most important central heartfelt desire? What was pulling them along? What were they desiring? Were they desiring to be good or were they desiring something else, and being good was unimportant? That was what I was experiencing.

BRAD LINAWEAVER: Well, let me narrow it down. Does God think Arabs are evil?

J. NEIL SCHULMAN: Brad, you're trying to impose upon my interpretation of the experience into something...

BRAD LINAWEAVER: I'm just trying to figure out if God loves all humanity or not, that's all I'm asking. You brought up love.

J. NEIL SCHULMAN: I wasn't experiencing it that way. It wasn't like this global, United Nations sort of thing, Brad. Maybe that's where I'm having my greatest difficulty conveying this. It wasn't like that. I wasn't thinking in terms of Arabs and Jews. Briefly, for a moment, I was thinking in terms of blacks — and just got the thought of a magnificent destiny — but that was only because that sort of drifted into my consciousness because I was working on the O.J. Simpson thing.

BRAD LINAWEAVER: Before I drop this, the only reason I'm asking is you once asked Dennis Prager, if he met God, what he would ask God, and Dennis Prager didn't have much of an answer. You were being very precise, asking Dennis Prager what Prager might ask God about Himself.

J. NEIL SCHULMAN: Right. That was what I was asking, what Prager would ask God about Himself.

BRAD LINAWEAVER: But still, if you asked somebody a question about himself it could involve opinions about others. If somebody asks Brad Linaweaver a question about Brad Lineaweaver, himself, it could actually touch on opinions Brad might have about...

J. NEIL SCHULMAN: I was getting some opinions, okay? I saw that God thought the churches were dull and should be fun. I was experiencing that God looked well upon libertarian writings and natural law, and He looked and saw that that was good. Okay? And I saw His view of how He views us as, what is our most heartfelt desire? In other words that was what He was looking at. Almost everything seems unimportant to Him other than what was in our heart to do. What was compelling us? Were we drawn to be good, and was that important to us? Did we feel that it was important to make a right choice or that we can simply blow off making the right choice for something else? Okay? That is what I was experiencing, and in terms of Arabs and Jews, or something like that, He wasn't looking at it in terms of some sort of collective conflict or something like that. He would simply, maybe, be thinking, if He saw a specific action, maybe the point at which a terrorist has to decide whether to execute a hostage or something like that. What is in his heart at that moment? Is there empathy for this person who is in his charge, or something like that? That's how God would view it. "Terrorist, what is in your heart? What do you want to make of yourself?" That is how He would view it.

BRAD LINAWEAVER: Well, I'll wrap up this sequence of questions by merely saying the people who read this book may wonder, if they had God's mind, or access to God, what they might ask or wonder. You can deal with it as you wish.

J. NEIL SCHULMAN: All I can say is that Neil Schulman wasn't phrasing it in terms of questions of God while the experience was going on because Neil Schulman was somewhere off away while this was going on. It was being recorded in Neil Schulman for later use, but the experience itself, I was not Neil Schulman thinking about what questions do I want to ask God. And if it happened to you, you wouldn't be Brad Linaweaver thinking of what questions you want to ask God because you wouldn't be Brad Lineaweaver during the experience. You would be God.

If what God was concerned about about each of us was our heart-most desire to do good and evil, and what we've become because of it? Then how is that not answering your question, that what He is concerned about is right choices?

BRAD LINAWEAVER: Because there's an emotional component missing in that answer of are we God's children or not?

J. NEIL SCHULMAN: Brad, if during this experience I'd come across Adolf Hitler and looked into his soul...

BRAD LINAWEAVER: — or Genghis Khan or Jack the Ripper....

J. NEIL SCHULMAN: — or Joseph Stalin or Jack the Ripper or anybody like that, then I would know the answer to that question, and be able to give you the visceral and emotional reaction that you're asking for. All I can say is the experience, as it was happening, was too short. I had too many other things going on, and I wasn't going out looking for it.

I was not fully revealed to myself. In other words, there were still things that were just a taste of what was going on.

Now, you and I have talked about this previously, but not during this tape series that we're doing right here, about an opinion that I expressed to you. Remember that I started out this section talking about Jesus, after His baptism, going into the desert for 40 days and then coming back. And then, according to the first three of the Gospels — not John, John is an exception to this.

BRAD LINAWEAVER: You talking about the ketosis?

J. NEIL SCHULMAN: Right. Jesus does not perform His first miracle until He gets back from the desert.

BRAD LINAWEAVER: That is correct.

J. NEIL SCHULMAN: And what I have expressed to you is that what happened to me was just a taste of the experience Jesus had and He had it for far longer, and far deeper, and was therefore able to deal with it over a much longer period and at a much more intense level. Getting to the point that He was able to effect miracles. I didn't do any miracles during those eight hours.

BRAD LINAWEAVER: But you had a taste of it?

J. NEIL SCHULMAN: I had a taste.

BRAD LINAWEAVER: That's got to count for something.

J. NEIL SCHULMAN: Right. So what I am saying is that I had an experience akin to what the descriptions of what Jesus...

You see, we don't have a Gospel According to Jesus. We only have the accounts written by the people around Him.

BRAD LINAWEAVER: True.

J. NEIL SCHULMAN: Okay? And so I don't recall that anybody ever asked Jesus what was going on inside Him.

BRAD LINAWEAVER: No, Jesus was not interviewed by Larry King.

J. NEIL SCHULMAN: No. It didn't occur to any of them to ask Him the sorts of questions that you're asking me, and the answers would be fascinating, wouldn't they?

BRAD LINAWEAVER: Well, if you put me in front of Jesus Christ I would ask these questions.

J. NEIL SCHULMAN: Right. Of course, and so would I.

BRAD LINAWEAVER: My questions is this, because I've been meaning to bring this up through the entire interview, I never have.

Thomas Jefferson is, I think, one of the most libertarian of all the founding fathers, and although he only related to Jesus

Christ in terms of His moral teaching, and tried to reject all the really important God aspects, from my point of view, he still argued that what Jesus was preaching was benevolent and sublime. I like that phrase, he says what Jesus brought to the world in terms of His teachings was benevolent and sublime and, he says, clearly preferable to all the ancient philosophers.

So, and this is always the problem I had when I was a Christian and when I lost my faith the problem remained with me, and remains with me to this day.

When Jesus Christ said to forgive your enemies, I've never fully been able to understand that. Whether I was in faith or out of faith, and since you've had this Mind Meld, I want at least to address that before we move on. This is the last Jesus Christ question I will ask in this interview.

Did you get any feeling or sense of what that really, truly means?

J. NEIL SCHULMAN: Yes.

BRAD LINAWEAVER: Then please explain it.

J. NEIL SCHULMAN: During the experience, I was taken out of myself. I was seeing Joseph Neil Schulman, to use my full name here — the little boy who had been Joseph, who at age 16 decided to use his middle name — from the outside, and looked upon him as somebody else.

I think that, at the point of God's Judgment, we will be taken out of ourselves and be able to look at ourselves from God's point of view.

We will be given His eyes to look at ourselves — all of us, not just me — for this period. That was just a special foreshadowing, or something like that, for whatever job I have to do here.

But I think everybody gets that, where you are taken out of yourself and you look at yourself as if you're judging somebody else. I think that what Jesus was saying there, about loving your enemy as yourself, it means that, at some point, you need to apply the same level of criticism for your enemy as you would apply to yourself. The exact same sorts of excuses and rationalizations and reasoning that you would use to justify yourself, you have to apply to your enemy as well.

That's what I think.

Chapter 8: Aftermath

BRAD LINAWEAVER: What happened next?
J. NEIL SCHULMAN: First of all, physically, for the next of couple weeks, I thought it was quite possible that I was dying. Again, after this experience, I found myself in the Emergency Room, had to rehydrated again with an intravenous drip.

Over the next week, physically, I was very weak. I had to stop dieting and start increasing my calories, simply to try to balance out my body. I felt wrecked, I felt drained. I felt like I needed to draw energy into me somehow and where was I going to get it? And so what I was doing, I went down to the beach with my shoes off — and remember this is February so we're not talking about balmy summer days on Venice Beach or something like that — but I felt I had to walk along the cool sand and crunch the sand beneath my feet and draw energy into me to survive.

I had an experience while I was driving in my car. It was like I was driving through waves of fire like through curtains of fire or something like that. Where suddenly, whoa! It's just enormously hot and I had that happen to me several times. It's part of the reason why, in writing *Escape from Heaven*, when I have Jesus doing His resurrection on Duj, He does it not with water, which would be the traditional Biblical imagery of Baptism, but with fire.

It was because I felt that I was going through some sort of transition and that fire was burning something out of me. Physiologically, this is what was going on.

Now, mentally what was going on, was like asking the question over and over again: was it real? Did this really happen? Did I have an experience that was real or did I just have a psychotic break with reality? Did I just experience some sort of naturally induced drug trip?

BRAD LINAWEAVER: Was it ever possible both could coexist in some way?

J. NEIL SCHULMAN: I was trying to ask myself questions like that. But the most important question that I was asking over and over again was: what does this mean? Okay? And the consequence of that question was: am I, in some sense or another, really God?

Because, remember, the experience was me having the mind of God, and now suddenly, when it ended that evening on February 18th, it felt like a withdrawal, like at the end of sex, or something like that.

BRAD LINAWEAVER: Or like drugs? Coming down from drugs?

J. NEIL SCHULMAN: No. I wouldn't know that, honest to God. I haven't really taken drugs to know that. But what it felt like was withdrawal at the end of sex. Okay? A softening. It was almost like post-orgasmic or something like that. This release of tension. But it was like God wasn't gone. He was still there but the volume was down. And that continued on, the feeling that God was still there within me, but with the volume down.

BRAD LINAWEAVER: Could it be, in a sense, we all have that contact with God, but we don't notice it because the volume is down so low? And you felt it because the volume was turned way up in your case and then turned back down. Is that a metaphor that works?

J. NEIL SCHULMAN: Yes, but the question was very individualist and poignant for me.

Since I saw myself from outside of myself with God's eyes — with His viewpoint, with His cognition — and since it was clear to me that there was a mission involved here, somehow, and I didn't know what it was, I had not been given the specifics beyond, "A circle will form around you."

BRAD LINAWEAVER: Explain that a little more, "A circle will form around you."

J. NEIL SCHULMAN: That people were going to be drawn around me, almost in the sense of disciples or apostles or something like that.

BRAD LINAWEAVER: You really felt that?

J. NEIL SCHULMAN: It was explicit in the message.

BRAD LINAWEAVER: Oh, wow! It's not a feeling. It's words, and concepts?

J. NEIL SCHULMAN: That was definite, "A circle will form around you."

And, by the way, I asked God, "When is this going to happen?"

He said — and it's like I'm saying to myself, remember always — "Soon."

Here's a strange question I asked. I guess I must have started to be individuating from God again by the point I asked this question, soon for you or soon for me? And His answer was soon for you. So there was already starting to separate going on at the point where I'm asking that. In other words that must have been sort of toward the end of it when we were already separating and I wasn't fully aware of it yet because I was already starting to think like Neil Schulman again, if I'm saying soon for you or soon for me? But I was told there was a mission and that it was not going to involve my getting executed like had happened when He had done this before.

And that, by the way, was when I started really taking seriously the idea that maybe Jesus was real. Because of that interchange, that memory, that there was something that it hadn't worked out well the last time.

BRAD LINAWEAVER: Something really happened 2000 years ago, it's not all made up?

J. NEIL SCHULMAN: Yes, that was part of the recollection. That was part of the access to the memory banks, the Tree of Knowledge or whatever we want to call it.

Okay. So I kept on trying to figure out: does this mean that in some sense I am God?

BRAD LINAWEAVER: How many hours are we talking about again?

J. NEIL SCHULMAN: The experience from beginning to end?

BRAD LINAWEAVER: Yeah, yeah.

J. NEIL SCHULMAN: Basically starting at around noon and ending at around eight o'clock in the evening. At the full volume, at the full volume. Then, at lower volume, for weeks after that.

And then you sort of get peaks and valleys. Some of the peaks being when I began writing intensely on *Escape from Heaven* again. Then the volume went up again.

BRAD LINAWEAVER: Oh really? You definitely felt it coming back in places?

J. NEIL SCHULMAN: Oh yeah, and we'll get to that.

But, I was trying to figure out, is this true?

I mean, I feel like a megalomaniac in even asking myself this question. I'm trying to phrase it in terms of where I was then. Okay. You know? Only a megalomaniac would think he's God. And yet what if it's true?

How could this be possible? I mean, coming from my background which only recently before I hadn't even believed in God, and now I'm asking myself if I am Him? And, by the way, I thought that was funny even at the time. That here I am — just recently an atheist — and I'm asking myself if I'm God?

BRAD LINAWEAVER: A way of saying that you don't believe in yourself.

J. NEIL SCHULMAN: Right! And that, by the way — the way that you just phrased it right now – "Do I believe in myself?" — was, in essence, saying, "I know God is real but am I real?" Because I had been pulled out of myself. Is this person — whom I've been since my birth — a real person, or is it merely a fictitious projection, as I was experiencing while this was going on?

Look. C.S. Lewis taught me a lot and one of the things he taught me, I believe this is a traditional Christian viewpoint here. In asking yourself "Is Jesus Christ the Son of God? He made this claim." — there's only three possibilities. One. "He's a liar, a charlatan." Two. "He's a madman, a psychotic who was having megalomaniac delusions." Or three. "He's telling the truth and He really is."

Now, I knew I wasn't lying, because it was myself, but that left me with two choices. One. What I had experienced was real and in some sense I was God. And two. I was out of my mind.

I had eliminated fifty percent of the alternatives and I was still left with the big one! "Am I out of my mind? Was this a break with reality?"

BRAD LINAWEAVER: Or was this experience real?

J. NEIL SCHULMAN: Or was it real?

Now, mind you, it was not the first time that I'd had experiences like this, okay? And so I was not able to get shut of the reality of it. As much as I was afraid of it, in some sense I had to almost — as an article of faith – say, "What has been given to me is real, and if what God is telling me is that I am God, then in some sense that I can't comprehend, nor am I willing to accept or believe, I am God."

I don't know what that means, and I don't know what I'm supposed to do with it.

And, by the way, what I started doing then was a search to try to find out, has this happened to anybody else? That was the most important thing on my mind then: has this happened to anybody else?

That's why I started reading books like *Conversations with God* by Neale Donald Walsch and started trying to basically read up in an area which I had no real interest in before then, none whatsoever. But I was simply trying to find out, am I the only person this has happened to or has it happened to a ton of people and I'm simply one of them?

BRAD LINAWEAVER: Well, of course some critics would say, "Oh, the insane asylums are full of people like this." Though, in fact, the insane asylums have more people who think they're Napoleon, or think they're some historical figure who's long gone. There are people who have what they call the God Complex in asylums, but there's not as many as people who think they're historical figures.

What I want to know is why, when a medium at a séance claims to channel a lost human being — a ghost, basically — why people don't freak out? Atheists just go, "Oh, well, what a fraud!" And religious people wonder whether it's true or not. And certain fundamentalist Christians say you shouldn't risk your soul in a séance. And others are willing to try for it. But nobody gets upset over the idea that some living person is channeling a ghost. But people get very upset when a living person claims to be channeling God.

J. NEIL SCHULMAN: Right. And I was simply curious to find out if there were others claiming to be channeling God.

Now, I need to point out something to you, since you mentioned the insane asylum. Okay? The crazy person goes around trying to convince other people that he is who he says he is-

BRAD LINAWEAVER: Napoleon or –

J. NEIL SCHULMAN: Napoleon, or Jesus Christ. As you say, the asylums are full of people who claim to be Jesus Christ or Mary or something like that. But the point is they're going around trying to convince other people of it.

The last thing I wanted to do was tell anybody about this. Because, if I thought I was crazy, certainly they would think I was crazy, too! I didn't want to tell anybody that I was considering — inside my skull — the idea that I was God. They'd put me away!

I was pretty much back to myself after the first few weeks, when I started feeling physically stronger again, and no longer

had this fear that this was an end-of-life experience. Because, by the way, people who I've spoken to about this experience since, say that, in some senses, it matches up with the near-death experiences of those who have had their hearts stopped or something like that and found themselves out of themselves. Because, when I would try to explain that I was out of my personality, people would hear it and think of it as an out-of-body experience.

I wasn't out of my body. God was in my body with me. That was different.

BRAD LINAWEAVER: No, it's definitely flipped from the normal. It's definitely different.

J. NEIL SCHULMAN: Right. So, again, I didn't want to go around telling anybody I was God. Not during the experience and not afterwards.

BRAD LINAWEAVER: You weren't floating around looking at your own body. You had decided that God had invaded your body –

J. NEIL SCHULMAN: No, it wasn't an invasion because it was welcome. The experience was entirely welcome.

BRAD LINAWEAVER: I don't know what verb to use but God had overlapped with, intruded upon...

J. NEIL SCHULMAN: How about had communed with me?

BRAD LINAWEAVER: Or double exposed, or whatever?

J. NEIL SCHULMAN: How about conversation in the Biblical sense? That it was a joining? Instead of a physical joining it was a spiritual joining? Or to use the metaphor which I came up with later, it was a Mind Meld.

BRAD LINAWEAVER: Well, I just used the modern term with double exposure, and you're using the *Star Trek* term, with Mind Meld.

J. NEIL SCHULMAN: Double exposure also works. An overlay. But also — during this overlay — being God was much more who I was than Neil Schulman. And then it reversed again when I was Neil Schulman more again.

But the question always arose: is there any truth to this? And then later on I started asking myself: is it possible that there's more than one interpretation of it? I know that there is an identity exchange going on but is that simply a consequence — an artifact — of the way that God communicates in this situation? And that I'm not really God. It's just that you have to think you're God while it's going on, to be able to get the experience? Was it, in fact, like a Vulcan Mind Meld?

Because, again, I wasn't Jesus. My flaws were very, very clear to me. My humanity was very, very clear to me. My imperfections were very, very clear to me, and my weakness — and lack of super powers — was very, very clear to me. I wasn't able to — like in *Bruce Almighty* — reach across the table and have the cream slide toward me. I didn't have telekinesis. I didn't have the ability to turn water into wine –

BRAD LINAWEAVER: Or beer!

J. NEIL SCHULMAN: Or beer. Or to heal, or raise the dead, or any this other sort of stuff. In other words, if what comes with the full package was being able to do that, I didn't have the full package. And how could I be God if I didn't have the full package?

BRAD LINAWEAVER: Allow me to make one stupid joke. You still had the power to turn wine and beer into water.

J. NEIL SCHULMAN: That's right. Yes, that is quite correct!

BRAD LINAWEAVER: I had to say that.

J. NEIL SCHULMAN: Very good! Okay.

So for the next year, there were a few people who I talked about this with. A very few. I talked about it with my sister.

BRAD LINAWEAVER: I seem to recall you talked to me about it.

J. NEIL SCHULMAN: I talked to you about it. I didn't talk to Dafydd about it.

BRAD LINAWEAVER: At some point you finally did tell Dafydd, but not at that time.

J. NEIL SCHULMAN: Yes, but I was very circumspect, and careful, and slow and deliberate. Part of it was simply I had to ask. You know I needed some professional advice here, of people who had the knowledge of theology and mysticism, and all this sort of thing which I did not have.

BRAD LINAWEAVER: I need to know this. Did you talk to Sam Konkin?

J. NEIL SCHULMAN: Yes.

BRAD LINAWEAVER: Did you talk to Victor Koman?

J. NEIL SCHULMAN: Not at any great length.

BRAD LINAWEAVER: Back in 1988 when you had the hand-on-the-heart experience –

J. NEIL SCHULMAN: Victor knew about that.

BRAD LINAWEAVER: Victor and I sat there, together with you at a hotel, and you told us all about it, together. Victor and I talked about it, long afterward. After that one, the year that Heinlein died — to this day Victor and I remember that. You were telling both of us at the same time in a hotel lobby. I just wondered if you've had the conversation with Victor, equivalent to the one you had with me, after the Mind Meld.

J. NEIL SCHULMAN: I don't remember at this moment.

BRAD LINAWEAVER: Okay. And any comment from Sam, do you remember?

J. NEIL SCHULMAN: Sam took it pretty well in stride.

BRAD LINAWEAVER: Give a sentence or two on that.

J. NEIL SCHULMAN: I'm not sure how relevant this is to people who don't know who Sam was. Sam, my best friend who passed away a couple of months ago, who was my libertarian mentor and a good buddy. He was somebody who I always bounced ideas off of, so in essence, I think I just gave him sort of an outline of the experience, just to let him know that this was what was going on with me, so he would have context of perhaps some odd behavior that he might be noting in me. Why I seemed to be more interested in certain things that I had been. But Sam wasn't judgmental about it. If he expressed the thought, "Well, Neil, that's crazy," I don't think he thought I was any crazier than I had been before. Because, again, I'd had the previous experiences, which I'd told him about.

He had the experience — going back to when we were living in New York — where we went on that trip, borrowing Bob Cohen's car and going to a Boston Tea Party demonstration of the Society for Individual Liberty in Boston. And, on the drive back, the car spinning out, in Rocky Hill, Connecticut. And none of us being hurt, going to the motel room, none of us making any phone calls. And the next morning, I called my folks to tell them what had happened and my mother said, "We already know."

"How do you know?"

"Well, your father leaned over to me around ten o'clock last night, and said, 'They've been in an accident in the car but none of them were hurt.'"

BRAD LINAWEAVER: Wow!

J. NEIL SCHULMAN: And Sam was a witness to that, so he knew he had been an actual observer to one of these psychic experiences in my family. So, going back to 1974, 1975, Sam knew that there was something going on with me.

BRAD LINAWEAVER: How did he ever account for that, being such a total materialist?

J. NEIL SCHULMAN: He remembered it. He never shied away from being a witness to it. Whenever anybody asked him about it, he said, "Yes, that's what happened." But he was never able to go beyond that and attribute any meaning to it, because he was an absolute materialistic skeptic.

BRAD LINAWEAVER: Right.

J. NEIL SCHULMAN: But he never shied away from being a witness to it and being an honest reporter of it. Sam was too honest for that.

BRAD LINAWEAVER: Yes!

J. NEIL SCHULMAN: So, yes, I discussed it with certain people. There was a summer after the experience — maybe even that next summer — where I visited my sister in Colorado Springs. And my sister is part of a spiritual community there with a lot of friends who have psychic experiences and mystical beliefs and that sort of thing. And I started talking with some of them.

Some of it was very confronting to me because they were saying, "Oh, yes, every mystic has this experience and you're just one." But none of them could lay claim to the experience that I had had. I always felt like they... this business: "Why, we all think we're God."

No! I hadn't thought I was God before this happened. And I was finding it hard to believe afterwards! As a matter of fact, if anything was draining my energy, it was my trying to fight the idea that I had to believe that. Sure, I'm willing to accept that I'm a prophet. That's easy. Fine. A prophet. No problem. Long history of that.

BRAD LINAWEAVER: Dime a dozen.

J. NEIL SCHULMAN: Dime a dozen! Prophet, mystic, one of God's soldiers. "I'm on a mission from God!" from The Blues Brothers. No problem with any of that. But, "I'm God!"? "Are you out of your freakin' mind, Neil? That doesn't track! That is crazy stuff! Neil, stop being a megalomaniac! You've gotta stop doing that!"

That's what was going on after this, then...

BRAD LINAWEAVER: Question, this is a good one. Is it possible that the people who truly meet God, ultimately have the experience of being God? Have you stumbled onto that perhaps?

J. NEIL SCHULMAN: Not personally, I haven't met anybody like that.

BRAD LINAWEAVER: I'm talking about all through human history. I don't mean here and now.

J. NEIL SCHULMAN: I kept on being disappointed because I really wanted to find somebody else who this happened to. That's why I read two of Neale Donald Walsch's books and was disappointed, when I'm reading this stuff, and he has God saying things to him that I knew God would never say. Because for one thing, he has God talking to Neale Donald Walsch, and having God refer to us as "you people" or something like that. "Oh, you people!" Like God is some alien from another planet or something like that.

What I experienced during this is that God didn't experience Himself as separate from "you people." That God thought of Himself as one of us.

BRAD LINAWEAVER: Do you find more truth in a Jim Carrey movie like *Bruce Almighty*, than in all these New Age mystic books?

J. NEIL SCHULMAN: Yes, absolutely! And that's also true of *Oh God!* I find a lot of truth in *Oh God!* and I find a lot of truth in *Bruce Almighty*. These seem to me closer to the spirit of what I experienced than what I was getting from Neale Donald Walsch. And I'm sorry, I don't mean to be critical and judgmental about it. I'm simply saying that I wasn't getting it from him. I wanted to be getting it from him and I was disappointed that I wasn't getting it from him. I wanted somebody else whom I could seek out, share the experience with, and maybe be able to understand it a little better by the sharing of it. And I wasn't getting that from anybody around me.

BRAD LINAWEAVER: These guys have not had the experience you've had?

J. NEIL SCHULMAN: That was the impression I was getting.

BRAD LINAWEAVER: And who was the guy on the CyberCity show Jack brought on?

J. NEIL SCHULMAN: John Hogue.

BRAD LINAWEAVER: I got the impression from listening to that exchange that whatever experiences he's had, they have nothing to do with yours?

J. NEIL SCHULMAN: My experience, I was not finding an analog for it in anybody else, except in one case and it scared the hell out of me.

BRAD LINAWEAVER: Which is?

J. NEIL SCHULMAN: Jesus Christ, Himself.

BRAD LINAWEAVER: Oh, nobody you met personally?

J. NEIL SCHULMAN: Right. The only thing I could find anywhere — not Joan of Arc, who heard voices, or prophets who had dreams — although I'd had dreams also and continued to have them — but I couldn't find anybody else, in looking through mystical experiences, other than Jesus Christ, who apparently had the same experience that I had — only He had it at a deeper level. In other words, I had just a spoonful of it and He had an ocean of it.

BRAD LINAWEAVER: Could you conclude though, in the last 2000 years, there's other people who may have had this spoonful of experience that you just don't know about?

J. NEIL SCHULMAN: Yes.

BRAD LINAWEAVER: Look at the trouble you're having getting your message out, isn't that a reasonable assumption?

J. NEIL SCHULMAN: Absolutely. But the point is that I haven't found them. And as a matter of fact, one of the reasons I put the license plate on my car, "*I met God*," is that I hoping that somebody who met God is going to see the license plate and say, "I did, too! Let's talk about it! I've been looking for you!"

BRAD LINAWEAVER: So, far from wanting to make some kind of exclusive-ist claim, you're looking for other people to share the experience with?

J. NEIL SCHULMAN: Yes.

BRAD LINAWEAVER: That's very important to stress in this book.

J. NEIL SCHULMAN: I'm searching. I'm searching for whoever else has gone through this, and fearing that it might only be me. What awesome responsibility that is. That, in a profound sense, sucks.

BRAD LINAWEAVER: Yes!

J. NEIL SCHULMAN: The sense of responsibility, if you are really chosen.

The next event that really happens is the writing of *Escape from Heaven*. And, as you well know, because you kept on encouraging me — here's where you come into the story a little bit more — is that I was having a very hard time trying to get going on this and a number of things happened to me in the meantime.

BRAD LINAWEAVER: You mean in *Escape from Heaven*?

J. NEIL SCHULMAN: *Escape from Heaven*. But things were happening in the mean time.

The first thing is that only a couple of years after February, 1997 — now we're into 1998 and 1999 — and Brad, that's the Pulpless.Com experience — when what happened?

BRAD LINAWEAVER: We'll never forget it.

J. NEIL SCHULMAN: A circle formed around me!

BRAD LINAWEAVER: Oh, that's true! It was your publishing venture but it was most certainly a circle.

J. NEIL SCHULMAN: Right. A circle formed around me and I was publishing books and meeting people who I was able to change what was happening. For the first time, I was starting to get a sense of being able to accomplish something.

And then that crashed, that didn't reach its full potential. But while look what we accomplished, the publication of over 50 books in a year.

BRAD LINAWEAVER: It did make some impact. It didn't go away right away.

J. NEIL SCHULMAN: Right. There was some impact and even some lasting impact to this day. For one thing it got all eight of my books, at that time, in print, and suddenly I was fully in print for the first time in my life.

BRAD LINAWEAVER: That's true.

J. NEIL SCHULMAN: And other people, other of my friends, were suddenly in print, including two books of yours, and four books by Victor Koman and so on and so forth.

BRAD LINAWEAVER: One book by John DeChancie.

J. NEIL SCHULMAN: Right. I was able to get into print a lot of books by people in my circle, the circle that was forming around me.

BRAD LINAWEAVER: Then I had a very bad year, the year 2000, in which, number one, I was trying to save Pulpless.com by starting another venture called Eazychair. That collapsed because it was built on representations being made to me which turned out not to be true. I don't need to get into that story. It's irrelevant here. But nonetheless, five months of my time, gone. And, then, the year 2000 was the year my father passed away after a long illness.

So all this was going on, distracting me from really doing anything else. Until finally, we get to the period approaching the anniversary of when my father passed away.

We're in 2001, and in August, 2001, I'm finally at the point where I'm able to start writing on *Escape from Heaven*. I've basically been wiped out of my business ventures and I have nowhere else to go as a businessman, so I go back to what my first calling was, as a writer.

I knew that it was going to have to be *Escape from Heaven*, that I was never going to be able to do anything else until I had that done.

BRAD LINAWEAVER: And you knew that because?

J. NEIL SCHULMAN: Because of something a prophet once said to me, Brad.

A friend of Barbara Branden's, in the 1980s, who told me at that time that the next novel I wrote was going to have a religious theme.

BRAD LINAWEAVER: Who was this person?

J. NEIL SCHULMAN: I'll mention his first name, Walter, who was a man that Barbara Branden was friends with, then. A very interesting man, a gourmet chef, and I found him very, very interesting. But he had told me that. He had said that he sensed that my next novel was going to have a religious theme of some sort, and for some reason I always knew he was right, that that was true.

BRAD LINAWEAVER: That was long before –

J. NEIL SCHULMAN: That was going back to the mid-1980s. So I knew, even during this long gap when I was not a novelist, because I was not writing any other novels during this period. And then after 1991 or 1992, I knew that the book was going to be *Escape from Heaven*. But then look how long after that it took to get to the point where I could write it, after that first outline which was, in essence, taking me in the wrong direction.

BRAD LINAWEAVER: And chapter one — which I have always maintained could be a stand-alone short story — which was a very powerful piece of writing. I remember, when you first read it to me, there was a long period between that first chapter and the rest of the book. Talk about that.

J. NEIL SCHULMAN: Because that opening was in the original, that was practically the only thing I retained from the original.

Now, there were other ideas which I transplanted forward, and I had to change and rework. When I started working on the book again, seriously, to try to actually break out, in August of 2001, one of the things I had to do was, in essence, decide which parts of the outline I was going to keep and which parts I was going to throw away.

Chapter 9: Collaboration

BRAD LINAWEAVER: And that's where the God voice — I'll call it that — turning the volume up, if you will, on the God broadcast — is that where the God voice made a crucial difference in guiding you through what was to be dropped and what was to be used?

J. NEIL SCHULMAN: Yes, and let me try to explain the process, the way that it was happening.

First of all, 9/11 happens. I am, at that point, maybe no more than three chapters, maybe four chapters, into the book. Okay, three or four chapters, right near the beginning. okay, 9/11 happens. I am up all night, writing on the book. I'm at my computer in the family room. On the couch next to me, my daughter is asleep. I have the TV on in that room, with the sound muted.

About six o'clock in the morning, I look over to the TV and I see –

BRAD LINAWEAVER: The Twin Towers?

J. NEIL SCHULMAN: I see the Twin Towers. I'm looking at New York live news footage as smoke is coming out of the Towers.

BRAD LINAWEAVER: They haven't collapsed yet?

J. NEIL SCHULMAN: Oh, way before they collapsed. And I turned up the volume, was shocked when they talked about the second plane having hit. Okay, I watched around a half hour, went upstairs, woke up my mother, and said you've got to see what's happening here.

Then around seven o'clock that morning, I called my daughter's mother and I said, "I'm keeping her out of school today." I said, "I don't know, they're talking about things hitting Washington. I don't know what's going to be happening here on the West Coast, if anything, but I'm keeping her out of school today."

I then got dressed and I went to the nearest supermarket and I did the sort of shopping I had done when everybody was talking about Y2K. I got canned goods, batteries, bottled water – basically, what, living in California, we refer to as earthquake supplies. And then the towers started collapsing while I was at the supermarket. I got back into the car and heard about it on the radio.

Okay. So, I did not see that happen because I was already in emergency mode, trying to protect my family.

BRAD LINAWEAVER: You saw it with the ten million reruns.

J. NEIL SCHULMAN: Yes, that's right.

Now, 9/11 did not stop me from writing the book. It wasn't like I'm going to stop at this point. I knew I had to continue more than ever.

BRAD LINAWEAVER: It even increased you motivation.

J. NEIL SCHULMAN: It increased my motivation. Now I really felt that I had to get this book done, and get it done quickly. And also, in the back of my mind, was sort of like a promise I had made to my father, that I was going to have this book done by his birthday, which was October 1st, which was only a few weeks away from 9/11. So I felt the pressure on me.

Now I had experienced this period of intense writing the last time in 1981 when I was writing *The Rainbow Cadenza*. I hadn't had anything like it since, even working on *The Frame of the Century*?

BRAD LINAWEAVER: Which is your O.J. book.

J. NEIL SCHULMAN: Right, my O.J. book. I'd had bursts of energy, where I was writing maybe 50 or 60 pages but a lot of that book was simply collecting various things and putting them together. It was, in many ways, almost more of an editing job than a writing job, from stuff I had previously written in discussion boards on the Internet, where I was arguing with people, and I was collecting pieces of data.

Writing nonfiction is, in may ways, much more about research than it is about writing.

BRAD LINAWEAVER: Fiction writing and nonfiction writing are different experiences, as you and I both know.

J. NEIL SCHULMAN: So this was like the first time that I was at this level of intensity of creation since 1981. Here I was, 20 years later. It had been 20 years since I'd done this. Plus, I didn't have the chemical aids which I'd had while writing *The Rainbow Cadenza*, because every day, my writing formula — when writing *Rainbow Cadenza* — was to make myself an Irish coffee – and only one Irish coffee because — the way that I said it — the caffeine was focusing my mind and the alcohol was calming down my fear of writing.

Well, I was doing it without the Irish coffee this time, and to get to that level of intensity without it took me a while, and that's one of the reasons it took me so long to get into the groove again.

So here I am, in the weeks following 9/11, with, of course you know, all this chaos and intensity. And of course, while I'm writing the book, I'm also writing four or five short articles about 9/11 and the impact. I couldn't disengage from it. I tried to and couldn't write anything for the first few days but then too much was going on that I couldn't stay out of it.

So while I'm writing the novel I'm also tossing off these nonfiction pieces.

And then, suddenly, something strange started happening. I abandoned my outline entirely and what was happening to me was that I would write a chapter and end a chapter, having put things in that I didn't know why I put it there. In essence, painting myself into a corner.

I was laying out problems for myself, putting things in there, and asking myself, "Why is that there?"

Let me give you some concrete examples.

Two things, in particular. I'll just mention two of them because I think it makes the case very adequately. One of them is that I have Lucifer's press conference in Heaven, when — having successfully won her coup to take over Heaven and driven God and God's palace out of Heaven — and by the way, the image of God's palace being missing from Heaven was directly taken from seeing the Twin Towers gone.

BRAD LINAWEAVER: I think it's one of the most powerful images in the novel. Please go on.

J. NEIL SCHULMAN: So after she has driven God and God's palace out of Heaven itself, Lucifer holds a press conference and I say, in describing her, here she was about to announce her victory but she looked sad, as if she had just been defeated.

BRAD LINAWEAVER: And what you mean by that was?

J. NEIL SCHULMAN: I had no idea why I wrote that. Why is that there? Why am I writing that, that she looks defeated even though she is announcing her victory?

Why? I had no idea when I wrote that.

Then, later on, a couple of chapters later, the explanation is given to me as if I'm a reader and I'm reading along and then suddenly I'm reading the answer. And the answer was, it was because — having made an arrangement with God to hold elections on Earth to determine who is going to rule Earth — she had to go back to God, humbly, hat in hand, and say, "Can you help me set up the election? I can't figure out a way to get the votes of everybody on Earth. Can you solve that problem for me?"

The way that I describe it in the novel, it's like a rebellious teenager who — having decided to move out in a huff — has to go back to Daddy and say, "Can I borrow your van to move?"

BRAD LINAWEAVER: Right, Right.

J. NEIL SCHULMAN: And that's why she looked so defeated. But I had no idea, when I wrote that sentence, about why she looked defeated, when she was about to announce her victory at the press conference, I had no idea. That's one example.

BRAD LINAWEAVER: It came to you later?

J. NEIL SCHULMAN: It came to me later.

Another example. I have Duj Pepperman, when the council forms around him — and again, I took that direct language of "A circle will form around you" and I put it into the novel and gave it to Duj Pepperman –

BRAD LINAWEAVER: It had been Pulpless.Com before and now it's in the novel?

J. NEIL SCHULMAN: Now it's in the novel, right. And, by the way, I wasn't even sure, at the time, whether that was the circle or whether that was simply part of a circle. I wasn't really sure again what "A circle will form around you" actually meant, and still, to this day, I'm not really sure.

BRAD LINAWEAVER: It has multiple meanings. In an occult practice there are circles that have certain arcane meanings as well.

J. NEIL SCHULMAN: Right. I have Duj Pepperman have all these famous dead people who become sort of his cabinet – the circle around him –

BRAD LINAWEAVER: H.L. Mencken and everybody else?

J. NEIL SCHULMAN: Right, everybody. Ayn Rand, Robert Heinlein, and that sort of thing.

BRAD LINAWEAVER: Even Charles Lindbergh?

J. NEIL SCHULMAN: And it is about Charles Lindbergh that this happens. Because I say, at a certain point, Duj had a special mission for Charles Lindbergh. But that doesn't come into the story yet.

Now when I wrote that I had no idea what the special mission for Charles Lindbergh was going to be. Not a clue. Why am I writing this? Why am I creating this problem? I'm trying to get this novel done and I'm putting things in there that I have no clue why. How am I going to pay that off? I don't how I'm going to pay that off.

BRAD LINAWEAVER: Right.

J. NEIL SCHULMAN: And yet, again, a few chapters later it turns out that what Charles Lindbergh's mission was, was to go into the tunnel, connecting Earth and Heaven, and basically slip in there, to be able to open it up at will when Duj needs to be able to get Jesus to Earth.

BRAD LINAWEAVER: Right.

J. NEIL SCHULMAN: But I had no idea that that was going to happen. I didn't know what that mission was. But it works out so perfectly when it happens.

BRAD LINAWEAVER: Right.

J. NEIL SCHULMAN: Now this was what was starting to give me the idea that God was active within me again, that the volume was up again. Because I was getting all these things and it was just coming through full force with such high pressure that it essentially carried me to the point where, in essence, I think I wrote the last ten chapters of the book in about four days.

BRAD LINAWEAVER: Writer to writer, that's impressive.

J. NEIL SCHULMAN: I couldn't sleep. I was only able to sleep a couple of hours a night while this was going on. I was, you know, at full intensity. But unlike what had happened with *The Rainbow Cadenza* when it was a fearful experience, this time I was ready for it and I was able to handle it. It was pleasurable this time just like it was scary the first time.

My first time where God is directly encountering me, He's putting His hand on my heart and saying I can kill you now. The second time, it's this benevolent mind sharing, totally different experience. And here again, I wasn't fully ready or understanding what was happening the first time. The second time it's a gas.

BRAD LINAWEAVER: We talked about this earlier, it's pain into pleasure.

J. NEIL SCHULMAN: Right, because I am becoming more the sort of person who is able to handle it. I'm being made into a person who's able to tolerate it and who actually enjoys it.

BRAD LINAWEAVER: Yes.

J. NEIL SCHULMAN: I'm the one who's changing, God isn't changing. I'm changing.

BRAD LINAWEAVER: I will want to ask about the screenplay. But I'll wait until we finish talking about the novel. This sets up my first question about the screenplay please continue.

J. NEIL SCHULMAN: I started finding out, piece by piece, that there were things put into the novel, great important central symbols, which my religious education had never told me anything about and why was I putting them in there?

BRAD LINAWEAVER: Kabbalistic symbology?

J. NEIL SCHULMAN: Right, two things in particular I have as a central part of the book that God has a wife and that that wife was also the mother of Jesus. In other words, and this I took in essence from the mythology of *The Book of the Holy Grail*, which J.R. Ploughman brought to Pulpless.Com.

BRAD LINAWEAVER: I've read it.

J. NEIL SCHULMAN: Okay, the idea that you have God who is Erebus, and His wife who is Yse, and that is the god and goddess who are the mother and father of the human race. In fact, they are also the mother and father of Jesus, because they come down and meld their spirits into two human beings. One of them Joseph, who God goes into — who Erebus goes into — and the other one Mary, who Yse goes into, and then as both gods and human beings they procreate and their son becomes Jesus — Yeshua — and that is how God and man, the bloodline is formed on Earth which they then go off — and here is where I become a heretic to *The Book of the Holy Grail* — they say at that point that the whole point was so this bloodline could be created and therefore Jesus is never crucified and it's a trick. I want no part of that! But nonetheless, here's the thing in meeting with J.R. Ploughman in the Summer of 1999, to meet with him and experience his presence, he is saying that he recognizes my God experience as real.

And other people who I met around my sister said they recognized my experience as real, they had a sense that this had happened. And also I started doing some things which almost came to the point of being miraculous. I sat with one of my sister's friends who is very, very psychic, and she would put a pebble in my hand and suddenly I was getting a flash of where the rocks were from. And this was a collection of rocks which she had taken from all over the place and she told me I was getting one hundred percent. "Yes, this is from there, yes this is from there" and it's like it was a total psychic connection.

BRAD LINAWEAVER: I remember you and Soleil talking about feeling somebody's heartbeat at a distance.

J. NEIL SCHULMAN: One of my sister's friends — a man named Art Barteldt — who was close to being a full blooded, I think, Apache — I'm not sure that that was his tribe. But he was able to do something, in which he would stand across the room from me — at least eight or ten feet away — put up his hand, and say, "Put up your hand, I'm going to send you my heartbeat." And then I would feel his heartbeat in my hand. Then I could feel his heartbeat thumping in my hand. And that was my first experience with actual magic.

So, in other words I knew that there were more things in Heaven and earth than even I had experienced. In other words I'd had some profound things happen to me, but this was also remarkable.

Okay. So all of this is going on during this period, and then I find out that I have these symbols, and this is post publication.

After the book is already published, after *Escape from Heaven* is in print, that's when I start discovering what I put into the book. What God has revealed to me without my even knowing it.

And two things in particular. One is that I got ahold of Leonard Nimoy's photographic book, *Shekhina*, and I had never heard the word *Shekhina* before then. But this is what was interesting to me, and here is the sequence of knowledge and learning here.

BRAD LINAWEAVER: Back to kabbalah...

J. NEIL SCHULMAN: Right. Leonard Nimoy was raised Jewish, in Boston, and when he was taken to the Orthodox synagogue, you had the ritual of everybody turns their back so they can't see the Holy of Holies and I guess the Rabbi holds up his hands and does the Vulcan greeting, as we know, with the two fingers separated into a "V" in the middle.

BRAD LINAWEAVER: "Live long and prosper!"

J. NEIL SCHULMAN: The "Live long and prosper" symbol, which is a representation, Nimoy explains in his book *Shekhina*, of the Hebrew letter "shin," if I'm not mistaken, which is the representation of *Shekhina*. *Shekhina* being the Holy Spirit, the feminine aspect of God.

And I am learning, when I start now researching this — having learned about it — that it's God's wife, the female aspect of God. And here's the important part: the advocate of man to God.

BRAD LINAWEAVER: I have to ask you a question.

J. NEIL SCHULMAN: But let me, before you ask me the question. I can't let this go by without emphasizing it too strongly.

We go back to 1988 where I had that dream, the dream that changes my life, where my attorney — my advocate — is God and she is a woman. God was a woman in my dream, okay?

I put that in *Escape from Heaven* and now I find out that *Shekhina*, the Holy Spirit in Judaism, is a central part of the hidden kabbalistic doctrines, and I've met her in my dream in 1988, and put her in a novel? And only now I find out who she is? That the defender of humanity before God, in essence, represented me?

This is — I'm starting to think — this is a central part of Judaism which I never knew about.

BRAD LINAWEAVER: I always thought it was a hidden part of Judaism.

J. NEIL SCHULMAN: Hidden, but you know it's not something I was taught in the year of Hebrew School.

BRAD LINAWEAVER: That's what I mean, I always thought it was kind of like secretive.

J. NEIL SCHULMAN: It is. It's secretive. It is deliberately secretive.

Here is Leonard Nimoy doing a book about it, telling me about it, starting me researching about it, and what I find out is that who *Shekhina* is, the Holy Spirit, the defender of man before God, was in my dream, defending me in 1988, after I had the experience where I had God — the male God — having His hand on my heart.

I'm blown away when I learn this.

Then something else.

In writing *Escape from Heaven*, I have the image of God's palace. Remember the palace that Duj is invited to, so he can have this conversation with God, and be sent back to Earth.

BRAD LINAWEAVER: Yes.

J. NEIL SCHULMAN: And I describe as a giant diamond, two pyramids — one the apex pointing up, the other the apex pointing down — and joined at the middle.

I then start doing a little research and here's what I find out. That symbol — if you just overlap it a little bit so that the bottom pyramid's base is sticking out a little bit -

BRAD LINAWEAVER: Star of David!

J. NEIL SCHULMAN: It's the Tree of Life symbol, and that, when flattened, becomes the two triangles of the Star of David.

BRAD LINAWEAVER: Right!

J. NEIL SCHULMAN: That's where the Star of David comes from, the three-dimensional representation of the two pyramids opposing each other, and that is the central image of Judaism. Now actually some would argue, some would say it's the Menorah, but nonetheless, I don't think we can discount the Star of David as being a powerful symbol, identified with Judaism, and certainly a kabbalistic symbol.

BRAD LINAWEAVER: Yes.

J. NEIL SCHULMAN: Okay, now why did I put that in there? I didn't know anything about that when I wrote that. One of the things that Sam Konkin, that actually impressed him about my description of my experience, is that he knew how little I knew about any of this stuff. That I was never interested in reading about Judaism or theology or any of this sort of stuff. No interest in it.

BRAD LINAWEAVER: In fact Sam and I discussed that on a number of occasions.

J. NEIL SCHULMAN: What did he say?

BRAD LINAWEAVER: What you just said, I'm providing you a third party witness.

BRAD LINAWEAVER: Okay. So, in other words, it's not like I'm trying to say, "Well this was in there and I was taught it in Hebrew School" or had read up a lot of it. I wasn't interested, never knew any of this stuff, and here it is, it's ending up in my book and I'm discovering that it's there after the fact, after it's written.

BRAD LINAWEAVER: No, you have me convinced that you did not have any of this kabbalistic background and yet work these images into your book. You did not have the background. You have me convinced of that.

Let me know when I can ask my next question. It does tie in to this.

J. NEIL SCHULMAN: I think we're at that point right now.

BRAD LINAWEAVER: Okay, here's my next question, why is it Christianity has been criticized for really being polytheistic by having the Trinity? Remember, there was a God view from various dimensional aspects.

J. NEIL SCHULMAN: And also the sentence that I did want to get out, and that is that I really think it doesn't matter whether, in my conception, God creates the other two parts of the Trinity, so that there's three personalities, or since He is fissioning Himself — and what they are are aspects that have always been God and been with God. As Saint John says in his gospel "And The Word was God and the Word was with God." He's saying both, so in essence what I'm saying is, is that my view may appear to be heretical to Orthodox Christianity, but I don't think it really is.

BRAD LINAWEAVER: My question is, why is Christianity criticized for sneaking polytheism back into a monotheistic religion if the original Hebrew religion has a God and a Goddess, the same as Zeus and Hera on Mount Olympus? That is my question.

J. NEIL SCHULMAN: Sure. Very good. And more than that, going back to Genesis, God never says He's the only God, and speaks as if there are other gods. He's almost talking as if some of the angels are gods.

BRAD LINAWEAVER: May I ask you something about the screenplay?

J. NEIL SCHULMAN: Yes, I think we can go to that point.

BRAD LINAWEAVER: When you were writing the screenplay for *Escape from Heaven*, was it purely your technical skill as a scriptwriter that elaborated certain sections? Dropped certain parts of the novel, then put in new material that's more dramatic cinematically? Was that just J. Neil Schulman the technician or did — to stick with the earlier metaphor — did the volume turn up again and were you hearing the God voice again, at any point during the screenplay, the way you were during the novel?

J. NEIL SCHULMAN: The volume was turned up again, and particularly in certain things coming together.

For example, in the novel, I have the Beach Boys' "Good

Vibrations" as the song which the angels sing as they take Duj to be transitioned over to Heaven. That's in the novel, that's written September 2001. So now I transfer that song into the screenplay for the same scene.

Then at a later point in the book, you see, the way that I structured the novel was not dramatically structured enough to be a screenplay. Too much of it is Duj, his narration, his exposition, his telling things at a distance of what happened. He's telling it like a storyteller, of events that have happened in the past, and really it's all in flashback, because he's a narrator.

So I have to make everything present and open it up and externalize it and make it... and Duj is still the viewpoint character but really, maybe from the standpoint of the novel, I don't have to have Duj's personal problems be at the center of it, but I do have to focus it so that we know what the central dramatic conflict is much more sharply in the screenplay than in the novel, and that's why I decided as a concept in essence to make it a buddy movie between Duj and Jesus.

BRAD LINAWEAVER: But why isn't that all Neil the technician?

J. NEIL SCHULMAN: Because we haven't gotten to what I'm talking about yet. That is all Neil the technician. What isn't Neil the technician is things coalescing around November, 1966, when suddenly things start happening. I suddenly find out that the Beach Boys' "Good Vibrations" came out in November of 1966. When I find out that there was an Elvis Presley recording from his movie Spinout, which came out in 1966, and the song is called "Adam and Evil." Then I found out that Howard Hughes moved into the Desert Inn, in November 1966.

Suddenly these all points start focusing in on November, 1966, so that I have a sequence in the screenplay of Duj having to time travel back to November 1966, as a centerpoint of the film, and all these sorts of things which become central plot points in the screenplay, particularly having to do with Howard Hughes and the Desert Inn and the song, "Adam and Evil," which really explicates and motivates the plot moving forward to the second-act climax, and setting us up for the resolution in the third act.

All this started coming together much more elegantly than I was ever able to plan it out.

BRAD LINAWEAVER: When did you write the screenplay, Neil?

J. NEIL SCHULMAN: I wrote the screenplay probably just about a year ago now.

BRAD LINAWEAVER: Okay. See, I view them as different works, and in a few ways I like the screenplay better than the novel, if only because it seems to answer a few more questions. Yet I don't think it would work as well if you ever tried to rewrite the novel to incorporate the new material from the screenplay. They're different media and there are certain things you can do in one medium better than another medium.

But I think some of the extra scenes you added to *Escape from Heaven*, the screenplay — especially some of the scenes in Vegas — and we're not that far from Vegas now. We're doing this interview in Pahrump, Nevada. We're about an hour away from Las Vegas, as I ask this question: did you do it all by yourself or did God give you a little help on the Las Vegas scenes in the screenplay?

J. NEIL SCHULMAN: Well, as I say, I was guided toward November, 1966, as the spacetime conclusion for this. For some reason, the idea of Las Vegas on the day Howard Hughes is moving into the Desert Inn, I seemed to be guided there and ended up there with the song "Adam and Evil" as a crucial plot point.

BRAD LINAWEAVER: Right. So do you feel that you now have expressed the full potential of the *Escape from Heaven* story concept between the novel and the screenplay? And yet there is a possibility of other stories, drawn from these same sources, in the future? This is a question for both Neil the novelist, Neil the screenwriter, and Neil, receiving these experiences.

J. NEIL SCHULMAN: I keep on getting flashes of additional imagery and different plot lines.

I think I know what the first line would be for the sequel to *Escape from Heaven*, which I list in the forthcoming books in the novel *Escape from Heaven*, itself, in the front pages, in which I say that the title is *Raising Hell*. I believe that the first line of that novel is, "Everyone in Heaven smokes."

BRAD LINAWEAVER: That's a great line.

J. NEIL SCHULMAN: Because, obviously, once you're in Heaven smoking isn't going to be damaging to your health anymore. How you can object to tobacco and people smoking, because it's bad for your health, when you're an immortal? That's pretty funny.

BRAD LINAWEAVER: Yes, it is.

J. NEIL SCHULMAN: So "Everybody in Heaven smokes" is a really funny first line for that novel.

BRAD LINAWEAVER: I agree.

J. NEIL SCHULMAN: Now I sort of indicate what the plot of *Raising Hell* would be, and to give just a little foreshadowing of it here.

It would be that *the great divorce* is over and Jesus, and Jesus' ex-wife Satan, are back together again — and are Adam and Eve again. And, in essence, Duj Pepperman has been the Jewish Messiah who is bringing Eden back on Earth by opening up the gates. So that Earth is now in full communication with God again and God can walk freely on the Earth again, not having been frozen out anymore during this great interregnum when Satan was able to keep God at bay.

That's the cosmology and the history I'm giving in the novel, the revisionist mythology. Now that Earth is Edenized again –

BRAD LINAWEAVER: That's the whole planet?

J. NEIL SCHULMAN: The whole planet, in fact I say: and Earth was returned to its original name, Eden.

BRAD LINAWEAVER: Oh, so you're arguing Eden was the whole world, not just the garden.

J. NEIL SCHULMAN: Right.

BRAD LINAWEAVER: People wandering around, trying to find the location for the Garden of Eden, are missing the point that Earth was Eden.

J. NEIL SCHULMAN: Earth was Eden, but then there was the Garden of Eden. But the Garden of Eden was a specific place on planet Eden.

BRAD LINAWEAVER: Beautiful, beautiful.

J. NEIL SCHULMAN: Now, the sequel to that, now that that problem is solved and Jesus and His ex-wife are back together again, and she is not in rebellion anymore, she has apologized, she has, in essence, rejoined the team. You still have the problem of what to do with this fallen planet that she has created. Where she, as a demiurge, to basically take the Gnostic heresy and turn it on its head, that in fact the really imperfect god who creates this really imperfect world — which is called Hell — is Satan. Now that she's good again, she has the job of saving her planet from its misery.

And who does she go to? She goes to her husband, Jesus, who is going to go with her to that planet, and now they have the job of saving Hell, of *"Raising Hell."*

Now, who do they call upon to help them? The same crew from the first book, starting with Duj Pepperman.

BRAD LINAWEAVER: I like it. Not everybody listening to this audio book may know, if I may have your permission to explain this.

J. NEIL SCHULMAN: Go ahead.

BRAD LINAWEAVER: The demiurge is the idea that Jehovah in the Old Testament is so wicked and evil He can't possibly be the God who is the father of Jesus Christ in the New Testament. It's basically trying to say the Jehovah is really another manifestation of the devil or Satan. That is one of the original Gnostic heresies.

J. NEIL SCHULMAN: And of course, it's the Gnostic heresy that Robert Heinlein explicitly plays with in *Job: A Comedy of Justice*.

BRAD LINAWEAVER: There are other very famous people in recent times who are into it as well.

J. NEIL SCHULMAN: Yes. But you see people are always coming at me with various different books before mine –

BRAD LINAWEAVER: The books are endless.

J. NEIL SCHULMAN: Yes. Dante's trilogy, Milton's *Paradise Lost*, C.S. Lewis's *The Great Divorce*, Robert Heinlein's *Job: A Comedy of Justice*, *The Last Temptation of Christ* by Kazantzakis. All these sorts of previous books. And they try to figure out, well, did I take this from this and this from that? And of course that wasn't my approach at all.

BRAD LINAWEAVER: No, it was not.

J. NEIL SCHULMAN: My approach wasn't even to try to make my book kabbalistic or Gnostic.

BRAD LINAWEAVER: No, not at all.

J. NEIL SCHULMAN: The logic of my story — not any of these other things — were what told me that Adam had to redeem his own sin, that the best loved of God would in fact be like an ex spouse. All of these sorts of things and then coming together and saying that would mean that, if Adam has to redeem his own sin, then Adam is Jesus.

And that means that there is this continual spirit that runs through the story, more than we know.

That in fact it makes sense for Eve, the fallen, to, in essence, be redeemed and that could mean that, after her disappointment with Earth, then she becomes Satan, and foments the rebellion because of her profound objection to Creation.

That she has been promised that there's going to be meaning coming out of it, and she hasn't found the meaning, and she thinks that God has basically sold her a bill of goods and is a liar.

That's the rebellion. It is looking at your parents and saying, "You're not perfect!" And what child hasn't done that?

When you get to the point where you realize that your parents — as great as you think they are – aren't perfect. And remember, I worshiped my father — but he wasn't perfect.

And I'm sure that I'm not perfect to my daughter.

Chapter 10: Heresies

BRAD LINAWEAVER: Neil, in one of your interviews with Jack Landman on CyberCity, you and he were discussing *Escape from Heaven* as a book about God, while at the same time being a novel or a work of fiction. The subject came up of the *Bible*, and also the Dead Sea Scrolls, and you pointed out that the holy books of the world are books about God written by human beings, but that doesn't mean God does not exist. Just as *Escape from Heaven* is a novel about God but that doesn't mean that God does not exist. The point you made was that human characters, people you've actually known, you could put into a novel that doesn't suddenly mean, if you're writing an historical novel, that all those people cease to have ever existed.

So you were arguing that books about God are interpretations of God but they cannot be taken as the ultimate experience of God in the sense that traditional religious people think they are. But they should be taken more seriously than atheists, who believe that God is a completely fictional construct. With that in mind, I would like to ask you after your experience your epiphany and what you have done in your post epiphany novel, which is *Escape from Heaven*, and the screenplay, I view those as two separate works. What I would like to know is do you now look at the *Bible* and the *Koran* and the *Talmud*, and all these holy texts of the past, with different eyes than before your epiphany?

J. NEIL SCHULMAN: My viewpoint is — I hesitate to use the word — "evolving." "Unfolding" might be a better word, for what's been happening.

I find, going back, looking at what I've written over the course of my career, back to when I was an atheist, several of my earliest short stories — two of them in particular "Benny Rich is Dead" and "For the Sake of Ten Men," both in my short story collection *Nasty, Brutish and Short Stories* — both of them are dealing with religious themes, with Biblical themes. "Benny Rich is Dead" is a fantasy story which takes place in the Court of God. "For the Sake of Ten Men' has to do with a general, on the brink of nuclear war, who takes Biblical text to decide what the moral choice for him to do is.

I find that I was dealing with this way back before I had thought of myself as having any religious impulse, or any God-driven impulse. I looked back at Contemporary American Authors, when they gave me the form to fill out in 1979, to describe how I saw myself as an writer. I remember the quote I gave: "It is the birthright of every storyteller to try to save the world ... we exist in a messianic competition."

So I was seeing the thrust of what I was doing — even though I thought of it in a secular sense — as being messianic, even back from the beginning of my writing.

I also have to say that part of what I'm doing here, I have had a great deal of difficulty of expressing, of being able to find the right words, which is strange for an writer who lives and dies by words, trying to find the right words to describe an experience which is almost entirely without external referents.

And the primary axiom of General Semantics, when Heinlein got me to read Count Alfred Korzybski and S.I. Hayakawa — the negative axiom that the map is not the territory, the symbol is not the referent — has been extremely useful to me.

I realize that both fiction and nonfiction are symbol structures. They're maps. And they are not so different from each other when it comes to the way that they reflect reality. One might be a topographical map and the other one a geopolitical map, but they are both maps of reality using different reference points.

It's almost like a novel is more algebraic than nonfiction and nonfiction is all particulars, where you attempt to draw every particular from reality, a particular time and place, a particular person. Whereas in fiction, what you try to do is, you try to draw a symbol structure, which applies universally, to a number of different points rather than one particular point, but they are both abstractions.

When you draw a particular in nonfiction, it is not the thing itself. It can't be the thing itself because you are leaving out a thousand particulars and choosing maybe two or three to focus on. You are editing. The very fact of editing makes every work of nonfiction a map and, in that sense, fictionalized.

The point is the way that I've come to view scripture is that part of it is history, part of it genealogy, part of it is myth, part of it is political observation, part of it is rhetoric, part of it is lists of laws, part of it is war stories — and it's all mixed together. What I'm saying is that we cannot look at it dumbly. We cannot look at it as just one level. We have to look at it as a rich tapestry of different things, and my criticism of my atheist buddies when they look at it, for the most part — and I have to exclude certain close friends from this who were very scholarly when it came to the *Bible* — but a lot of them simply take the dumbest possible interpretation of the *Bible* and then they try to debunk it, without seeing the richness of the levels, not merely metaphor, not even taking into account the experience of the peoples at that time, the historicity of it, who were part of the context, you understand, aside from anything else.

Now, I am not a Biblical scholar, I have read scripture, reread parts of it. But I have not read it from cover to cover. I've read the important parts of the Old Testament and I've read the Gospels and I've read some of the latter parts of the New Testament, certainly The Revelation of St. John the Divine. So seeing the *Bible* as all these different things, I try to interpret them according to what it is.

When I'm reading Genesis, I actually regard Genesis as possibly the most important book of the entire Old and New Testament, put together. It seems to be the one which tells us the most about God. Exodus also tells us a lot about God, but Genesis tells us, almost directly, the most about God and what His original intents were. What His original creative purposes were, what He was like as an artist. Which is how we first meet Him, as an artist, as a creator, as a parent.

I draw a lot from that and when I'm writing, now, *Escape from Heaven*, I'm taking a lot of what I think was — I'm trying to find the right word here — conveyed to me. The word "conveyed' is nice and loose and doesn't really focus on the means by which I gained this knowledge. But information came to me, was implanted in me, was conveyed to me, was told to me — whatever word you want here — went from there to here — and then I am again drawing my own symbol structure, my own map. I am creating a mythology and — as I have said — it may be a revisionist mythology, because I am disagreeing with some particulars of the way the myth has been told in scripture.

BRAD LINAWEAVER: I'll get to that in a second. Now, I agree with you that Genesis one of the most interesting things of any religious text. The reason I asked you the question, though, about books as interpretations of God — without being necessarily the Word of God — is when you were being interviewed briefly on Jack's CyberCity, you were asking John Hogue, regarding his epiphany experiences or spiritual or mystical experiences, what some of the concrete details were. You were looking for a "something" out of that. His response was classic Buddhist Nirvana stuff, to tell you that you were off base to look for something, that his first true spiritual experience was nothing — he experienced nothing — and then Jack –

J. NEIL SCHULMAN: Yes, but it was not that I was looking for something. It's that I was getting something.

BRAD LINAWEAVER: Yes, but what I wanted to ask you –

J. NEIL SCHULMAN: I did not try to initiate that experience. That experience was initiated from the other end.

BRAD LINAWEAVER: No, you made it very clear that you did not go seeking the experience that you were on the receiving end, just like Lewis maintained when he was tracked down by a God intervention in his autobiography, *Surprised by Joy*.

J. NEIL SCHULMAN: Precisely!

BRAD LINAWEAVER: I don't think this guy ever fully grasped that, how much you said you were on the receiving end. You did not seek it out. But when he talked about the big mystical nothing, I realized that, from my point of view, the atheist tracts of the nineteenth century, these superficial, free-thinking tracts, strike me as of more value than this mystical big nothing.

You have never claimed, out of your experiences, a big nothing. On the contrary, you seem to have had an increase in the data inputs from your epiphany, not a decrease or an absence of it.

J. NEIL SCHULMAN: The reason I like the word unfolding or flowering of the experience, is that it's like certain kernels of very basic axioms were given to me, certain observations, on a very crucial fundamental base level, were given to me. And as these seeds grow, I am able to see more and more of what they grow into.

BRAD LINAWEAVER: Do you have a profound shift in how you view morality from a religious perspective before your experience and after your experience, or is it the same? Because you were a libertarian before — as you and I define the term — and you are a libertarian since, as you and I define the term. So, I'm assuming that nothing in your epiphany experience fundamentally shook or distorted previous libertarian ethics, which I assume you got from natural-law beliefs, which are to some extent religious.

J. NEIL SCHULMAN: I think that the Creator of natural laws would choose as somebody possibly worth talking to, among us, a believer in natural laws, a person who believes that you could look at the universe we're in and derive the fundamental premises of moral behavior, as Ayn Rand did. It is possible to observe certain fundamental things, which are the roots of morality, without reference to the Ten Commandments. I am chagrined, frustrated, not sure what word I want to use here, when I hear people like Dennis Prager say that our morality comes from the *Bible*. That without reference to the *Bible*, people aren't going to behavior morally. Now, in a practical sense, it may be true. In some practical sense, people with a religious education may have more of a moral sense, simply because they think about it, because morality is on their mind.

And I have to say, simply as an observation, I have not been particularly impressed in the overall world at people who say that their morality is derived from Objectivism, and they go out and cheat and steal, and do not act in a moral sense. But nonetheless, it's hard to make comparisons because it's all anecdotal. There's certainly no shortage of Christians who act shoddily, or people who call themselves Christians, who act shoddily. It's no guarantee.

But nonetheless, as a believer in natural law, as a believer that the universe is intended — it was created — to be comprehensible, it puts me more on the side with the atheists than with the superstitious religious person who thinks that the universe — and God's mind — are fundamentally incomprehensible, and therefore all we can do is look at this rule book and do what we're told like good sheep.

BRAD LINAWEAVER: So you were a natural-law libertarian before and after your epiphany experience.

J. NEIL SCHULMAN: And what's more, one of the things that came out of the — I'm not sure epiphany is the right word, but I'll use it — one of the things that came out of the experience was, in essence, God conveying to me that the reason why He was there, or we were together — whatever you want to call it — was because of what I was and where I had come from. That it wasn't a random sort of thing where in *Oh, God!* George

Burns is talking to John Denver's character and he says "Well, you're like the millionth guy through the bridge gets to meet the governor." It wasn't random.

That God was looking for something specific and I fit the job description. I had gone through — to use a much more contemporary reference — the winnowing out to become The Apprentice. There were other candidates who I had to beat out, much like I said. We were in a messianic competition.

BRAD LINAWEAVER: Do you think the fact that you were a natural law libertarian –

J. NEIL SCHULMAN: — crucial to it!

BRAD LINAWEAVER: — beforehand, made the experience easier to get through? Because what's found, from your point of view, is a very strong vindication of the natural-law belief.

J. NEIL SCHULMAN: Did I take comfort that God agreed with me? Yes!

BRAD LINAWEAVER: Well, the natural-law God position?

J. NEIL SCHULMAN: Yes.

BRAD LINAWEAVER: Now what I want to ask you — because that means that you've got things to separate people religiously — certain areas of rule-keeping and laws for their own sake. You don't have that problem with your C.S. Lewis in terms of the Tao, the Golden Rule, the basic morality level of religion, where different religions have an area of real agreement. A lot of them have an area of agreement.

What I want to ask you, now, is one of the areas that separate people in religion — that mystics sometimes argue against — are the various specific claims that religions make historically. So I want to begin with, do you believe, before or after — I don't care which or both — do you believe there was an historical Jesus Christ?

J. NEIL SCHULMAN: Yes.

BRAD LINAWEAVER: Do you believe he came out of the tomb three days after crucifixion?

J. NEIL SCHULMAN: Yes.

BRAD LINAWEAVER: Okay, take it from there, because right there, a lot of people from a Jewish background are going to be screaming for your head at that moment.

J. NEIL SCHULMAN: Where I differ from the Christians, I guess what makes me a heretic and not a Christian accepted by any of the churches today, is that I do not believe that there was or is an eternal Trinity. I take the idea of One God seriously and the reason I take it seriously is that it fits in with my metaphysical approach.

My metaphysical approach is that the words "God" and "existence" are two different words for the same referent and there is only one existence.

BRAD LINAWEAVER: Right.

J. NEIL SCHULMAN: No matter how many universes, no matter how many parallel universes, no matter how many probabilities, it all comes down to one existence.

BRAD LINAWEAVER: I Am that I Am, and God being the Alpha and the Omega.

J. NEIL SCHULMAN: Right, there is one Existence.

Therefore, how is it that we now have multiple minds?

To me it means that God fissioned. He started splitting off parts of Himself into their own little universes so that they could have free will. But what I'm leading up to is the idea of an emergent Trinity, one which starts out with God fissioning Himself into male and female and then God and Goddess and then out of that, the first angel and the first angel would be the soul which we would identify as Jesus. But who I believe we know Him by the name Adam before then. Because only Adam could redeem his own original sin, and that makes me a heretic to the Christians –

BRAD LINAWEAVER: — and the Jews –

J. NEIL SCHULMAN: Well I'm not sure it makes me a heretic to the Jews because it's almost a Jewish thought.

BRAD LINAWEAVER: Well, every Jew I've run it by, who claims to be a religious Jew, claims you're a heretic. So I think you're a heretic to the Jews, the Christians, and the Muslims, as far as I can tell. But that makes your theology original.

What I want to ask you is this, because I followed everything you just said, but what I want to ask is this: you really don't even need the Trinity.

The Trinity was cobbled together for the Nicene Creed, to answer what they deemed to be some contradictions, in problems in terms of how much adoration do you give the Son and how much power does the Son has after He's Risen and all of this. Isn't it fair to say that the Neil Schulman theology as applied to the Christian beliefs — I'll get to some others things in a minute — that the Neil Schulman theology, as applied to the Christian beliefs, is that Jesus is distinct from the Father, to the extent that we ourselves are. To use the old Jewish phrase that upset the priests of the Temple so badly, "the Son of Man," which only the Jews understood the full significance of "the Son of Man" when Jesus said that.

Isn't it arguable that Jesus Christ had these supernatural powers, and was therefore able to do things that "normal" human beings couldn't do, and was truly in that sense more the Son of God than the average Joe — Joseph, the average Joseph — but despite that, is still distinct from the Father? That's my question. Because you don't even have the problem of the Trinity, if you have the pre-Nicene Creed approach.

J. NEIL SCHULMAN: I'm not sure that it makes a difference for the following reason: being in flesh, being in a corporeal body, has its own logic because of it, its own consequences, its own effects. God — You take that Mind, and you put it in a human body — and God looks out of the eyes from the body like anybody else, can feel pain, can die, can be mutilated, can eat, can fall in love, can have sex, can suffer dandruff or psoriasis or boils, impotence — any of these things which flesh is heir to — you take God Himself's soul and figure out a way to put it in flesh — which is, by the way, the reason why Jews consider it blasphemy to consider that, this is what they reject more than anything else — the idea that that Soul could be put into flesh –

BRAD LINAWEAVER: Yes, that's clear. Every educated Christian knows that's the ultimate heresy to the Jewish belief.

J. NEIL SCHULMAN: That is the heresy to Jewish belief, that it could happen. But nonetheless, if you believe that God is powerful, that God is a genius, that God who created the Heavens and the Earth might want to experience that — He might figure out a way to do it.

Given that — once He has done it — He is a man and, as a man, He thinks as a Man, He feels as a man — and He's still God.

BRAD LINAWEAVER: But can there still be a supernatural dimension intruding on that tent of flesh, which are the miracles of Jesus Christ? Yes or No?

J. NEIL SCHULMAN: Yes, and I will say exactly how I know. I think that what Jesus experienced was something akin to what happened to me on February 18, 1997 only it was longer and deeper. I had just a taste of it for a few hours, of what it was to have that mind of God inside me.

BRAD LINAWEAVER: So if you had it for 30 years of a mortal life?

J. NEIL SCHULMAN: How about three years? How about His ministry, three years?

BRAD LINAWEAVER: Yes, okay the three years of the ministry.

J. NEIL SCHULMAN: Suddenly, He wakes up one day, and He's the genetic candidate for that time and place. He's the clone. He's the chip off the old block.

BRAD LINAWEAVER: The stars are in alignment and into Him it comes.

J. NEIL SCHULMAN: Right. And He has, for the next three years, what I had for eight hours, and that means that He has time to develop the powers that I wasn't able to do in eight hours.

BRAD LINAWEAVER: I consider that a perfectly legitimate view which a lot of traditional religions would call a Gnostic heresy, that I consider a perfectly valid, plausible scenario, every bit as reasonable as anything argued by the orthodox religions. But I repeat, to repeat an earlier statement, I maintain that it's heresy to the Jews because it's not just your normal "wizard." It's not your normal magic. It's not Moses having God stuff channeled through him for the purposes of a miracle. It is that full God consciousness in the full human body that you just expressed so beautifully a few minutes ago. It is that that was so heretical to the priests of the temple and made Jesus Christ the ultimate heretic to the Jews. Therefore, I maintain that you are a heretic to all the religions.

Do you see what I'm saying, do you follow this?

J. NEIL SCHULMAN: How dare Man — whether Jew, Christian, Muslim or any of them, these children of God — how dare they instruct God what He may not do?

BRAD LINAWEAVER: That's exactly right. That's what they all do, all the traditional religions every last one of them. Sometimes it gets almost funny, with the levels of bureaucratic rules.

It is hilarious that the human institutions pretend to know God's mind so well, so intimately, and in such excruciating detail, that they can do precisely what you just said. Which makes no logical sense, because these are the same people who turn right around in the next second — you've heard it from Dennis Prager — and say that God is unknowable. So how can God simultaneously be so unknowable, and yet all the Jews can know all the rules, all the Christians can know all the rules, all the Muslims can know all the rules? How can you know all the rules and, at the same time, say that God is totally unknowable? That is a total contradiction.

J. NEIL SCHULMAN: Right. Here's the thing, and this is why I love Genesis so much, because Genesis has God telling us about Himself, and by the way so does Exodus. Let's just talk about those two books, Genesis and Exodus. Forget about the other three books in the Pentateuch. What does Genesis tell us about the nature of God?

Number One, it tells us that he's not a perfectionist. He looked at His creation and does he say "Perfect"? No. It says, "He looked at it and saw that it was good." "Good" is good enough for God. "He looked at it and saw that it was good." That tells us something about His personality right off.

BRAD LINAWEAVER: If it was perfect there would have been no choice in Eden.

J. NEIL SCHULMAN: Right and tells me something else, leading into another...

BRAD LINAWEAVER: Point one.

J. NEIL SCHULMAN: But let me make the point with full force. I maintain that perfection is a verb, not a noun. As a noun, it is without referent — including God Himself — because God — being dynamic, being alive, being a chooser, being an experimenter — is a risk-taker, and all action has the risk of imperfect results. Because, if you did not have that possibility, action would be futile.

The very nature of being a living, active, consciously volitional God, means that you have taken this idea — that you've had possibly for eons before — of being perfect and whole, and thrown it out for this Grand Experiment called Creation. And that means You're a risk taker, You're an experimenter, You're a scientist, You're an artist.

You start out being a scientist, and then being an artist. Which, by the way, is the same evolution we see in children, where they come out, and the first thing they do is start exploring and being a scientist, and then later they become artists and they become creative.

BRAD LINAWEAVER: Right

J. NEIL SCHULMAN: Well, I say that God went through the same sort of thing. That at the moment He decided to make minds, souls, other than His own who could disagree with Him, results uncertain — experiment started — God at that point is no longer one soul, He has given up being the only one existing. There are now multiple existents, the very multiplication of souls itself makes God's soul part of a community and is the first step to Him becoming a human being.

Going back to what God tells us about it so that we know Him so that He isn't ineffable and unknowable.

I just had a Passover service a few ago, and I noticed something that I never noticed before.

God says, I am not going to send my angels to do the tenth plague, the killing of the first born of the Egyptians. I will do it myself. Now, what is the word "Passover" about? It means that God asked the Jews to put a symbol on their doors so that He would "pass over" their doors.

Now, let's think about this for a second. God's doing this Himself.

Excuse me? If God's omniscient, what does He need anybody to mark any doors for Him? If God's omniscient, He doesn't know which are the Jews and which are the Egyptian firstborn? He's going to make a mistake?

No! It means that God is operating within our sphere, within this universe, within the rules of this space-time continuum, and He is capable of making a mistake and so He wants a backup there.

Then why does every atheist use God's "omniscience" and His "omnipotence" as a contradiction to hang their atheism on, and why do so many theologians demand that if He's not omniscient, omnipotent, and omnipresent, that He can't be God?

BRAD LINAWEAVER: Right. Yet Gene Scott was the first TV Christian I ever saw who said there's no claim in the New Testament, there's no claim in the Old Testament, there's no claim in the official holy text of Jews, Muslims or Christians claiming any such thing. You cannot find the verse, because Scott says it does not exist. Now do we agree with Scott on that?

J. NEIL SCHULMAN: We sure do.

BRAD LINAWEAVER: Okay. Now let's go somewhere with this. When do theologians start coming up with this poison and then when did the atheists start figuring that if they could answer the poison they would have answered the claims of religion? It's worthy of research.

J. NEIL SCHULMAN: You know what it is? Oh, I don't know when it happened but I'll tell you the purpose for it. It's inflation. If you can blow God up so much that the word becomes meaningless, you no longer have something concrete to deal with. You're now dealing with the phantasm, or as I like to say, it's not the worship of God, it's the worship of Fog.

BRAD LINAWEAVER: So I don't know where it all began but it's definitely poison, it's theological poison, and atheists for generations have felt if they could disprove this crap they'd disprove religion.

J. NEIL SCHULMAN: Atheists prefer an impossible definition of God because it makes God impossible. Theologians prefer an impossible definition of God because it makes God whatever they want Him to be for their own political purposes. You really have to have met God before you're really interested in who God is and what He is, and at that point He's not ineffable, He's not malleable – any more than meeting anybody else. Everybody who you meet is somebody, and so is God.

You see, the two hardest things I have, in conveying my experience to people, is that what makes me convinced of its reality is that God is real. He come across to me like a real person — a personality, opinions, thoughts. Not the physical body. The one thing that I didn't meet was the physical body. It's not like on Joan of Arcadia where there's this person showing in a different guise every time, I haven't had that. I haven't had the John Denver and George Burns experience where you could see Him and feel Him. It was something inside, behind my eyes.

But everything else is exactly the same as meeting somebody. That means, a person with thoughts, opinions, a style, a sense of life, a sense of humor. And that's what makes me convinced.

BRAD LINAWEAVER: It seems to me that the God experience you've had — and your belief that He split off all these entities that we are because He didn't want to be alone, He wanted to have other beings to share existence with and to have free will, your origin of us as the fissioning of God model, for want of a better term, I think God fissioning is a good way to describe what you've got — is it not possible that God could have performed this operation whether He created space-time or not? In other words, I'll state it slightly differently. That what we call existence could be eternal and not in need of creating — like the atheists say — and there could still be God creating all of us? Or God could have created the space-time continuum but the essential thing about God's relationship to us exists independently of whether He created space-time or not? I can rephrase it you want.

J. NEIL SCHULMAN: I understand the question but I'm not sure in reality there's a distinction. Because I see certain necessities involved. The necessity for free will requires, I think, some sort of actual physical separation from God. Now I'm not sure what the word "physical" means in this context but it may mean in some sense an extra dimension, or an extra universe, an extra continuum. I'm not sure of the right word to use. But for the separation to exist and be real, for us to have a will free from God's will, thoughts free from God's thoughts, real actual freedom of choice, that it would require creation of an independent universe for us to exist in.

BRAD LINAWEAVER: Which can logically imply the creation of the universe, but it's not essential.

J. NEIL SCHULMAN: Right, but that's my thought of why.

BRAD LINAWEAVER: You don't have a firm certainty on it?

J. NEIL SCHULMAN: No.

BRAD LINAWEAVER: Because you don't think it's essential ultimately, to your real discovery.

J. NEIL SCHULMAN: Let's just say it's above my pay grade.

BRAD LINAWEAVER: Or it's not essential to your real discovery is another way of putting it.

J. NEIL SCHULMAN: Well, not yet, but right now it's above my pay grade. It's beyond the detailed understanding that I have.

BRAD LINAWEAVER: Very good. Good answer. You obviously believe there are creatures that are more supernatural that God creates in addition to us. In other words you have no trouble believing in the angels of various religious traditions?

J. NEIL SCHULMAN: Right. But as I portrayed in *Escape from Heaven*, not necessarily superior. Possibly cognitively or physically superior, but not necessarily superior in the sense that we may have capabilities that they don't have.

BRAD LINAWEAVER: But they may have some we don't have?

J. NEIL SCHULMAN: Right.

BRAD LINAWEAVER: Now having said that, can you accept the idea that, from our human perspective, there's good ones and bad ones, which we can call angels and demons, for want of a better term?

J. NEIL SCHULMAN: Well, inasmuch as angels would have free will –

BRAD LINAWEAVER: That's a reasonable idea.

J. NEIL SCHULMAN: It necessitates what we would call "good ones" "and bad ones."

BRAD LINAWEAVER: Now, you don't doubt that Moses had a God experience, with the burning bush? And Exodus — just like Jesus Christ is an example in human history of a God experience

— Moses is an example in human history of a God experience. Do you believe Mohammad was in a cave, as I remember, and he's supposed to have had contact with angels in a cave?

J. NEIL SCHULMAN: Did Neale Donald Walsch have a God experience? Did Mohammad have a God experience? Did Joseph Smith have a God experience? Did David Koresh have a God experience? Did Joan of Arc have a God experience? All of these are different people who, at one time or another, have claimed God experiences.

Now the *Bible* is the writing of writers. The *Koran* is the writing of writer or writers. So is *The Book of Mormon.* So were whatever David Koresh thought he was unsealing. So is what Neale Donald Walsch is writing. These are the writings of writers, writers other than me.

Now I've had my own experience, and I have my own interpretations, and I have my own writings, which have come to me because of these. It is with things done by other people who claim contact with God, I am in an odd situation.

I do not do what most religionists do, such as Dennis Prager, or Pat Robertson, or Billy Graham.

BRAD LINAWEAVER: Which is?

J. NEIL SCHULMAN: Which is judge their experiences by the written down revelations of other people. I do not judge the reality of what happened to me by what other people have written down. I do the opposite, which is, I judge the reality of what I see in those writings by what I know to be true from what has happened to me.

BRAD LINAWEAVER: You do not let traditions influence your first-hand experience.

J. NEIL SCHULMAN: Correct.

I do judge the tree by its fruit and the problem I have with Islam is that any club which says, "Join, obey — or die" — as far as I'm concerned — is not a respecter of free will and not a respecter of God.

I am looking for the truth. I am doing it by trying to extract meaning from my experiences, and apply logic to them, and try to tie them in to the vast writings and cultural experience and all these other things. That's why I find something like Genesis or something like Exodus or the Gospels relating what Jesus did, to be informative to me, because I find things that have happened to me which has meaning there.

BRAD LINAWEAVER: My earlier statement though — the area where you become a heretic even to the Jews — is I've known a lot of Jewish Kabbalistic believers, in science fiction over the years, and their imagination shuts down at the precise moment that your imagination catches fire. You know where that is?

J. NEIL SCHULMAN: Where?

BRAD LINAWEAVER: The Jesus story.

J. NEIL SCHULMAN: It's because I see God as an Artist and, particularly, I see God as a Storyteller and that tells me something crucial.

Genesis, the Creation, is a First Act. It tells the story of a creation. It tells a story of a fall.

Now, I will tell you this much. The granting of a patch of land in the Middle East — surrounded by a billion hostile enemies, without any oil on it — does not strike me as a good Second Act.

BRAD LINAWEAVER: Amen, brother!

J. NEIL SCHULMAN: If you're going to tell the story of a creation and a fall, you have to tell the story of a resurrection, and Judaism does not tell that story.

Chapter 11: Doctrines

BRAD LINAWEAVER: We've talked about when you were an atheist. We've talked about when you were an agnostic. We've talked about when you became a theist. What I want to suggest to you in this question — which I think is the most important question I will ask you in this series of questions in this entire interview: isn't it right to say that after you had contact with God, and started making these discoveries — or started having these experiences — that in one extremely specific sense, when you became a theist you also became an atheist again about one thing?

You are now a more-convinced atheist than even most atheists, of knowing certain beliefs of what God is to be false. In other words, when a person has an experience of God, doesn't that force him into knowing certain views of God must be untrue. And if that is so, isn't that the ultimate irony, that the deep experience of God must make you an atheist about other people's absolutely false impressions, if it runs too counter from what you have experienced?

Clearly your view of traditional religion's misinterpretations of God, from your experience, would make you an atheist toward many traditional religious views of God, only because you've experienced God and he's not that guy! That is my primary question in this book.

J. NEIL SCHULMAN: It's a brilliant question. I love the irony of it.

God is an existent. He has His own identity. The law of identity says both what a thing is and what it is not. It is the sum of its characteristics, the sum of its particulars.

And God is the sum of His own particulars, He has a specific identity. The Law of Identity says that a thing is its characteristics.

BRAD LINAWEAVER: Yes.

J. NEIL SCHULMAN: And God is His characteristics. He is a specific thing. Just as you, Brad Linaweaver, cannot, at the same moment, be both a communist and an anticommunist.

BRAD LINAWEAVER: Right.

J. NEIL SCHULMAN: You cannot both be a libertarian and a non-libertarian. You cannot both be wearing charcoal pants and red pants — unless you're wearing one over the other.

BRAD LINAWEAVER: Right.

J. NEIL SCHULMAN: But the point is, the sum of whatever you are — the fact that you wear glasses, the fact that your hair is a particular color and is a particular pattern — these are the specific particulars that make you you.

BRAD LINAWEAVER: Sure.

J. NEIL SCHULMAN: The choices that you make, the decisions that you make, the opinions that you have, the jokes that you tell. All of this sums up the particulars which become Brad Linaweaver.

BRAD LINAWEAVER: Yes.

J. NEIL SCHULMAN: And God is the same way.

The particulars of His choices, of His thoughts, of the consequences of what He does, are the particulars that make God God as a person.

BRAD LINAWEAVER: But when you meet Brad Linaweaver, you are meeting somebody, and noticing some of those characteristics and noticing some of those particulars, that make up that character. Is that not true?

J. NEIL SCHULMAN: Yes.

BRAD LINAWEAVER: And therefore, having an experience of God starts giving you an impression of God in the same way that having contact with a fellow human being gives you an impression of that fellow human being, correct?

J. NEIL SCHULMAN: That is correct. My experience of meeting God is the same as meeting any other human being

I've ever met with the one difference that there was not, outside of me, an observable physicality.

BRAD LINAWEAVER: So here's the logical corollary to the other question: here it is.

You are not a New Age mystic, though many people might consider you that, who do not pay attention to what you're saying. Even if this book is being sold in that part of the bookstore, you are not New Age because you are being Aristotelian and Randian about the Law of Identity. When you are saying that God cannot be a certain thing and its opposite, simultaneously, or anything you want God to be — to be more precise I'll repeat that, anything you want God to be — at that moment you part company with most of the so-called New Age mystics and it puts you in the company of traditional orthodox religion.

But you are not done because Part Two is that your encounter with the "characteristic particulars" of God show you — from your point of view, which is the only point of view you have to work with — that the claims which traditional orthodox religions make about God are mistaken. They are wrong. They are not talking about the God you have encountered.

And for the same reason, that you cannot be a New Age mystic and say God can be kind and cruel, and wet and hot, and tall and short, all simultaneously — for the same reasons you reject the New Age God–can–be–anything position — you are in direct conflict with all the traditional religions of the world to the extent that the God you have discovered — a God who's a libertarian, a God who is even subject to natural law himself — is not the God of the Christians, the Jews, the Muslims or any other religion I have ever studied.

That is the corollary to my big question.

J. NEIL SCHULMAN: The God who I have met is the God of the Jews, the Muslims, the Christians and all the others. But they run away.

The doctrines — the articles of faith that you must adhere to – "I accept Israel along with God!" to be a Jew, "I accept Jesus as my personal Savior!" in order to be a Christian. All of these things are external to the attempt to accept the reality of what's going on.

In the same way, we are told in the Old Testament that the Hebrews went to Moses and said, "Don't have God talk to us again! Have Him talk only to you! We can't take this!"

A lot of religion is substituting tradition, ritual, form, performance — anything — to give them the impression that they are obeying this God, but the last thing that they want is the personal contact because that's dangerous — that's scary.

Let me put it another way.

Suppose you had a child who was orphaned, and that child always wanted to meet his parents, and then, some day, discovered that he wasn't, in fact, orphaned, but that he'd been placed in an orphanage and his parents were still alive.

Over his entire life, he has built up all these expectations and beliefs and ideals, and images and stories and fantasies –about what his parents will be and who they will be ... when he finally meets his parents.

And he leaves the orphanage, and moves in with them, and his parents are real.

His parents are grownups, and when he does something that they don't like, they spank him. They're capable of delivering pain.

And he realizes something about his parents that he didn't fantasize about: his parents are fundamentally dangerous.

Now C.S. Lewis — when he describes Aslan in *The Chronicles of Narnia* — a phrase over and over and over again throughout *The Chronicles of Narnia* is: he is not a tame lion.

When Jill Pole in *The Silver Chair* meets Aslan — not knowing who He is, she asks, "Do you eat girls?" and Aslan says, "I've swallowed up entire kingdoms, boys and girls, men and women."

This is not somebody who's trying to make you comfortable with the situation.

BRAD LINAWEAVER: That's Jehovah's destruction of people in the Old Testament, isn't it?

J. NEIL SCHULMAN: Yes. God — if real, if not merely a myth, if not just a story, if not a creation of religion — is fundamentally dangerous because He has power and His own will, and we are less powerful and our wills can be conquered by His decisions.

BRAD LINAWEAVER: You know where the phrase "God fearing Christian" comes from?

J. NEIL SCHULMAN: Yes.

BRAD LINAWEAVER: They're afraid of God and think that God is scarier than the devil!

J. NEIL SCHULMAN: Right, right. Okay. And the fear of God is, in some sense, something that must be overcome in order to meet God.

Now, let me go back to your original point — which I love — the idea that I'm an atheist who knows God, and is an advocate for God.

If you take it, I am not an a-Deist — I'm not without God — I am an a-theist, in the sense of...

BRAD LINAWEAVER: Without theology! You are without theology!

J. NEIL SCHULMAN: Without theology, right!

BRAD LINAWEAVER: This would be a different definition of "atheist" that would actually make more sense than how the word is normally used.

J. NEIL SCHULMAN: In other words, if we look at it not in the metaphysical sense but in an epistemological sense, that I am not rejecting God. I am rejecting the maps.

BRAD LINAWEAVER: Right.

J. NEIL SCHULMAN: That regarding religion's maps of God, I'm being a cartographer and I'm laying them out on a table. And I'm saying, "Yes, this is right here. This is right here. No, that's wrong!" I'm correcting the maps.

I'm looking at the maps, and I'm saying, "This matches up with my experience, with what I know. This is wrong. This is impossible. God couldn't possibly be this, or this, or this."

So, in essence, I find myself outside the religious traditions, even though I am at the center of all of what they say their core belief is.

Because, I reject Judaism but I accept the God of the Jews.

I reject Christianity but I accept the God of the Christians.

BRAD LINAWEAVER: You can say the same for Islam too.

J. NEIL SCHULMAN: I reject Islam but I accept the God of Islam.

I have been less concerned with labels for a while now, and I had to be, because I realized that I was more concerned with being true to my principles than being true to my label. And again, this is a theme which goes through a lot of what I'm going to say.

I was not concerned: am I still a Jew?

I was not concerned — if I bring Jesus Christ into the picture — am I now a Christian?

It's interesting to contemplate, but it's not important to me. What's important to me is: am I accurately apprehending the reality of what God is and what He is saying?

Both Jews and Christians, today, act as if God and Jesus are historical figures and not active in our daily lives. If you pray, maybe a very tiny miracle might happen, occasionally. But it's not something to be expected in the same way that you are a blind man walking around when Jesus is doing His ministry. You heard the rumor that here is this man who can cure the blind, and you actually find Him.

And He goes up to you and He can.

Chapter 12: Supernatural Law

J. NEIL SCHULMAN: I think that God, in His original state — I talked about the original state and then the developed state – God in His original state was the one being who violated the first axiom of Korzybskian epistemology. When God was both the only Consciousness and the only Existent, the map was the territory.

At the point where God allowed Himself to think fantasy, in other words to think thoughts which He did not put into effect — for Him to contemplate without taking action — those became in essence, images, maps, those became unreality. I do see a distinction. And that, in essence becomes the beginning of the development.

In other words, where God starts thinking free from His own body, starts thinking of possibilities other than His reality, in essence He becomes non-mundane.

BRAD LINAWEAVER: Okay.

J. NEIL SCHULMAN: So that would be a crucial dividing line between before and after, in God's time-line, in His own individual personal time-line.

Now after that, however, the idea being that when He fissions off other souls from Himself — or fissions them off and allows them to develop independent from Himself — we're real. I do not believe that you can have a living intelligence which is not real. I do not believe that you can have an intelligence which is only virtual. There has to be some physical reality to it.

BRAD LINAWEAVER: Well, once you give birth to a child, you can't just suddenly recall it. And you're saying, in a way, if we're all God's children, we're all real once we exist. You can't just suddenly recall your children — well maybe God could but He doesn't — because you also believe God operates under natural law.

J. NEIL SCHULMAN: Yes. And let me explicate on that, since we're bringing that out.

While I agree with the traditional view of God as the Creator — that God creates natural law, that God is the author of natural law — He is not the author of all natural law.

I can see Him when He, perhaps, goes into the primal atom — or whatever the current scientific paradigm is — before the Big Bang, and in essence designs into it what's going to happen when the fireworks go off. What the chemical compounds are going to be, whether you're going to have atoms and electrons and molecules and physics and gravity and space and time and all these sorts of things within a particular closed space-time continuum — or another sort of continuum which may not even have time or space as part of it. Now I can't conceive of that. Maybe God can. But nonetheless, when God creates a closed continuum, God is the author of the natural laws of that universe and if those natural laws have as part of the primal mathematics within it that it will reach a point where life will evolve, then God is the author of life within that continuum.

I can see a universe in which all of the development of life is in the seed, that God, in essence, puts the DNA for us in the very DNA of the universe itself. I can see that as a possibility.

But where I differ from most theologians — it may even be all theologians I don't know any other –

Again we have to keep in mind that I'm not a religious scholar. I'm simply a guy who thinks, and who says that God talked with him. So there are vast areas of ignorance in me, dealing with some of the technicalities of other viewpoints, of traditional religions or theologies.

BRAD LINAWEAVER: You have less to unlearn.

J. NEIL SCHULMAN: I have a lot of Zen going for me in that sense.

But what I'm saying is, where I think that I disagree with most others who conceive of God, is that I see God being subject to the Law of Identity, because He exists.

BRAD LINAWEAVER: Which means there's a meta-natural law that even God subscribes to?

J. NEIL SCHULMAN: Right. And we could call that, perhaps, a supernatural law because it is above the natural laws which God creates.

So therefore, the supernatural law is, perhaps starting with some of the laws which Aristotle identified — the Law of Existence, the Law of Non-contradiction, the Law of Identity — these would be laws that God, being an existent, would be subject to, and would not be able to violate.

And I think C.S. Lewis accepted that. When Lewis says that not every sentence that starts with "God can" is a possible real sentence, Lewis himself is putting forward the idea that God can't do something which is self-contradictory.

BRAD LINAWEAVER: Yes, that's right. He's at least suggesting it very strongly.

J. NEIL SCHULMAN: Yes. So again, this is why all sorts of theology which as we have discussed — not necessarily in these recordings but which we have discussed — are not necessarily even scriptural, making claims of God of being Omnipotent, Omniscient, and Omnipresent –

BRAD LINAWEAVER: — which you're not the first to point out –

J. NEIL SCHULMAN: I say He was in His primal state, but not now.

BRAD LINAWEAVER: Yes, you're not the first to point out those three things can not coexist, in terms of the universe we know.

J. NEIL SCHULMAN: And when I say that the concept of creation out of nothingness — creation ex nihilo — is ridiculous, that it violates the Laws of Existence and the Laws of Identity to which even God is subject, I say that God can create out of very little. He may be able to create out of quantum probabilities — in other words, something that would look to us like practically nothing, like waves or dust or even subatomic something — but nonetheless, He would be starting with something and imposing pattern on it, imposing form on it, and the void would not be totally void — it would just be formless.

So the creation is taking the formless and imposing a new form on it or taking an existing form and reforming it.

BRAD LINAWEAVER: Well, as a matter of fact, the opening line of Genesis describes God "re-creating" the Earth. There is no Biblical scholar worth his salt — Lot's wife not withstanding — who does not admit that the opening lines of Genesis — "The Earth was without form and void" — it is describing the re-creation of the Earth. There is no doubt.

J. NEIL SCHULMAN: Well, I wouldn't necessarily have to use the word re-creation, in the sense of, would you say that a painter who starts with a blank canvas is re-creating a painting?

BRAD LINAWEAVER: It's not a blank canvas, "The Earth was formless" suggests that material of Earth is already there.

J. NEIL SCHULMAN: Right, the material. In other words, in the same sense that a sculptor comes to a block of marble –

BRAD LINAWEAVER: If you paint a painting on top of an older painting, isn't that the use of the materials that are there?

J. NEIL SCHULMAN: Absolutely! But it is also true that if God were starting with a tabula rasa — if He were starting with a blank slate that –

BRAD LINAWEAVER: It's works just as well for a re-creation of Earth.

J. NEIL SCHULMAN: It works either way. It's not a distinction that we find it necessary to concern ourselves with.

BRAD LINAWEAVER: It doesn't tell us whether this Earth was the only Earth God has created.

J. NEIL SCHULMAN: Right. Now, again, I believe that this is possibly His earliest creation of this sort. That He had never done something like this before. And the reason I think that is that His learning curve is so steep.

Chapter 13: Heaven

BRAD LINAWEAVER: Neil, given your experiences, and how you've used them to help produce this current work, in terms of novel writing and script writing, why do you think there are almost no stories, at least none that I can find, where a character goes to Hell and can just come back the way characters seem to go to Heaven and don't stay there?

J. NEIL SCHULMAN: Well, of course, there's one classic version of it, and that's *Orpheus in the Underworld*, which has been made into various operas. That's where I first encountered it. I suppose *Inferno* — both Dante's version and then the later re-doing of it by Larry Niven and Jerry Pournelle — is precisely that of a human being who gets to go to Hell and then come back, maybe not necessarily to Earth, but in the case of Dante you manage to get out and go to Heaven.

But in terms of modern stories, I guess the only one I can really think of here is Richard Matheson's What Dreams May Come, where the hero follows his wife from Heaven into Hell to rescue her, which again is an Orpheus story. But in terms of why it's not done, I don't know.

BRAD LINAWEAVER: Well the Persephone story and in the case of Dante's *Inferno* you're kind of getting a tour of Hell, there are the exceptions admittedly. But it seems like there are a lot of stories about people going to Heaven and they don't stay, which confuses me because if I ever got to Heaven I would not want to leave. And then you have lots of stories, horror stories especially, nobody gets to leave Hell.

I guess the idea is, if you get to leave Heaven, why would you ever choose to? I guess, maybe, you don't get to leave Hell because it's a punishment, like you don't get to leave prison. But why would anybody choose ever to consciously and deliberately leave Heaven?

J. NEIL SCHULMAN: Well, only when the writer writes Heaven in such a way that it's not worth staying. Which means essentially that what we are doing is we're encountering stories in which Heaven is a device written by a writer who doesn't believe in it.

BRAD LINAWEAVER: That's the thing about your novel. You're very pro-Heaven, and you very much have the idea that Heaven is a place that you want to stay, and yet the title of your novel is *Escape from Heaven* because of the plot situation that you've got, and the ultimate fate of Earth with the political campaign between Jesus and Lucifer.

But it's interesting that people who might pick up your book, or see the movie that will eventually be made of *Escape from Heaven*, could expect this more typical modern idea that when you get to Heaven you can't wait to leave it. I guess it's dull or something. That is the opposite, actually, of what you've written, despite the fact that your work is entitled *Escape from Heaven*.

J. NEIL SCHULMAN: Well, that's because my fundamental premise about Heaven is different.

Heaven is supposed to be "perfect."

Well, if Heaven is "perfect," we know that perfection means that there is no moving forward. I mean, once you are perfect, why do anything except basically sit around and sip tea? You know, there's nothing to do. You don't have to do anything. All your needs are fulfilled. You don't have any wants. There's no excitement. And it does come across as dull.

In the same way that when we have the concept of God being "perfect" it makes Him static as well, why should God take any action whatsoever? Why should He create? Why should He do anything, if everything is perfect?

Perfection is death. Perfection is an ending. Perfection is saying you're done.

BRAD LINAWEAVER: But your Heaven is not perfect.

J. NEIL SCHULMAN: Right! "My" Heaven is not perfect. My Heaven? My portrayal of Heaven, my map of Heaven.

BRAD LINAWEAVER: You know what I mean.

J. NEIL SCHULMAN: Yes. The Heaven in which I am mapping is not mapped to be perfect. The God who I am saying that I have been in communication with is alive, and dynamic, and makes choices, and, therefore, there's a before and after, better or worse. But there is none of this static idea of perfection. Everything is still alive. Everything is still in play — and I play it that way.

Now. It's interesting that my view is actually scripturally correct, because not only does the Old Testament show us God changing His mind and "repenting the evil that He thought to do unto His people" — as it says in Exodus — but also, in the last book of the *Bible* — The Revelation of Saint John the Divine — we are told that there is a war in Heaven, and Heaven is destroyed, and a new Heaven is created afterwards.

People don't remember that there is a re-creation of Heaven, very much the same way as the restoration of Eden is supposed to be the re-creation of Heaven. There is a fall of Heaven itself, and then a re-creation of Heaven itself, or a new Heaven, a new and better, improved Heaven.

Well, that's what I portray in my novel.

We have a war in Heaven, which goes back to the dream I had, in which Heaven falls under attack and, in essence, is devastated in this war.

Well, a Heaven which is devastated is not a nice place anymore. It's not Heaven in the way that we think of Heaven.

BRAD LINAWEAVER: It's not "Heavenly?"

J. NEIL SCHULMAN: It's not "Heavenly," right. But again, this is playing with words.

If Heaven is a real place, then it is a place that can suffer the same destruction as other real places, such as New York City, being hit on 9/11 and having the Twin Towers disappear.

So when Duj goes there — and he has to escape from it because it's a war zone — then that accounts for both the experience that I had in my dream in which I had to escape from Heaven which had fallen under attack, and then, in the novel, Duj has to escape from Heaven because it's fallen under attack.

But the title is also a more general metaphor than that, because — in essence — aren't so many of us in effect escaping from Heaven?

If, in fact, we don't like the meal that is set before us — and we reject it — if we don't like the idea that Earth is not perfect but it is perfecting — it is designed to be a tool to perfect us, an environment in which we play a game to get experience points — to use an old gamer's metaphor — and what happens afterward is a goal we don't want, we don't like God's plan — how many different ways do we escape from Heaven everyday?

If God says that it takes sperm and ova to have babies — and sperm come from a penis and eggs come from an ovary — and the two of them getting together is what sex is — and yet somebody chooses two women or two men, well, that's an escape from Heaven.

Not that I'm condemning it as evil or anything like that. I'm simply saying it's not part of the plan because you don't get babies from it.

BRAD LINAWEAVER: Unless you go to the lab or something like that, which is another escape from Heaven.

J. NEIL SCHULMAN: Well, we could argue whether it's a diversion or part of the learning process, whether it's Science Lab or not.

Remember, I do believe that we are intended to become gods under God. That is part of the cosmology, and part of the eschatology, that I'm portraying in *Escape from Heaven*. That, in fact, the whole point of this exercise, both for angels and humans, is that we are going on paths to make us into gods who are capable of having these enormous powers, and using them, and living forever. With all the challenges of that, the challenge of living forever, you have to be the sort of person who can survive living forever without going crazy, in the same way that God had to figure out a way not to go crazy, not to be bored, not to accept perfection as an end.

BRAD LINAWEAVER: Right.

J. NEIL SCHULMAN: So, in essence, it's also an escape from perfection, and that's where the story begins.

That's when things become interesting. And if you believe that we live forever, it basically means that we go through perfection, as a verb, but not end up in it as a noun.

BRAD LINAWEAVER: In other words, *"Escape from Heaven"* can also mean "escape from the idea of perfection," because that is static?

J. NEIL SCHULMAN: Yes.

BRAD LINAWEAVER: Now, my last question in this sequence, and this is a psychological question, not scriptural, not based on any of the world's holy texts.

Neil Schulman, before, during, and after these experiences – psychologically — never seemed to accept the idea of Hell. Give me psychological or philosophical reasons but not scriptural reasons — why do you think there is no Hell?

J. NEIL SCHULMAN: Wow. Well, for one thing, I guess I'm optimistic enough to think that God, sooner or later, will get through to us. I don't believe in a punitive or penal philosophy to begin with. I don't think that God goes out of His way to administer punishment. I think that, sometimes, He steps out of the way and lets us suffer the consequences of our own actions, and that is in fact punishment. But there is no necessity for creating the prison called Hell, to condemn prisoners forever, to accomplish that because what, in fact would be the point?

Let's look at it in terms of capital punishment here on Earth. Capital punishment is a contradiction in terms, because if you are killed the punishment is over. In fact, you have destroyed the punishment by ending the person who is capable of regret or perceiving it. Once you have eliminated that which is capable of perceiving punishment, you have eliminated punishment.

So, in the same sense, that it is only something which is able to reform the criminal or, in this particular context, the sinner, would there be any meaning to the concept.

Now if you want to argue that Hell is a reform school, a penitentiary — with "penitent" being the root word — that you reach the point where you are penitent for what you have done and attempt to make reparations — if you want to argue that is what Hell is then, okay, I don't have a problem with Hell. I think the Roman Catholics would call that Purgatory though.

BRAD LINAWEAVER: Yes, I like what you're saying. It's like when we talk about libertarian as capital "L" or little "l" or the State as capital "S" or little "s". What you're saying is small "h" hell, you can see that, but capital "H" Hell, you don't see why that would be necessary, and what purpose it would serve for God. Is that right?

J. NEIL SCHULMAN: That is correct. In other words, the idea of eternal punishment — I have said this before — seems to me to be such a dumb idea that only someone who lives a short human lifespan could have such contempt for the idea of eternity as to think of eternal punishment.

BRAD LINAWEAVER: That sets up my final question for *I Met God* by J. Neil Schulman. Here is my final and obvious question: do you think, expect, or hope that you will meet God again in this lifetime or do you think the next time you meet God will be after this lifetime?

J. NEIL SCHULMAN: You're asking me about my hope and my expectation.

Well, of course my hope is to meet God anytime I can, and if I can do it while I'm still alive, great. And if I have to wait until after I'm in the next life, great.

I still feel I have work to do here and so, if I were to die soon, I would die regretfully because there are still things I need to do. I have a daughter who I want to see to adulthood. I have a mother who I'm still taking care of. I have works which I still want to write and — very frankly and very selfishly — I want to be here to see *Escape from Heaven* produced as a movie and done right. That's something I want to hang around to do.

Also, when I die, I want to die thin. That's just a very vain thing and, dumb as it is, I'd like to get myself back into shape before I go. Leave a beautiful corpse, as they say, for the short amount of time before it turns back into dust.

But, I'm not ready to go, but if I do go, then I know that where I go next is going to be exciting, and I'm confident that God's going to be there and it'll be a return home.

I've already been shown my home on the other side. So I know that it's going to be someplace that'll be very much like a kid being offered dessert and then turning away from it. You know, "You don't want dessert?" "No, I don't want dessert! I want to stay here!" That kind of thing.

So, again, I may not have my phobia about death anymore, but I'm not ready to embrace it yet.

BRAD LINAWEAVER: Thanks, Neil.

J. NEIL SCHULMAN: Thank you, Brad.

God's Libertarian Prophet?

An Interview with *I Met God* Author,

J. Neil Schulman. Conducted by Gary York

Introduction

Many years ago, needing to feed my science fiction habit, I bought the book, *Alongside Night*, written by an author new to me: J. Neil Schulman. I thoroughly enjoyed the book and welcomed and enjoyed his second novel, *The Rainbow Cadenza*. Thereafter I visited his web-site at intervals and loosely followed his career. I cheered for him as he published work after (non-fiction) work on strongly libertarian themes. After an absence of a few years I returned to his site to discover that his latest book was titled *I Met God*. Oh, dear!

How could someone who was an atheist, as was I, who was a libertarian/Objectivist, as was I, who seemed so completely dedicated to rationalism – just like me — go so utterly and completely off the rail?

He had written a new science-fiction book, *Escape from Heaven*, so I bought it and read it. It was a splendid, funny book. Sure, he used religious themes but so did many of my favorite SF authors; more importantly, he used those themes well and brought to the table a basket of fresh ideas. Clearly his religious views had not corrupted him as a writer.

And so began a furious exchange of emails.

J. Neil Schulman first appeared on the libertarian movement's radar when his 1979 novel, *Alongside Night* – which portrayed a near-future where a libertarian cadre battled a

U.S. government crumbling from hyperinflation – received endorsements from Milton Friedman, Thomas S. Szasz, and Anthony Burgess.

His 1983 novel, *The Rainbow Cadenza* – which portrayed a future that replaces conscripting young men for military service with conscripting young women for sexual service – received accolades from Nathaniel Branden, Robert A. Heinlein, and Colin Wilson.

Neil didn't begin his sojourn into libertarianism by writing fiction. Before J. Neil Schulman had published his first novel, he had been a libertarian activist on his college campus and later organized libertarian dinners and conferences; he had written the review of Murray Rothbard's *For A New Liberty* in Rothbard's own journal, *The Libertarian Forum*; and he'd been an active partisan in Samuel E. Konkin's neo-Rothbardian "radical caucus."

Schulman has never held back on his libertarian intentions, and in a career that has taken him from New York to Hollywood, he's often paid a price for it. After breaking into network television writing with script sales to *The Twilight Zone,* Neil found his TV writing career cut short. Apparently his 1992 Los Angeles Times Op-Ed piece, favoring private ownership of handguns, was received so unfavorably by prime-time TV producers who had promised him a writing job on their Emmy-winning network show that he was immediately blacklisted.

Undaunted, Schulman decided to do what one of his literary heroes would have done, and if Neil didn't stop the motor of the book publishing industry, he at least gave it a long overdue oil change. Schulman founded two book publishing companies – SoftServ Publishing and Pulpless.Com. They used new technology to bypass traditional bookstore distribution and made books available for immediate download or after on-demand printing. The books were sold through computer bulletin boards and, later, through the Internet. Both the *Wall Street*

Journal and *The New York Times* have recognized Schulman as a pioneer of the eBook.

Schulman also wrote one of the most effective books defending the individual right to keep and bear arms, *Stopping Power: Why 70 Million Americans Own Guns*, and counts Charlton Heston among his celebrity fans. Dennis Prager, who hosts a nationally syndicated radio talk show, once an advocate of gun bans, credits Schulman's writing as the reason he now favors gun ownership.

A sequel, *Self Control Not Gun Control*, collected his libertarian essays on a wide range of other topics and won him an endorsement from Walter Williams.

Post 9/11, Schulman departed from the mainstream libertarian movement in two respects: despite his anarchist and isolationist roots he elected to support President Bush's War on Terror; then, even more iconoclastically, Schulman abandoned his life-long atheism and revealed that on February 18, 1997, he had met God. Literally.

The results of that encounter – and the lifetime of mystical experiences leading up to it – came out in J. Neil Schulman's two latest books: his 2002 novel, *Escape from Heaven*, and his latest autobiographical book, *I Met God*, released in 2005 as an audiobook and being prepared for release as a printed book.

In 2006, J. Neil Schulman expanded out of screenwriting into producing, directing, acting, and even songwriting, with his feature film, *Lady Magdalene's*, with *Star Trek* icon, Nichelle Nichols ("Uhura") starring in the title role. As of this writing the film will be completed in a few weeks and will be submitted to major film festivals before seeking a studio to distribute it.

A movement coalesced in modern times around the fiction and drama of a single Russian-born novelist, playwright, and screenwriter. Arguably, Ayn Rand is as much responsible for the character of the modern libertarian movement as any economist or political figure. While the Left has always considered artists, musicians, and writers to be essential personnel in their push for social change, both the Right and the libertarian movement are underrepresented in the battle for hearts and minds.

Since Ayn Rand, few libertarians seem to have enlisted in the Culture War, and why should they? The left rewards its culture warriors with Academy Awards and Nobel Prizes. We don't. Guess who's standing on the high ground?

J. Neil Schulman has been for the last three decades, and continues to be, one of our leading cultural commandoes.

We conducted this interview by email and by telephone.

GARY YORK: You've come out in support of the War on Terror. Why the change from your original anti-war position?

J. NEIL SCHULMAN: I understand the roots of opposition to war thoroughly. As a matter of fact I opposed both the original Gulf War and President Clinton's bombing of Iraq.

What changed me were the 9/11 sneak attacks, which I consider really were acts of war, as much as the Japanese attack on Pearl Harbor. Unlike previous wars, the enemy is not a nationalistic state but an ideological cadre. I wrote about exactly that sort of ideological cadre in my novel, *Alongside Night* — albeit my cadre was dedicated to libertarian goals achieved by libertarian means, not attacks on civilians as part of a desire to kill anyone who can't be coerced into converting to your religion.

The madrasas and other Islamic extremist propaganda are brainwashing Muslim children with an Islamic variation of the Hitler Youth's anti-Jewish-hatred, and because radical Islam's position that any non-Muslim can be sold into slavery or killed at will, these Islamic extremists equal the Nazi contempt for anyone not fitting their approved racial profile.

Regardless of how badly anyone thinks the U.S. and the U.K.

may be at prosecuting the war on terror, it would be a fatal error to think that anything short of marginalizing the Islamo-Nazis' ability to launch effective attacks can save modern civilization from these evil psychopaths. It's a mistake to think they're attacking us because of our foreign policy. They're attacking us because free trade imports our modern culture and out-competes their own push for cultural world domination. Western-style civilization, while leaving much to be desired from a libertarian's standpoint, is far more protective of individual rights than any other human civilization, past or present. I'm not going to apologize to my fellow libertarians for thinking it needs to be preserved, even at the cost of allowing the Department of Homeland Security to get their hands on my Amazon.com bill.

Let me be clear, however, that the trade-off for my support is contingent on the government actually using its powers to defend our country, rather than using 9/11 as an opportunity to promote other agendas, such as internationalism or the further disempowerment of the individual. The way to win a "war on terror" is to identify those enemies who want to kill us and either kill them first or make the price for killing us so high that they will quit trying.

The United States prevailed in World War II against industrial powers in Germany and Japan and in the Cold War we prevailed against a Soviet military superpower. Radical Islam is truly a threat because it is within the ability of terrorists to obtain and deploy WMD's against our cities, but the way to meet that threat is not by making us take off our shoes before we get on an airliner but by making it clear to the rulers of Iran, Syria, and Saudi Arabia that the cost of them not eliminating radical Islamic terrorists will be an American thermonuclear strike against them should another 9/11 attack succeed.

It's not the job of the American government to diagnose and cure the psychotic worldview that leads some believers in God to think God wants their specific religion to be the only brand of faith on this planet. It is the job of the American government to defend our freedom.

That said, I also want it to be understood that I do not regard Judaism, Christianity, and Islam to be three separate religions, but a single religion. They all worship God. None of them worship Odin or Zeus. Any war between any of these three artificial partitions of God worship by religious texts, doctrines, and organizations is the equivalent of domestic violence. It may be necessary to engage in a lethal response against a family member attacking with deadly force but one should never do so with glee. Jews, Christians, and Muslims are all children of God, and if any one of them thinks God is about to play favorites, they are out of their fucking minds.

GARY YORK: How much were you involved with Ayn Rand, her circle, and Objectivism?

J. NEIL SCHULMAN: I was a little late getting to Objectivism because I was 15 years old and living in Massachusetts in 1968 when Ayn Rand split with Nathaniel and Barbara Branden, and the Nathaniel Branden Institute shut down. There really was no formal Objectivist movement by 1971 when I moved to New York City and met up with those libertarians most influenced by Rand and Objectivism. Due to the influence of Robert Heinlein's books, I was already a libertarian rationalist by the time I encountered Rand's writings and the Objectivist remnant. I read *Atlas Shrugged*, and was hooked. I'd found my philosophical home.

GARY YORK: Where would you say you most passionately agree with Miss Rand?

J. NEIL SCHULMAN: To start off with, her reliance on Aristotle's axioms of Existence exists, Non-Contradiction, the Law of Identity. Her Introduction to Objectivist Epistemology is fine as far as it goes, but is incomplete and does not allow for sources of data not deriving from the five senses, since she never would have considered anything beyond that capable of being validated. I agree with Rand's philosophical attacks on selflessness, forced self-sacrifice, collectivism, and on Kant's demand that moral behavior has to have no personal benefits. Rand was, I think, annoyed that the Christian author C. S. Lewis, agreed with her on all of this.

I agree with Rand that an observation of the nature of man as rational, volitional beings is sufficient to derive an objective moral code, with no reference to religious documents or mystical premises. Such a moral code would apply even to immortal beings, although with somewhat distinct moral imperatives, since physical survival would likely not be at stake for an immortal.

Ayn Rand was one of the best thinkers to identify the anti-life nihilism, and envy-based hatred toward the thinker class, at the core of all variants of socialism, and anticipated both the entire political correctness movement and the loony left's ever-morphing fetishes. She was a brilliant and funny satirist, if too bitter late in life when I finally met her. And there was a hot Russian siren buried somewhere in that little Russian babushka. All in all, if I'd met her when she was younger, I would have wanted us to fuck our brains out.

GARY YORK: What are your strongest disagreements with Objectivism?

J. NEIL SCHULMAN: Interestingly, my disagreements with Objectivism as a formal philosophy are fairly minimal, partly because Rand never developed Objectivism into a full philosophical system. I find what she wrote to be true in its own context, but her context was too provincial and time-bound to encompass the possibility of an afterlife. Her dismissal of paranormal experience as sources of data about the real world negates the possibility of learning about additional continua beyond our conventional sensory experience, which is limited to local knowledge gained from our own bodily existence.

If I have more of a problem, it's not so much with Objectivism, per se, but with the cultish behavior of her admirers, who in their worship of *Atlas Shrugged* mirror Evangelical Christians worship of the *Bible*. I also have a problem with Objectivist-influenced atheists who raise skepticism to the level of religious dogma.

GARY YORK: Neil, you say you met God. What exactly do you mean by that?

J. NEIL SCHULMAN: God didn't call me for an appointment in an office building like in *Oh God!* or *Bruce Almighty*. But I've had two distinct waking experiences where I can say with confidence that I encountered God's presence.

The first time I recognize for sure was on April 15, 1988 when God put his hand on my heart and threatened to kill me.

The second encounter was February 18, 1997, when God merged his own consciousness with my own for the better part of a day, and for that short time let me share his own mind and superhuman cognitive powers.

Both were life-changing experiences, and when my abstract skepticism came up against my actual experience, I could either conclude that I was out of my mind or eventually accept the reality of it. After a thorough analysis of my previous life's experiences, and later experiences that lent validation, I concluded that the reality was that what had happened to me were really encounters with God — therefore proving God's existence to me — and that sanity would lie not in denying the truth of my experience by dismissing it as a psychotic break but in embracing the reality of it, maintaining my rational faculties, and proceeding accordingly.

GARY YORK: Presumably you once believed in the separation of Church and State; has your personal encounter with God changed your opinion?

J. NEIL SCHULMAN: No, but that's because I've never been much of a fan of either church or state. I see both types of institutions as degraded functions. Both churches and states exist as attempts to channel human behavior to their own vision of the good. Combining church and state – just like combining a single political party and state, as did communism and Nazism —multiplies their power to impose conformity to their vision. The flaw is that any institution wielding the power to enforce conformity attracts Bizarro Supermen who want to remake men in their own image. Kept away from the levers of power, churches often encourage self improvement and end up being a more-or-less good thing. Libertarians, being curmudgeons, see the glass as half empty. Since my encounter with God, I'm more of a glass-half-full guy.

GARY YORK: You claim to have met God, to have "mind melded" with him and so you feel free to say what God would and would not want. But what about all those others who weekly proclaim from pulpits their version of God's demands and desires? Should something be done about them? Surely, if God in fact exists, He must deplore this incredible cacophony of error!

J. NEIL SCHULMAN: That's easy. My answer is, don't take anything religions say on faith and don't take anything I say on faith, either. Test second-hand knowledge for its truth. Existence — or God, if you prefer — will give you independent validation. Ground your beliefs in testable reality. Find me a church that has the confidence in God's craftsmanship to make the same disclaimers I just did, and I'll consider joining it.

GARY YORK: What do you think God wants taught in the classroom?

J. NEIL SCHULMAN: What makes you think God finds classrooms the best place for education?

OK. Maybe classrooms, like factories, are useful for mass-production. I don't tend to like the products that come out of a lot of classrooms. I do like the products that come out of the Internet, talk radio, and late-night libertarian science-fiction beer-fed bull sessions.

GARY YORK: Doesn't "freedom of religion" necessarily imply "freedom from religion?"

J. NEIL SCHULMAN: It implies that one should be free to practice religion. Demanding others join you is where freedom ends. Demanding that others stop their own practice because you feel excluded is tough shit. Everyone needs to lighten the fuck up.

GARY YORK: You once were a rationalist; you claim that you remain a rationalist. How, as someone who now believes in God, a supernatural entity, can you simultaneously espouse a belief in the supremacy of reason?

J. NEIL SCHULMAN: Because I don't believe the supernatural is unreal, therefore reason can eventually discern supernatural operations and supernatural laws.

GARY YORK: Perhaps you can both believe in a God and remain a rationalist because you had personal experience of a nature that was convincing to you; but what about someone who adopted a belief in God because of reports of your unverifiable personal experience? Wouldn't that be irrational? In other words, wouldn't it be irrational to believe in God because of what you say?

J. NEIL SCHULMAN: Sure. Nobody should take anything I say on faith. But I think an ungrounded belief in God is a self-correcting problem. If you don't have some personal experience that has convinced you of the reality of God — if you only accept the existence of God based on other people's assertions — then you don't really believe in God anyway. You only believe in whatever propaganda you've been fed, and that's not really making good use of the independent soul God gave you. I think God has use for people who question his existence, so long as they're willing to be open to however the personal evidence plays out.

GARY YORK: I've heard you claim that God is a libertarian. On the face of it, this seems absurd; what do you believe that makes this seem true to you?

J. NEIL SCHULMAN: God gave up being the only person who existed so he could live forever after as a less-than-omnipotent person within an existence containing other individual persons. And those he created with the power to disagree with him. How fucking libertarian is that?

GARY YORK: In what respects would you say that God is not entirely libertarian?

J. NEIL SCHULMAN: From the standpoint of someone who's been around forever, even the smartest among us are just precocious children. It's hard to be entirely libertarian in dealing with beginners who are going to harm themselves and others through their own inexperience and ignorance if the parent doesn't set some outside limits. Here's where I differ from most religions. God doesn't expect us to stay children. The more we increase in wisdom and power, the more God can deal with us like grown-ups.

GARY YORK: I know that there are people who profess to be "Christian libertarians." Some libertarians are pleased to welcome them, at least as fellow travelers. Others chuckle, and some do not care to share the same room with them. Has your perspective on Christian libertarians changed since you met God and if so, how?

J. NEIL SCHULMAN: Both Christianity and libertarianism are, in essence, worldviews with their own base premises, leading to moral conclusions. There is room for overlap, but they are not the same and there are divergences, particularly because much Christian scriptural interpretation is dogmatic rather than analytical. Conversely, many libertarian atheists are as smugly dogmatic in their dismissal of Christianity as some Christians are in their conviction that anyone who doesn't accept their script is deceived by demons. It requires particularly tolerant individuals to be open minded enough to embrace both.

GARY YORK: You have long been a libertarian activist; how do you see your role changing?

J. NEIL SCHULMAN: I no longer think all, or even most, of the problems of the human species can be solved solely by replacing coercive governments with private and voluntary institutions. Pushing as much as possible into the private sector brings economic forces into play that are often corrective, but I'm no longer a utopian "Marxist of the right" who thinks the private sector can solve all human problems. Not all human behavior is motivated by economics because economic behavior is a rational calculation, and much of the human experience is simply not rational.

GARY YORK: Have you significantly altered any of your libertarian positions since meeting God?

J. NEIL SCHULMAN: Yes.

I've come to the conclusion that when human beings are determined to be free, no institution can chain them; and when their hearts no longer crave freedom, no institution can preserve it for them.

I no longer accept as a basic premise that just because someone works within the State that they are necessarily or irredeemably evil.

I see important differences between Western democracies, republics, and federations with reverence for the individual, and tyrannies that attack the individual with ideology, theocracy, and crude gangsterism. I prefer what we tag Western Civilization and think it's worth preserving.

I continue to regard much that American government does as shoddy, unthinking, unimaginative, and short sighted, but I've met enough politicians at this point to know that many of their hearts are in the right place.

GARY YORK: With the understanding that you say nobody should take it on faith alone, what are you trying to get the readers of *I Met God* to believe?

J. NEIL SCHULMAN: That God is real, funny, warm, and very, very human.

That we have free will.

That what we choose to do will be with us forever.

That religious prophetic writings can't tell us what will happen in the future because that is not predetermined by some master plan but by our free will choices.

That God is good and wise and our creator and eternal, but God is not all powerful and all-knowing because He has chosen to share his power with us and we are free to hide from Him and ignore our highest interests.

That God's creation was an act of experimental invention thus the outcome was unknown to Him when He did it, and there were and still are enormous personal risks for Him.

That for any intelligent being – even God — "perfect" is not a noun but a verb, and any perfection is only a temporary way station in an unending adventure.

That denying God because he takes risks and his experiments don't always pan out is like a child finding out that his parents aren't perfect, and while God isn't perfect, he's still way smarter, better informed, wiser, and better at making the hard choices than the rest of us are.

That God is our Biggest Fan, because while he wants us to win, we have to do it.

GARY YORK: With the same caveat, what are you trying to get the readers of *I Met God* to disbelieve?

J. NEIL SCHULMAN: To disbelieve that life on earth is finite and that death is real.

To disbelieve that we don't have a real chance to win the brass ring.

To disbelieve that misery is our natural state and fate.

To disbelieve that the afterlife is an end to strife, growth, adventure, grief, and pleasure.

GARY YORK: Based on your experience, what do you think God wants people to do?

J. NEIL SCHULMAN: To choose to do good rather than do evil.

To act rationally and benevolently.

To be smart and think outside the box.

To try to be as good at making excuses for those who screw us up as the excuses we make when we screw up ourselves; but that does not mean that we have to be tolerant of great evil or great fraud.

GARY YORK: Based on your experience, what do you think God wants people to stop doing?

J. NEIL SCHULMAN: Stop killing in God's name.

Stop thinking that God cares more for land than he does for people.

Stop thinking that scripture puts a muzzle on God, and that your holy book is the last holy book and that your prophet was the last prophet and that your religion is the answer to everything.

Stop thinking that you get the kind of God that you want rather than the one who really exists.

Stop thinking that just because you can't understand how God could be real doesn't mean that other people don't have a better handle on it than you do.

GARY YORK: Given the lack of personal revelation (such as yours), why should someone believe in God?

J. NEIL SCHULMAN: They shouldn't, until they're convinced.

GARY YORK: Others have often held religious faith to be a virtue; it seems to be little more than believing in something because you want to believe in it. On the face of it, this practice seems a massive violation of personal integrity.

J. NEIL SCHULMAN: It depends on how you define the word "faith."

Rand usually used the word (and Heinlein did, too) to mean

the acceptance of a fact without proof or other adequate reason. (Some things, being self-evident, don't require proof.)

C.S. Lewis talked about faith in the sense of obstinacy in belief after already being convinced.

The first stage of faith, in my path, was "willing suspension of disbelief," on the theory that if I was living in a created universe, it would make sense to extend its author the same initial courtesy as the author of a novel I was reading — or as Johnny Carson used to say about a joke, "You buy the premise, you buy the bit."

The act of faith I made was praying to God to see if he answered. When I started identifying the answers I was getting as being other than a conversation I was having with myself — bicamerally or not — I was more in a position of taking seriously the possibility that the person at the other end of the conversation was the person whose phone number I had dialed (so to speak).

From my current perspective, faith has nothing to do with an acceptance of something without proof or reason. I feel I have plenty of both. The problem is that I can't lend my experience to someone else because it's internal/subjective.

GARY YORK: Given that one is already doing the right things and not doing wrong things and not believing wrong things, what's the benefit in believing in God?

How is that going to change anything?

J. NEIL SCHULMAN: The last thing I think God wants is for anyone to believe in him if they think they shouldn't. But one of the things that I gleaned from my experience is that God can use just about anything to start up a conversation. A chess club works as well as a church, if that's the symbol structure you're used to. As to what's the benefit to discovering a primary fact of reality, I think even Ayn Rand would argue the benefit of knowing the nature of existence, even if the truth is unexpected or personally discomfiting.

GARY YORK: Does God care if we believe in him?

J. NEIL SCHULMAN: Well, it's hard to talk to someone when they're thinking, "I don't believe I'm hearing this." Disbelief is inconvenient for God.

GARY YORK: How might our belief advantage God?

J. NEIL SCHULMAN: The advantage for God is like a parent who gets a call from a child who went away and never phones. But there is a point to God's customary invisibility. Not knowing how we got here is an irritation that can stimulate pearls of wisdom.

GARY YORK: Would that belief also advantage the individual?

J. NEIL SCHULMAN: Beyond being grounded in the truth, the upside is having God as a buddy, which I can tell you is way cool.

GARY YORK: Does God care if we disbelieve in him? Is our disbelief detrimental to God or us?

J. NEIL SCHULMAN: Well, God's not going to stop existing or going about his business because you don't believe in him. As for the disadvantage to you, think of it this way. It's like not having Internet access.

GARY YORK: Given that personal revelation is somewhat rare, how is one expected to know God and God's will?

J. NEIL SCHULMAN: Once you're looking at the universe around you as an artifact that has a creator, one can deduce a great deal of the author's intent and personality by looking at the art.

GARY YORK: Why do you think God chose you to communicate with?

J. NEIL SCHULMAN: Maybe God was sick of working with amateurs and I have a Writers Guild card?

Okay, more seriously.

I think God got particularly interested in me because while I was praying I started asking God questions he wasn't used to hearing, like, "Is there anything about yourself that you can't know?" Most religious people don't seem to be interested in God, personally — and of course the atheists are even harder for God to talk to. For example, I think it's hard to read the *Bible* and not feel sorry for God. I think God found it unusual that anyone was feeling sorry for him rather than blaming him for everything that goes wrong in their lives.

GARY YORK: That's original. I never before heard it suggested that, to get God to answer your prayers, it's helpful to make yourself into enough of a good conversationalist that God will take your call. Is that why you made God's earthly avatar in *Escape from Heaven* a radio talk show host?

J. NEIL SCHULMAN: Jesus. H. Christ. I only spent a dozen years writing *Escape from Heaven* and I never thought of that! Just chalk it up to one more case of divine inspiration.

GARY YORK: Surely a few thousand years of experience relying on "holy" scriptures, organized churches, and word-of-mouth transmittal has shown this to be a really, really poor technique for God to get his message out! Even one with the leisure to dedicate his life to discovering "God's will" could easily end that life aged, forlorn, desolate and discouraged. Granted that someone so dedicated would probably do little damage but it's far from clear he'd do much good either.

J. NEIL SCHULMAN: Well, there's a bunch of things I could say here. Maybe God is biding his time until he reveals himself. Scripture promises a restored earth someday. Maybe the people God really needs to recruit are the ones he's getting through to by other means, and they just aren't blabbermouths about it the way I am. Or maybe being on our own most of the time is the point of this experience. You can't grow up until you leave the nest.

GARY YORK: How is one more voice, yours, "crying in the wilderness" supposed to help?

J. NEIL SCHULMAN: Well, I'm not in the wilderness, am I?

I'm media savvy, can express myself effectively, and have spent years with teachers like Robert Heinlein and Ayn Rand developing my intellect, my imagination, and my communication skills. I think I am pretty well suited to the job I've been given. God is suffering not from underexposure so much as overexposure, and he doesn't need a new church as much as he needs a new publicity flack. I guess I see my mission essentially as giving God a PR makeover. It's as hard to live down bad publicity as to generate new publicity.

GARY YORK: If God's so powerful, why doesn't everyone like him already?

J. NEIL SCHULMAN: Power has limited usefulness and tends to drive people of independent minds away, leaving the zombies who don't like the hard work of thinking for themselves. Isn't this what we've seen in every cult?

GARY YORK: As a libertarian, I could get by for a very long while with one commandment: "Thou shalt not coerce!" Aren't ten commandments really too many?

J. NEIL SCHULMAN: Actually, like the Bill of Rights, ten seems about right. And in Hebrew, it's not the ten "commandments." It's the ten "blessings."

GARY YORK: Is God entitled to use force to defend his own rights?

J. NEIL SCHULMAN: God owns stuff and offers use of it under certain specified conditions. I think he has the right to defend his property from interlopers and enforce contracts made with him by withdrawing his protection when we fuck with him.

GARY YORK: Well, "withdrawing his protection" is not at all equivalent to using force. Full agreement on that. Did you have something else in mind?

J. NEIL SCHULMAN: Sure. What obligations does a child have to a father who loves him and has given him everything he has, and what may such a father rightfully do when that child uses force to break into the father's office, hacks into his private business and banking files without permission, steals from the father, screws things up not only for the father but for the rest of the family, and so forth?

Sound familiar? If this were a comic book, you could call this our origins story.

GARY YORK: If we understood paranormal phenomena as well as we understand physical science, might we not become as gods?

J. NEIL SCHULMAN: Absolutely.

GARY YORK: Isn't that – hubris? I thought God didn't like competing Gods.

J. NEIL SCHULMAN: Depends on what we mean by a god and what a god would do with it. God never says anywhere that he's the only god, and in fact — by demanding that no other gods are placed before him — acknowledges there are others whom he considers inferior to him.

What makes God unique is that he was the Eternal even before the creation of other conscious souls. Before God began creation, existence and consciousness were two words for the same fact – Existence itself was conscious, and the only consciousness. But even God's eternal consciousness evolved, because a living mind can learn and alter its views and opinions based on experience. Even God has a learning curve, and that's what makes his consciousness ultimately of the same kind as our own.

Now, if God spun off parts of his own soul into "free spirits" – independent souls, each free spirit with its own independent will – then these created spirits have a beginning that starts with their new identity but, like God, can be eternal spirits from that point onward. You can call these created spirits gods, angels, supermen, whatever – and this would be true even if they put on human bodies and lived for a time in a finite, closed-in universe as mortals. And if, like God Eternal, we will have the power to create closed universes of our own — or even planets with designed self-conscious life forms — the word "god" would be descriptive and useful.

Now here's where I distinguish myself from Milton's concept of Satan, and from Nietzsche's concept of the superman/god.

When you live forever and have the powers of a god, one must adhere to a degree approaching perfection to a code of conduct that subordinates one's desires, goals, and actions to an understanding that the consequences are inescapable, last forever, and sooner or later must be accounted and paid for. With the powers of god comes the necessity for the wisdom and self-honesty of a god. The antics of the Greek pantheon won't cut it; they are portrayed as capricious and petty brats.

GARY YORK: Story idea? The Greek pantheon (and a plethora of other gods) did exist and do and are walking around today being (with perhaps a rare exception) humans with bodies who think they're bodies. Why? 'Cause God got tired of cleaning up after them and basically said, "That's it! I'm finished playing janitor for you guys. Come on back when you can rent a clue."

"And God waxed wroth with them and cast them down from the heavens, saying unto them, "Be ye now subject to such as ye have wrought." He made them bodies of stone and clay and bound them up with a terrible Geas that they might trouble the Earth no more. Thus did He diminish them; in love and loneliness did He deliver them unto their fate."

J. NEIL SCHULMAN: That's wonderful! And that may well have been a description of the angels/gods that needed the lesson of coming to earth, where our natural laws could give them a finite classroom/playground to learn a code of values suitable for an immortal. If "Thou Art God" then "Thou had best not screw up." Even the consequences of a Hitler, Mao, or Stalin are limited in scope because they were confined to one planet, one continuum, and the victims were not permanently destroyed. An immortal Hitler might be able to destroy self-conscious beings permanently, and God can't allow those sorts cruel and foolish gods to play in his eternity.

------------I Met Ayn Rand------------

GARY YORK: Did you meet Ayn Rand personally? Did you like her?

J. NEIL SCHULMAN: I met her. I worshipped her. I didn't much like her.

In August, 1973, after I'd interviewed Heinlein for the New York Daily News, George Nobbe, the Sunday editor who'd commissioned my Heinlein interview, asked me who I wanted to interview next. I chose Rand, and proceeded to get in touch with her through her office. She had been burned by the press so often that she was hesitant to do a newspaper interview, but made an exception because at the time — hard as it sounds to believe — Ayn Rand was doing television commercials advertising the Daily News! She did, however, want total approval of the final printed interview, and demanded letters of agreement signed both by my editor and myself. We agreed, although my editor was astonished; he'd never been asked for such a thing for what he saw as a friendly puff piece written by a fan.

Rand telephoned me and asked to speak to me before she would invite me over to interview her in person. She asked me, "Are you a libertarian?"

I said, "Yes, Miss Rand."

She said, "Out of courtesy to the Daily News I will not hang up. You will please explain yourself."

Which I proceeded to do. "I agree with your metaphysics, your epistemology, your ethics, and your theory of esthetics," I said. "I just think your philosophical opposition to any compulsion more logically leads to private enterprise taking over all government functions, rather than to limited constitutional government."

"In this system with no government courts," Rand asked me, "what will be the final arbiter when men have disputes?"

The Heartmost Desire

I quoted John Galt's speech: "Reality will be the final arbiter."

"Don't utter bromides!" Ayn Rand said to me contemptuously.

We spoke on the phone for another four hours. Rand initially would not agree to let me interview her, but by the end I brought her around.

She interviewed me during that phone call as much as I interviewed her.

She told me that she watched *Star Trek* and Spock was her favorite character.

I told her that my favorite classical composer was Brahms, which apparently did not bother her the way answering "Beethoven" would have.

She asked me who else I had interviewed and I told her that it was Heinlein. She was familiar with him and thought well of him.

I asked her if she objected to *Atlas Shrugged* being called science-fiction, and she said she had no problem with that.

She criticized the nascent Libertarian Party for "using my ideas without giving me credit for them" and I told her that although I was not a member of the Libertarian Party, I needed to point out to her that the first platform of the Libertarian Party explicitly, by name, credited her philosophy as its foundation. "I did not know that," Rand said curtly. A few months later I saw her interviewed on television where, once again, she criticized the Libertarian Party for using her ideas without proper credit.

By the end of that conversation, she was ready to make an appointment to let me do the newspaper interview with her, but imposed an impossible condition on me. She would not agree to allow me to tape record the interview, as I had tape-recorded my interview with Heinlein. "But I'm not fast enough to take accurate notes and listen to your answers at the same time," I said. "You already have final approval of the text of the interview and I don't want to be in a position where I might misremember something you said and misquote you. Why do you object to my tape recording?"

"I don't want you to give the tape to Murray Rothbard," she said.

"I have no intention of giving Murray Rothbard a copy of the tape," I said. "This interview would belong to the New York Daily News." She would not change her mind. "Okay," I said, "how about if you have someone from your office record it and provide me with a verbatim transcript?" Once again she refused. "Then why would the Daily News even need me to interview you?" I asked, "Since you have final approval of the text, and without my having some objective record of our conversation, in essence you'd be writing the interview, yourself. I can't work under those conditions."

So we ended our conversation there amicably and she said, "I wish you good premises."

About seven or eight years later I managed to get my hands on Rand's home phone number, and called her. She remembered me and we chatted in a more or less friendly way, since I was now a published novelist, myself. I asked her if I might send her my novel for her to read. "I read an interview with you recently," I told her, "in which you said you had a hard time finding any new novels you could enjoy reading. Since we share the same esthetics, I thought you might like mine."

"Oh, you poor boy!" she said. "I meant I wished I could read something new by Agatha Christie."

I got mad. "I'm better than Christie," I said.

Apparently my arrogance wasn't enough to impress her.

Maybe a year later I phoned her again. I don't know what set her off, but this phone call didn't last long. It ended with her telling me, "I despise all libertarians." Then after a pause, "Including you."

Those are the last words I ever heard from Ayn Rand.

Well. Those are the last words I heard from Ayn Rand while she was alive on earth. I've since run into Ayn Rand on the other side, in one of my dream-state crossings to the afterlife. She was a whole lot friendlier.

By the way. None of these conversations were tape recorded so I've reconstructed the conversations from memory. The quotes are therefore not word for word.

Escape from Heaven

GARY YORK: I've read *Escape from Heaven* and was delighted by it; however, I can't help but wonder about that title. It's catchy and intriguing — we don't usually consider Heaven as a place from which we would choose to escape — did you select that title as a signal to non-believers that this was not a traditional book?

J. NEIL SCHULMAN: I wish I could claim that it was that well thought out. I chose the title simply because my having to escape from Heaven was my original 1991 dream that inspired the novel — and the irony of having to escape from Heaven — rather than escape to Heaven — struck me immediately.

Recently I did come up with a new tagline that plays on this: "War is hell — even if it's in Heaven."

GARY YORK: The book is full of ideas most of them fresh and some of them no doubt original to you. If God granted you the power to select just one idea that every reader would take from this book, what would that be?

J. NEIL SCHULMAN: After sitting here for ten minutes trying, it's apparent to me that God hasn't granted me this power. What do you think the one idea that sticks out is?

GARY YORK: I keep returning to this (expressed as an admonition): be lighthearted; there is a way to view these concepts that is not heavy and that does not portray God as a fundamentally evil being.

J. NEIL SCHULMAN: That works for me.

GARY YORK: I know *Escape from Heaven* has proven controversial and it seems unlikely that any current religion or sect would wholeheartedly endorse the theological positions you take in this book. With that a given, then — who's your audience? Unbelievers? Atheists? Heretics?

J. NEIL SCHULMAN: God only knows. OK, cheap shot. I think the real answer is my audience has to have a sense of humor, or a sense of adventure, that doesn't see their religion's truths as embalmed and God visible only through stained glass. I'm hoping that my book contains enough of the spirit of God that those recognizing God's influence will be friendly to it.

GARY YORK: Some people will read the title, *Escape from Heaven*, and think, "Oh, another God book," and promptly give it a miss and thereby deprive themselves of a good read. No problem, really. But who might be inclined to read it and then become furious with you? Of those who might actually read the book, who would really hate it?

J. NEIL SCHULMAN: The only person I can think of who told me he read it and hated every bit of it was C. S. Lewis's stepson, Douglas Gresham, which is ironic because I learned much of my sensibility for treating religious themes in fiction from C. S. Lewis. Douglas wrote me and said, "It is so sacrilegious in content that I have not yet found it at all funny." My intent was not sacrilegious and I don't believe I committed any actual blasphemy in the book. I do take license with traditional interpretations of scripture, but I consider my revelation gives me authority to do so. I admit that's a hard sell to those committed to existing dogma.

GARY YORK: Has your mother read, *Escape from Heaven*, and, if so, what does she think?

J. NEIL SCHULMAN: Her eyesight isn't what it used to be so I read it to her. She enjoyed it quite a bit.

GARY YORK: Have other family members or friends become more or less distant after reading this book or hearing of it?

J. NEIL SCHULMAN: I have not received negativity from those family members and friends who have read it. I do have some family members and friends who have not yet read it and appear considerably resistant to doing so.

GARY YORK: Does the publication of this book mean you've returned for a time to the science fiction genre? Can we look forward to more SF books or a sequel?

J. NEIL SCHULMAN: My usual problem is triaging the time necessary to undertake new long-form writing. Right now I'm trying to produce as feature films half a dozen projects — with *Escape from Heaven* at the head of the list.

GARY YORK: Do you think *Escape from Heaven* will appeal to fans of your previous SF books, *Alongside Night* and *The Rainbow Cadenza*?

J. NEIL SCHULMAN: Well, considering that you're an example of a fan of my previous books who liked this one, I'd say I have a good chance. Heinlein warned me back in 1973 that there are always fans of earlier books who don't like new ones as much, but sometimes one is lucky enough to gain enough new fans that one can stay in the business.

GARY YORK: How do you think your non-fiction readers will receive it?

J. NEIL SCHULMAN: I'm trying to get through to people who read only fiction with the novel *Escape from Heaven*, who read only non-fiction with *I Met God*, and who don't read at all with the audiobook of *I Met God* and the film version of *Escape from Heaven*. So I'm covered, even if there's no cross-pollinating. But there usually is. Certainly reading C. S. Lewis's and Ayn Rand's fiction led me to reading their nonfiction as well.

GARY YORK: I know you and Robert Heinlein had become good friends; if he were still alive he would surely have read the book. Have you considered what he might say about *Escape from Heaven* or what advice he might offer?

J. NEIL SCHULMAN: Remember, I believe in Heaven and that I'll someday get the chance to ask Heinlein what he thought of the book. But I'm pretty sure from his comments to me on my novel *The Rainbow Cadenza* that he'd laugh his ass off when reading this one, too.

---------------*Lady Magdalene's*---------------

GARY YORK: Personally, the most interesting question for me is, "Why?" Why did you make this movie?

J. NEIL SCHULMAN: For my entire life I have been at least as interested in film as an expressive medium as I have been in the purely literary forms I've written in, novels and short stories. My dad, as a concert violinist, was a performing artist, and that led me to an early interest in the performing arts. I always tried to be a dramatist when I was writing novels and short stories, so it was a natural transition for me to become a screenwriter. Then I spent two weeks on the shooting set of the produced *Twilight Zone* episode I wrote, "Profile in Silver," and I was hooked. It's only this year, though, that I determined to direct one of my own scripts — and that required me to produce as well.

So, I wrote a film outline for *Lady Magdalene's* early this year, and Nichelle Nichols — my producing partner in the development of *Escape from Heaven* — agreed to play the lead role. Prior to writing the script, I did location scouting — even doing some Handicam shooting of possible locations— then I wrote the script with those locations in mind — in effect, using my location footage as storyboards.

I started pre-production of the film as soon as I had a completed screenplay, and we started principal photography on May 23rd, wrapping June 12th. We just completed editing a rough cut and intend to have the film completed in September.

I made *Lady Magdalene's* for the same reasons I write novels. It is interesting, though, that the part of the process where I felt most like being a novelist wasn't writing the script or even directing the film, but in the editing of the movie. That felt to me like being an author.

And, I should mention that I learned editing a movie is the best training for directing one — and directing a movie is the best training for writing one. The later stage tells you what you need to be looking out for in the previous one, so you avoid making silly mistakes. You should have heard me during editing, cursing out the stupid writer and the idiot of a director!

Now, with one feature film under my belt, I look forward to producing and directing my screenplay of *Escape from Heaven*.

GARY YORK: If such a thing were done, would *Lady Magdalene's* bear a label "Warning: strong libertarian content!"? I'm really asking, I suppose, if I might particularly like to see the film; I should be asking, rather, why should anyone want to see the film — or, perhaps, who do you see as it's audience?

J. NEIL SCHULMAN: Well, let's see. In *Lady Magdalene's*, the heros are two federal agents — one of them from the IRS — and the madam of a legal brothel. On the surface, I'm only batting .333 from a libertarian standpoint!

But this is, after all, a movie written, produced, and directed by the same guy who wrote *Alongside Night, The Rainbow Cadenza*, and Stopping Power — the same guy whose favorite writers include Ayn Rand, C.S. Lewis, and Robert Heinlein. You might expect that surface appearances can be deceiving. On the surface, it might be hard to find any political point of view in *Lady Magdalene's*. But beneath the surface lies the heart of an iconoclast raised on Mark Twain and Jonathan Swift, who loves Monty Python and the Marx Brothers. *Lady Magdalene's* contains a lot of comedy, a lot of irony. Some of the early reactions have compared me to Fellini, and the phrase "black comedy" has shown up a few times. Shakespeare's tragedies — Hamlet, as the best example — contain some of Shakespeare's best comedy writing. So even when I have an overall serious purpose, it doesn't mean you're in for a somber time. Does *Lady Magdalene's* have strong libertarian content? Let me answer this way: if you don't know what to look for, my political point of view is buried under the comedy — just the way it should be.

As for who the audience is? As a writer I've never targeted a specific audience. The only category I ever wanted to be in as an author was "best-seller." But I'm doing some unusual things in *Lady Magdalene's*.

To begin with, for a movie centered around a brothel, there is not a single sex scene and the F word is never heard. I think the sensibility of this movie in many ways is more 1956 than 2006. The movie is cut more the way Alfred Hitchcock, Otto Preminger, Stanley Kubrick, or Orson Welles would have cut it, rather than any contemporary director whose sense of timing comes from TV commercials and music videos. I believe movies should be both suspenseful — which means that you have to give the audience things slower than they want it — and poetic — which means you don't cut to the chase. I hope there's still an audience out there that's not so addicted to fast food that they can't take a leisurely meal when I lay the whole seven courses in front of them.

GARY YORK: Was the film inspired by *I Met God*, or in some other way related? Is it more like a 'finger exercise' before tackling the film version of *Escape from Heaven*?

J. NEIL SCHULMAN: *Lady Magdalene's* was not inspired by *I Met God*, however both projects reflect what inspires me. As far as being a finger exercise — no way. I've never approached any of my longform projects with limited expectations or with less than a full head of steam. Now, it's true that if *Lady Magdalene's* succeeds, *Escape from Heaven* stands a better chance of getting made, and I stand a better chance of the money people allowing me to direct it. But the reverse is also true: if *Lady Magdalene's* fails, I'm less likely to get the chance to make *Escape from Heaven*.

------------How to Talk to God------------

GARY YORK: How should one talk to God?

J. NEIL SCHULMAN: Maybe this will help.

Get somewhere you're sure no one can overhear you. In the Sermon on the Mount, Jesus recommended using a closet for praying.

I think any room with a lockable door — or somewhere isolated and remote — might work. For an atheist trying this as an experiment, isolation limits the embarrassment factor, and you can always tell yourself it's not praying but just a form of meditation or a creative exercise or an experiment or anything that makes you less uncomfortable.

Next. Forget everything you've been taught about how to pray. You feel more comfortable jumping up and down on one foot or laying back and looking at the stars, or whatever, do it, if it helps. You don't have to be on your knees. You don't have to simulate the posture of a praying mantis. You don't have to use "thee's" and "thou's." You don't have to ask for anything or make any confessions or apologies.

Then just start talking, as if you're dictating a letter. Say whatever the heck is on your mind. Ask the questions you've always wondered about. Pretend you're applying for a job or a loan or a college admission.

I don't know in what form the response will come, or how long it will take, or how many times you have to do this before you connect (in fact, one of the questions I wonder about is whether God has voicemail of a sort and how often he checks stored messages) but I'm pretty sure you'll eventually get a response.

GARY YORK: Having read Rand and Heinlein for years I felt intellectually inoculated against kooky God stuff. Won't that be a real problem for me if I try to talk to God now?

J. NEIL SCHULMAN: No. Being a fan of Rand and Heinlein puts you so far ahead in conceptual mapping that it should make the conversation quite direct. A reading of Rand and Heinlein provides excellent paradigms, thought experiments, brain exercise, intellectual Drano. God may live forever but he's a busy man and is not adverse to saving time

GARY YORK: I've tried talking to God but never heard anything back.

J. NEIL SCHULMAN: Maybe the problem isn't that God isn't answering but that you're wearing earplugs. The first question anyone has to ask when wondering about a possible response to a prayer is: what should I identify as the answer?

Most people don't even realize the spam filters they have in place. A lot of atheists are atheists because anything originating from a source labeled "God" or containing a long list of banned words like "soul," "heaven," salvation," etc go directly into the bulk mail folder and get deleted without examination.

---------------Religious Do's and Don'ts--------------

GARY YORK: Is smoking a sin?

J. NEIL SCHULMAN: Smoking is a perfect place to start.

Why would God consider smoking to be a sin? Because it's calming and pleasurable? Or because it increases the odds of getting sick?

We on earth live in bodies that decay and die. Our souls are immortal but our bodies are mortal. They get sick, break down, eventually cease their ability to contain our souls.

Smoking is at worst something that contributes to the breakdown of our bodies. But so does a thousand different things. The difference is that smoking, for some people, compensates by giving small pleasures in return.

I can't see how God could possibly see smoking as sinful. If it is sinful, so is cheesecake ... and I don't know any religion that condemns that!

GARY YORK: Are dietary laws important; is it a sin if you don't "keep kosher?"

J. NEIL SCHULMAN: If you feel you need to do these things to keep yourself centered, go for it. Otherwise, not.

I've never been one for regularity in my life, and that has up sides and down sides. I sleep odd hours — sometimes going to bed early and sometimes going to bed late, sometimes getting a good night's sleep and sometimes being dog tired. I don't eat at regular mealtimes, and have had days where I eat five meals and some where I eat one. I've spent years as a vegetarian and years where I ate mostly meat. Some days I'm productive, some days I just screw around. The idea, for someone like me, that one day out of seven is a regular Day of Rest from the other Six is absurd to me — who says I worked the other six and deserve a day off?

I figure if I eat something and it doesn't poison me or make me fatter than I already am, that's more important to me than whether I'm eating a bacon cheese lobsterburger during Passover on a leavened low-carb bun, and I don't think God cares one way or the other. And I don't eat anything smart enough to be bothered by the fact that I'm eating it.

I have two Dietary Laws in my home. I don't have the right to make my daughter eat anything she doesn't want to eat, and she doesn't have the right to tell me what I shouldn't be eating. I keep the Law better than she does.

GARY YORK: What is a Spiritual sin?

J. NEIL SCHULMAN: A spiritual sin is one that transcends and outlives the physical body. Being cruel to someone or murdering them may follow them into their next life. All the serious sins are felonies against the immortal soul, as opposed to waste of the body's potential – gluttony or self-neglect, a sterile sex life, which can include both homosexuality and celibacy, spending one's life getting drunk or stoned – which rates on the sin scale somewhere between a parking ticket and a night in the drunk tank.

To the extent that sexual behavior is harmful to the soul — breaking solemn oaths, being callous to someone's feelings, putting someone else at risk of harmful consequences, molesting children, creating new life without taking responsibility for that new life or destroying life carelessly — sexual behavior can include spiritual sins. But merely engaging in sex-play outside of traditional marriage –even if it's gay sex-play or the pursuit of other harmless fetishes — isn't in and of itself sinful.

The one thing that strikes me about conventional religion is that it spends more effort preventing people from violating its sexual code or eating things not on its menu than it does with the important sins. But then again, the secular moralists these days seem more outraged by smokers than by murderers.

GARY YORK: Do we exist eternally?

J. NEIL SCHULMAN: If we don't do destructive things that

rate a real death sentence, then yes – we can live forever ... if we can become strong enough to endure it.

God will render a judgment on whether the soul is recoverable or whether it must be isolated or destroyed to protect the rest of existence. And I don't assume that even the most evil among us is necessarily a throw-away. God may know where the damage is and where the hidden keys to recovery are. Remember, with all of eternity at his disposal, God can afford to be patient.

---------------Abortion---------------

GARY YORK: Since you met God, has your opinion changed about abortion? Do you believe abortion to be wrong, a sin or an error?

J. NEIL SCHULMAN: I don't like abortion, personally, however I have always been and still am pro-choice. But I think a lot of the modern feminist rhetoric regarding a "woman's right to choose" is hogwash. Why should a woman have the sole right to choose whether or not to have a child, but the father — who is expected to be responsible for it — has no right to participate in the decision? That sort of feminism offends my libertarian view that there can be no duty where there is no choice. If women want the sole right to choose whether or not to have an abortion, and no man should be able to tell a woman what to do with her body, then women should lose all moral and legal claims for child support from the men whose semen they appropriate to achieve fertilization. But I also think a lot of the "pro-choice" movement has a hidden agenda: to eliminate human reproduction and kill off the human species. It's just another facet of the left's fundamental nihilism.

GARY YORK: Most religions agree that killing is wrong and that the killing of babies is particularly egregious. Some would say that "abortion' is just a polite term for "killing babies." Do you agree?

J. NEIL SCHULMAN: Well, what is a fetus? Is it a human body being prepared for the arrival of a conscious soul, or is it a living being itself from which a conscious soul emerges? The older view is that the soul is not yet present until the first breath of life, so a developing fetus is just a body part. I don't see why the modern revisionist view that the soul is present from the moment of fertilization should be automatically adopted by those who believe in reverence for life. I don't see the religious right picketing blood banks. The part is not the whole. A fetus does not necessarily have a soul, and without a soul there can be no murder.

GARY YORK: If the fetus is just a body part, why would you dislike abortion?

J. NEIL SCHULMAN: Because even though the body isn't fully alive without the soul, it's designed in the image of God and shouldn't be regarded cheaply. It's the same reason I have esthetic objections to body-piercing and self-mutilation.

By the way, I do think it's ironic that the right-wing arguments for fetal rights and the left-wing arguments for animal rights are exactly the same arguments ... and both of them fail to ask the fundamental question of what identity or nature is required for a thing to acquire rights.

GARY YORK: What is so special about birth – exit from the womb – that makes it proper to kill the prospective child before that moment and improper afterwards?

J. NEIL SCHULMAN: The old answer to that is that's when the soul comes into the body. The libertarian answer is that's the first moment when you have a free individual with its own independent identity.

A Non-Christian's Prayer To Christ

Of course
You already know what happened.
So I'll just tell it
for the audience.

I'm at the Abbey.
The place where You have the monks.
Only I was at a conference
and it wasn't one of the monks
I was arguing with.

This guy
and I don't have to bring names into this
You know who it was
and so do those who were there
and it's not important for the rest of you
he's a preacher
an official spokesperson
for Jesus
and the Word of God,
particularly the newer stuff.

But the reason I'm listening to him
is that he was close to somebody
whose opinion I really respected
and he really knows his stuff.
Also, I like him a lot
on the first meeting.

Anyway, he's selling me that
the *Bible* says
You took the bullet for me
And if I don't say it's so
naming the right Names
I don't get into Heaven.

Let me tell you,
I want to get into Heaven.
Eternal rest has no appeal for me.
Neither does swimming in fire.

I say, what about the Jews?
No go, probably, he tells me.
They say God but they don't mean
Christ
and that's a rejection of what
You did
for them.

Some,
the real religious ones
might slip through, though.

And the Mormons, I ask?
You ever look into them?
he asks me.
A scam job, he says.

But the idea, he tells me
Is that if they had the choice
to accept You by name
and they didn't take it,
it's one ticket to a customer.
And the theater is cleared
between shows.

Now, it was late.
I'd been up since early morning
and I was in one of those places
where you take an idea seriously
and run with it.

And I'm thinking,
Okay, God's always been straight with me.
I'll pray again
and if I have to use the name Jesus,
what's the big deal?

Then it hits me.
My parents aren't going.
Neither of them is ever
going to pray to Jesus.

That's goes for all my relatives, too.
Well, maybe except my sister
since I've never been able to
figure out
what she thinks
or who she prays to
or for what.
But I want her in Heaven, too.
It just wouldn't be the same
without her.

My grandmother
the biggest heart I ever knew.
Not there, waiting for me.

My aunt
a great heart
even if I always thought she was
a Communist
if the words Jesus Christ ever
left her lips
it was as a curse.
Probably not in Heaven,
according to my preacher friend.

And there's my ex-wife.
Okay, I admit I didn't make the
smartest move in marrying her
it didn't work out
but, damn it, she has a hard time
believing in You
so that means she's not going either
and if my daughter gets in
she's going to miss her mommy.

My friends.
My beloved friends.

One wrote a book
in which You Killed Yourself.

Another used to believe in you
but doesn't now.

Another one pulls stuff
that even I think is crap
but he's done a lot of good stuff too.

I can't think of three friends
who make it past Your gate
under these rules.

If I ask to go
I'm leaving behind
everyone I loved.

Then I think about the Mormons.
They want so much
to make sure everybody gets into Heaven
that they get genealogies on everybody
then baptize them
even if they're already dead.
Maybe some people are offended by this
but not me.
I think it's sweet.
Looking out for the other guy
particularly the ones who are ready to dump on you.
Now that's Christian charity.
You have to love the Mormons
for making maximum effort.

This was starting to put me in a panic.
Let me see if I have this right
I say to You
In LA Times letters page style.
Someone who doesn't love anybody here
they don't care if anyone's left behind
so it doesn't cost them anything to
use one particular name
and get into Heaven.
No problem for the guy who never

learned to love
he gets in.

Somebody who's a coward
and would sell out his family
because they didn't use the right name
but because this moral cripple uses the right Name
he gets in?

What sort of God
I ask You
would set things up this way?
This would be really lame.
I'd cry for the Universe
made out of such cheap materials.

And I think of Heinlein's story
where he already looked at this problem.
You could always count on him
to get to the point.

Hey, Heinlein wouldn't be in Heaven either,
under these rules
and there goes the most interesting man
I ever met.

So cowards go to Heaven
and it's not the home of the brave?
Lovers and families
are split up for all time
with those who use Your Right Name
left in eternal grief
or worse
given some forever heroin?

I know.
That's not how C.S. Lewis
played it
in his book about a visit to Heaven.

He stacked the deck
so everyone who's there
is happy

and everyone who's left behind
is drained of all that was good
about them.

You know what?
That sucks, too.

I don't believe it.
That's not how God would set things up.
That's the kind of universe the devil
would think up.

Then it hits me.
If you have to make this choice
between being a selfish coward
looking out for Number One
and getting into Heaven
or rejecting You
because friends and lovers aren't going?

It's a test.

It's like the gag You pulled on Abraham
to test his faith.
Take your son
and sacrifice him to Me.
Only at the last minute
You tell him,
Good Job,
Just kidding.

That's got to be right, right?
If I love
You have to love more than a mortal, right?
You've had more practice at it.

If I don't want to go to heaven
if all the good guys aren't going
if those I love won't be there
then that's out of respect
for an absolute standard of
good and evil

that even God would have to obey,
right?

God has to be better than I am,
and care about good and evil
more than I do
Don't You?

And if I
cheap as I am
would cut some slack
to let the marginal cases in
You know
the ones who tried
but didn't get it completely right
but they must have some good in them if
other people love them
then you'd cut an ever better deal,
right?

Because that's what God would do.

Listen, God.
You've got a p-r problem down here.
You've got people spreading bad news
about You.
Saying that you're cheap
and grumpy
and bureaucratic
and mean.
And they say Your Own Book said so.

The same people say
if I take this attitude
I'm choosing to reject You.
I'm in the devil's teeth.
I'm just a crackpot
heading for the kiln
for refiring.

I think it's a slander on You.
I think this is a libel.
I think that THIS is Satan's lie.

Not my creator, buddy!
He wouldn't be like that.
Take it back!

God is good
it says so right on page One
and if You ask me
somebody better take a blue
pencil to the stuff
that says otherwise
no matter what title it says
on the Book cover.

So, God.
By any Name.
Including Jesus Christ.
I don't believe that about You.
You take the good guys to Heaven
No matter what name they say
or even if their lips don't move
or maybe even if they don't believe
what they don't see
because that, after all, makes sense too.

And, I pray, I'll be seeing you
and all my lost beloved
just like You promised elsewhere
when it's my time.
Amen.

June 29, 1995

Who Is God and What Was He Thinking, Anyway?

I really should have considered just shutting the heck up. I should have known that if I started writing essays about basic principles, there would be someone with at least half a brain coming along and figuring out that I was holding back some of the premises upon which I was basing my writing.

Am I "a law unto myself," not accepting any authority except my own mind — as I have been accused of being by more than one advocate of traditional religious scripture — or do I have some other way of validating what I've been writing?

When I write that I have no fundamental objections to adult men and women engaging in sex play, even within their own gender, have I abandoned any possibility of sexual behavior adhering to a moral code — and if that code is not derived from Jewish or Christian scripture, then from where?

If I ask a boundary question — merely ask the question without providing my own answer — whether all individual members of a sapient species have the rights accruing to the whole of that species, irrespective of whether sapience is present in an individual or subset — have I opened myself up to permitting eugenics, genocide, and human vivisection on a scale practiced by the Nazis and the communists?

It's time for me to put up or shut up, right?

Okay, fine. I'll show my hand. If I'm going to be burned at the stake or nailed to a cross, I'll at least give you a good reason.

To begin with, I start with the assumption that the rest of you are often crazy. There it is. I don't trust any of you as far as I can throw you. As far as I can see, you're out of your freaking minds.

Some of you say you're followers of God, then demonstrate your devotion by endlessly murdering each other over a few square miles of desert real estate where God is reported to have made some personal appearances a couple of millennia ago. Well, I guess this shouldn't be any surprise. If Elvis fans and soccer fans act crazy, why shouldn't God's fans? I've seen film of the mob chaos at the Rolling Stones concert at Altamont and The Who concert in Cincinnati, and at soccer games. If people are going to act that crazy over musicians and athletes, why should I expect sanity from them when it comes to how they feel about God?

There it is. Bring out the stake and the gasoline. I think organized religions are no closer to being infallible than any other celebrity fan clubs. They collect relics, erect shrines, fantasize relationships with the object of their affection, are willing to go to war to defend their own idiosyncratic vision of the star.

But I have never made the mistake that atheists make of blaming God for the crazy things His fans do.

I also don't expect those journalistic writings called scriptures, including purported eyewitness accounts of God's personal appearances, actions, and sayings, to bear any close relationship to the reality of where God has been, what He has done, and what He said. I've seen what human reporters have done with more recent events to which I've been a personal participant or witness. I've seen how reporters spin. I know how rumors and propaganda get reported as established fact. I've seen history being written then rewritten.

Sorry. I place my trust in God, but not in the 'zines written by His fans.

But unlike atheists, just because the fanzines can't be trusted, it doesn't mean God never made those personal appearances, did at least some of the things He's said to have done, said some of the things He's reported to have said. Even The New York Times gets it right on occasion. But if a report doesn't make sense, I'm not going to believe it just because someone tells me to.

The thing is, God isn't dead and He isn't retired. Jews act as if God hasn't done anything worth reporting on for the last four or five thousand years; Christians act as if God hasn't done anything worth reporting on for two thousand years. Then they throw a fit if anyone says God's been around more recently.

I have news for you. God is still here among us, He is still talking to anyone who is actually curious enough to take the time to listen to Him, and you don't need any musty books to find out what He's thinking.

I know this because He's been in touch with me. More than once. Clear as a bell. Better connection than I've ever gotten from AT&T.

Bring out the cross-bars and the nails. Schulman's a blasphemer. Call the shrinks and get him restrained. Schulman thinks he's hearing God's voice. Schulman thinks the *Bible* is full of crap, but he knows what God is saying. This megalomaniac is so far removed from reality that he thinks he's sane and the rest of us are crazy. We'd better restrain him not only for his own good, but as a simple measure of public safety.

J. Neil Schulman is armed and dangerous, right?

Now you know why I haven't used my home address on corresondence for years, why I screen my phone calls, why I've never put a picture of any living family members on the web, why my preferred method of communication is email, why I'm armed to the teeth and have spent some effort learning how to shoot straight. I've been convinced that once I started letting you people know what was really going in my head, that the mobs of villagers with pitchforks were only a matter of time.

Let me get a few things straight before I get where I'm going.

I'm not setting myself up as a spokesman for God. God hasn't ordered me to deliver any prophecies to you. You have a question about what God thinks, ask Him, yourself. I'm not going to broker God's words.

I'm not guaranteeing that He'll feel like answering you, or

will answer you the way you want Him to. That's between you and God. All I'm saying is that when I had questions and made it clear that I was really interested in His opinion, God had no problem at all getting inside my head and letting me know how He saw things.

So what you're getting from me is the opinions of J. Neil Schulman. You're free to consider what I have to say is the ravings of a diseased mind. I don't expect you to trust me any more than I trust you.

But if something I have to say makes sense to you, even if it doesn't go along with something you read in some book that some other men have told you is holy scripture, I'm here to tell you that you're empowered by God to use your own brain and decide for yourself what is true and what makes sense. If you're worried that you're not smart enough for this, take comfort in knowing that God is perfectly capable of getting inside your head, too, and helping you with your homework.

Don't expect me to believe you if you say He has spoken to you, any more than I expect you to believe me when I tell you that. I certainly don't believe Neale Donald Walsch who keeps on writing bestselling books about his *Conversations With God*. That guy is certainly not having conversations with the same God who I've been in touch with.

But if God wanted us all to have a universally consistent and self-evident experience of Him, God would go on Oprah.

What, you think God couldn't get the booking if He wanted it? Let's move on.

God is a whole lot smarter than you think He is. You think He couldn't figure out that if He gave us brains, we would eventually use them to figure out how to fuse hydrogen atoms, or decode DNA sequences? You think He didn't know if He designed the male body to have a penis in the front and a rectum in the rear, that some men wouldn't figure out they could use the rectum as a surrogate vagina? You think God didn't pay any attention to what could happen if the hormonal balance during gestation got out of kilter on occasion and occasionally we ended up with brains that were oriented female in male bodies, and vice versa?

Give God a break.

Inserting semen into uterine accessways is how God designed the human mammal to conceive babies. That's why mammals have two sexes in the first place. Anything else we do with our sexual organs isn't making babies. To that extent, God favors heterosexuality over homosexuality.

But then you people go off the rails.

Listen. My mother hates rock music. She was raised listening mostly to classical music, and when she was a teenager popular music was Glenn Miller or Benny Goodman. So when she hears music with a rhythmic drum backbeat, or a standard E-A-B chord progression, she is repulsed by it.

My mother's revulsion by certain sorts of music doesn't make that music an abomination in God's ears.

And J. Neil Schulman's revulsion upon seeing two men kissing each other doesn't make it an abomination in God's eyes, either. That's my problem.

God designed all sorts of operating parameters for the human species which we alter all the time. If two men engaging in sexplay with each other is operating outside of what God intended, then so is transplanting a kidney from one human to another. Neither one is a "natural" act. Both are acts of invention. They are artificial in the sense that they require artifice.

And guess what. God knew when He gave us brains that we were going to be inventive, that we would be artists, artisans, and do the artificial.

Merely being artificial is not enough for something to be an abomination in God's eyes. You have to do something evil.

You want to know what are abominations in God's eyes? Murdering innocent people. Deriving pleasure from cruelty.

Stealing or vandalizing what someone else has worked for. Getting someone else in trouble by lying about them.

But getting all bent out of shape just because some grown men or grown women enjoy rubbing their private parts against each other? God is not as irascible about that as my mother is when she hears rock music. He's not that pathologically obsessive. That, my fellow human beings, would be you.

Now I can see that you get particularly bent out of shape when you think people are breaking God's laws. We all have a bit of the hall monitor in us and can't wait for our chance to scream for the teacher.

God says "don't murder" — and in this case I have no doubt that God really did say that — and you decide that this includes unfinished human beings still in the womb.

You know what? You might be right. It's not a bad argument. Neither do I happen to know what God's personal opinion on this is. I had other things on my mind the last time we conversed and didn't get around to asking Him about this.

But you might be wrong. The question that you keep forgetting to ask is when a soul is present in a human being and when it isn't. I don't happen to know how souls are made. Do they grow out of a living body or are they created somewhere else and move into them? Are souls the same thing as spirits, or is there a clear distinction? Is soul merely a software program in a mortal body until it's ready to be uploaded into permanent media?

These are questions that, lacking a direct answer from God, I'm not prepared to accept anyone else's opinion as a final answer — so the answer to the question of whether abortion is murder is not clear in my mind. But I suspect that if abortion was always murder, God would have been a lot more in my face about it up to now than He has been. I think this is just another one of those things that God wants us to figure out for ourselves.

And here we go with my main point.

God is father of the human race. He made us. He made us smarter than anything else we have encountered so far. He gave us brains that can figure out how to destroy all life on this planet and brains that are on the verge of designing new life forms. He gave us brains which will, by applying logic and imagination to our observations of the universe around us, eventually figure out how to control time and space.

Don't you get it yet? You keep on worrying that men are taking on the powers of God, that we play God, that we act as laws unto ourselves. Well, look at kids on a playground. They play at being grown-ups. They fight, they get unruly, they misbehave. Every once in a while a teacher needs to pull one of them off the playground and give him what-for. But that doesn't mean that this little snot-nose isn't going to grow up to be the fellow who figures out how to make a jelly that will regenerate broken spinal cords.

God has big plans for us when we grow up and become, like our father, gods. New and bigger worlds await our arrival on the scene.

We can't remain children forever. We have got to grow into the responsibility of using our own brains to figure out hard problems, and we can't find all the answers by flipping through a textbook, even a textbook which has some lessons from the Teacher. Some of the things in scripture are deliberate mistakes that we're supposed to figure out for ourselves.

You think God gave you a brain and various moving parts because He doesn't want you to use them?

What, you think God couldn't come on TV and just settle the abortion controversy by telling us how souls are made, and when? If God wanted sexual behavior to be merely procreative, you don't think He couldn't have designed the ejaculation of spermatozoa to be no more pleasurable than sneezing?

You must think God is an idiot in the way He made us. You must think He's orphaned us, leaving nothing but some old books behind.

You want the gospel of J. Neil Schulman? I'm willing to tell you this much.

God is real. He thinks. He's smart. He's a lot like us in a lot of important ways. He comes across as human. The first thing He looks at about a human being is what desire is in his heart. And, He realizes that He is powerless to make us be good or evil; the most He can do is encourage us to be good and give us the keys to His house if we are.

You think of God as all-powerful. From God's point of view, His power ends at the frontiers of our own ability to choose for ourselves. ... and that makes Him as powerless as any parent when it comes to dealing with their kids. When we were a younger race, God was more hands on in how He dealt with us. Now that we're a bit older, we have to handle more things by ourselves. That's the way of things.

Okay, you know how crazy I am now. You think I'm as nuts as I think you are. That's okay. I'm not looking for any followers. I don't believe in the New Age. I'm not about to get a TV show on the SciFi channel and start chatting up your dead relatives. I'll be happy if you just use your God-given brains to think a little more critically about what you're told you have to believe, and stop using scripture as a justification to act so crazy. It also wouldn't hurt if you grew up a bit, since that is our common destiny.

And don't worry that I haven't had a lot to say here about people who don't believe in God at all. I'm nowhere near being ready to shut up and have lots of words left for them.

But just because you've read a book, even a fancy book with gilded pages, don't expect me to follow you, either. I know way too much about how books are written and published.

One more thing. Happy Channukah and Merry Christmas!

The Heartmost Desire

J. Neil Schulman
December 22, 2000

MY AMAZON.COM REVIEW OF THE GOD DELUSION BY RICHARD DAWKINS

MARCH 18, 2007
"RICHARD DAWKINS' CENTRAL FALLACY"

If one agrees with Richard Dawkins, as I do, that concluding God's existence should not rely on an act of faith, but should survive a rational thinker's potent skepticism, one comes to consider Dawkins' central argument against the existence of God as the creator of our universe.

Dawkins submits to us that the complexity of our universe requires a long chain of prior events to become so complex.

Dawkins further submits that beings capable of creative design are not at the beginning of such a long chain of events but follow such a chain of events.

Dawkins sees human beings as being the result of a long chain of prior events, and sees us as creative designers. So, Dawkins and those who regard God as a creative designer are at least in agreement that such preconditions for a creative designer to exist can be satisfied, since here we are. But could a creative designer create an artifact as complex as an entire universe?

Dawkins submits that for a creative designer to have designed the universe, the creative designer, himself, would have had to have undergone a long chain of events prior to the creation of the universe.

If we regard the universe we perceive as the totality of that which exists, Dawkins has ended the discussion by reducing the thesis of a creator of the universe to absurdity, and his denial of the very possibility of a universe-creating God is justified.

But if a cosmology is possible in which that which we regard as our universe is not the whole of that which exists but is merely a part of existence, the paradox vanishes followed close order by the absurdity of the proposition that the universe could be a created artifact.

The Hebrews identify God in their scripture as being Eternal — as having always existed. If there exists a being with this trait, we can derive from that premise:

1) An eternal being would have sufficient time to develop his intellect, imagination, and other prerequisites of creative design;

2) Such a being would have time to learn a great deal, try out different philosophies, paradigms, methods, and so forth.

The possibility of the Eternal Hebrew God, so long as God's existence is something additional to the universe as we regard it — that existence is more than that which we regard as The Universe — therefore survives Dawkins' challenge to our reason.

Dawkins is free to demand a proof that such a being exists, but if, like existence itself, consciousness is a property of existence itself — then like existence, itself, there is no basis to demand a proof for that which would be the self-evident foundation for all further proofs.

We would not therefore be looking for proof of God in the sense of a mathematician deriving one, or in the sense of a scientist conducting experiments to test a thesis, but in the sense of seeing if we encounter such a being who can present us with experiences sufficient to satisfy our doubts.

Dawkins has not had such experiences. I have. Dawkins hasn't convinced me that my conclusion that my skepticism was sufficiently satisfied was irrational. Unless Richard Dawkins has experiences that personally convince him that his skepticism has been satisfied, it is reasonable for him to continue disbelieving in God until he has experiences satisfactory to his reason.

But Richard Dawkins demand for reason to be applied to the

question of God existence is, itself, quite godly, seeing as how to create a universe as complex as the one we find ourselves in one would require a being who is himself a scientist.

J. Neil Schulman, author

The March 27, 1993 proposal for *Escape from Heaven* sent to editor, John Douglas.

ESCAPE FROM HEAVEN
A Novel Proposal

by
J. Neil Schulman

Category: Novel

Proposed Length: 70,000 – 90,000 words

Settings: Current day America, Heaven, A Suburban Universe, Hell-on-Earth.

Logline: A man dies and goes to Heaven, only to find himself not at peace but back on Earth as a partisan in the ultimate War.

Major Characters:

Duj Pepperman, a dead radio talk-show host. Saviour of humankind, the universe, and God Almighty.

Caulinn Helms, lead singer of the rock group Seminal Lunch, whom Duj falls in love with when he returns to earth after his death.

"Manchu" Ellins, homicide detective with the Culver City, California, police department.

Myron Kaplowitz, a boyhood friend of Duj's who died when Duj was in college.

Sally Pepperman, Duj's daughter. She was two-years-old when Duj died; when he meets her in Heaven, she's a grown woman.

God (Jesus H. Christ, Cineman Hulls). Creator of the universe and the smartest, nicest, and all-around best person you ever want to meet.

Satan (Sun Amen Chill, Uncle Nimlash, Iceman Shnull). A rebellious angel. As smart as God but not nearly as nice.

Lucifer, Satan's alter ego. An unfallen angel, still on God's side. Go figure.

ESCAPE FROM HEAVEN
Outline

Duj Pepperman, our first-person narrator for this story, is not the sort of guy you think of as a hero. He's in his middle forties and looks it. He's less than a year out of a bad marriage, has one two-year-old daughter, and lives in Southern California, where he makes a decent living as a talk radio personality, fifteen hours a week.

It's not a bad life. But it is, by most of our standards, too short. On his way home from the studio, one night, Duj is walking to his car when out of the blue, something hits him in the head, fast. It could be anything from a small meteor to a bullet. Duj never finds out what it is. But suddenly, he's floating slightly above his body, which is now lying face down on the concrete, with blood oozing out of his head.

It takes Duj a few moments to figure out that this isn't a dream, then a bright light appears above him, and he realizes he has a choice: to climb back into his body and continue living on earth, or to follow the light. He realizes that, for him — now that he knows there is continued consciousness after the body dies — he is more interested in finding out what happens next than hanging around on Earth.

He floats up toward the light.

It is, as reported, an ecstatic experience. And when he gets to the end, he finds a welcoming committee made up of an old friend of his from school, Myron Kaplowitz, and a young woman whom he doesn't know right off but looks familiar. He soon learns that the young woman is his daughter, Sally, who was two-years-old when Duj died.

The source of the light is an immense, luminescent-crystal palace off in the distance but immediately before him are the streets of what looks to be the commercial district of a great city at night.

Myron and Sally help reorient Duj to his new existence. He learns that his new body has many more "options" than his old body, and he delights in exploring them: the ability to change hair or skin colors, body type — even gender — metabolism, and resist or repair damage by drawing on an unlimited supply of power. Going to Heaven is a lot like being from Krypton and finding yourself on Earth.

He starts by morphing his body into better shape, then learns that his new brain has a direct access to the Tree of Knowledge, giving him virtual-reality access to almost all the knowledge of the universes — just a question away. He works a bit on smoothing out the interface parameters, so that he can ask a question and decide in what form he wants it answered: holographically, visually, a spoken answer, or even text display.

But the new power that delights him most is his ability to fly like a superhero, which he's dreamt of his entire life. He gets the grand tour of the heavenly city. Unlike the Heaven in Heinlein's Job, there are no angels handing out traffic tickets to unlicensed humans.

From his bird's eye view, Duj has a panoramic view of the city. It's an island, but surrounded not by ocean but by empty space, unbroken even by stars. Duj finds he has the ability to see distant things at different magnifications at will. He can see the palace, glowing incandescently in the blackness below.

Duj lands for some closer-up sightseeing, and learns what Heaven is. It's essentially a multidimensional port city. It functions much as cities do on Earth for people who live in the suburbs: it's where eternal souls come to meet each other, share public entertainments, debate politics, engage in commerce.

It's also the capital of the many universes, where God lives, and is the home of the all-knowing universal library, known by mystics as the Akashic Records or the Tree of Knowledge. Hardly anybody except for some angels live there; everybody else is off in their own universes, and only come into town to meet, or if they need to see God, or need to do extended direct research in the downtown branch of the Tree of Knowledge.

The city design isn't completely different from cities as we know them, but this city makes Rodeo Drive or Fifth Avenue look like slums by comparison. The use of precious metals, crystalline structures, and ornamental jewels as ordinary construction materials is overwhelming. Special effects of the sort you'd see in theme parks — only done with a three-dimensional reality we've encountered in our lives only as flat images on movie screens — are routine. Duj's first thoughts are that what Heaven resembles more than anything else is Disneyland done for real.

Duj learns that it's mostly angels on God's payroll who live in the heavenly city itself; most everybody else goes into their own time-space continuum to create their own universes. Being able to create your own universe — design and furnish it as you please — is private property with a big bang.

But Duj does see some celebrities in Heaven. He passes a cafe where JFK is having lunch with Jackie. Duj is surprised because Jackie was still alive when he died; Sally explains that time loops — like the one that has her a live two-year-old on Earth when Duj leaves, and a grown up eternal soul when he arrives — are routine in Heaven, so he just might as well get used to them.

They pass a Heavenly Hyde Park with a heated debate between Thomas Jefferson and Richard Nixon, and another between Martin Luther and C.S. Lewis, and pass a panel discussion on philosophy with Aristotle, Ayn Rand, and Emmanuel Kant, in time to see Ayn Rand leap at Aristotle's throat after Aristotle casually mentions his opinion that all women are good for is slavery.

There's also a wild discussion going on among angels, who are charging that God's not a Trinity, but has a crazy fourth personality, and that God is suffering from Multiple Personality Disorder. This, they claim, explains God's bizarre behavior with regard to Earth. The angels also have a bunch of complaints regarding God having limited their security level in the Tree of Knowledge, and there's some wild talk about storming the Heavenly Palace and subjecting God to a sanity hearing. In another seemingly bizarre time paradox, the two angels who are the most antagonistic debaters are Lucifer — who is arguing that God is sane — and Satan, who's actually Lucifer at a different age, who's the one arguing for putting God on trial. Which one of the two is the older soul is something we don't know.

Sick of political discourse, Duj and Sally stop off for a movie, written by Woody Allen, directed by George Lucas, music by Beethoven, and starring Woody himself, "Slick Willie" Shakespeare, Charlie Chaplin, Greta Garbo, Donna Reed, Robin Williams, Sarah Bernhardt, and the Marx Brothers.

Duj and Sally also take a trip to visit Duj's parents in their own universe. Sally's visited before. Unlike most married couples, Duj's parents found they had enough in common to want to team up again, and have collaborated on building a universe together. It's a small and brand-new universe, but well-along because it wasn't created from scratch; it's based on a lot of build-a-universe shareware downloaded from the Tree, with only one Earth-like planet inhabited by humans. On this particular planet, it's day all the time and nobody ever sleeps; all the cultural institutions and customs are strange to us because of that one difference. For example, there's hardly any imagination – no concept of lying or fiction — no sense of "home" or privacy. Duj finds out that his parents, as gods, are a lot more interesting now than he ever thought they were when they were alive.

As Duj and Sally return to the Heavenly City after the visit, they stumble into the middle of an angelic riot, led by Satan, and triggered off by God — having heard Satan's remarks – deciding to drop the angels' security access level to the Tree even further — far below that of human beings. Satan has told his troops to round up as many human souls as they can get their hands on, both as shields against attacks God might make on them, and also to try using humans to hack their way back into the Tree again, the secrets of which they need to stand a chance of victory.

Escaping from the rioters, Duj and Sally meet up with Myron, and the three make plans to *escape from Heaven* by jumping back into Earth's time line at various points. Even on Earth they can uplink to the Tree, and by leaving messages for each other in T-mail, they can figure out a way to rendezvous and figure out further plans later. But they'll all have to be careful and keep their uplinks short and untraceable; if the rebels jack into the Tree, any of their uplinks could be instant capture.

With Satan's angels hot on their trails, Duj, Sally, and Myron each dive back down toward Earth. Of course, since Duj is our narrator, we stick with his point of view.

Duj dives out of Heaven back to the moment of his death. We replay his death scene, only this time, when the women trips over Duj's body and screams, Duj slips back into his body, gets up, and tells her he was just stunned; he's okay.

As soon as he's gotten rid of her, he steps behind a truck, exits his damaged body again, and lets it fall to the ground. Then he rematerializes next to it in his new body, says, "Save," and zaps his old body, so it instantly disappears.

Outwardly, Duj resumes his life on Earth as if he'd never left it. But his perspective is different, and sometimes he lends us his heavenly perspective. He tells us about watching an AIDS benefit on MTV, only to have it transform before his eyes into Stars Against Death on TV. ("Over two million Americans die every year," says Cher. "Few of us haven't lost someone near and dear to us. It's a disease that hits young and old alike, and we all know it's in store for us. Yet, what has the President done to stop this awful plague?")

Until Duj can rendezvous safely with Myron and Sally, his main problem is simply keeping a low profile. Which isn't all that easy, when you're a young god resuming your old life on earth. The misery we take for granted seems stupid and wasteful; yet, for Duj to fix things too visibly leaves the possibility of his being detected. Even a short flight is out of the question; he can make himself invisible to living people easily, but not from hostile angels.

Also, he realizes how much unseen goings on there are on Earth, enemy territory held by Satan's angels. Obviously, Satan's angels have entered earth's timestream far into our past, and now treat it as occupied turf. There are entire cities of fallen angels on Earth, visible to him but invisible to us. Duj has to pretend that he doesn't see them; masquerading as human, Duj has to avoid reacting to the devilish cruelty that invisible angels routinely impose on humans.

Duj realizes that most of human history starts to make sense when you realize it's a several-millennia's old hostage crisis.

It comes time for the uplink, and Duj learns that both Myron and Sally have been captured by the enemy. However, Myron has left him a message: God wants to meet with him.

The rendezvous instructions are included in the message. The City of the Angels, Souplantation Restaurant, the next afternoon at two.

It is only by very careful blending in that Duj avoids

being detected by enemy angels when he uplinks to get this information.

Duj has trepidations about meeting with God. He was an atheist most of his life, and even when he decided that he believed in God before his death, he wasn't sure what kind of God he believed in. Reading the Old Testament, in particular, has given him doubts. If the *Bible* is at all accurate, then as far as Duj is concerned, the spirit inside the Ark of the Covenant, talking to Moses, couldn't have been any worse to the ancient Jews if it were Adolf Hitler traveling back in time.

But when the meeting happens, God puts Duj at ease by treating him as an equal, and discussing all of Duj's doubts rationally and calmly.

After God recruits Duj to his army, Duj is given his mission. He needs to recruit some living humans as a commando squad, and pull a raid on an earthbound concentration camp, where fallen angels are keeping immortal humans and loyalist angels prisoner. There is one prisoner in particular that Duj must get out: Lucifer. Not Satan, but Lucifer. Lucifer and Satan are two time segments of one being, but which one will prevail in eternity is in doubt, the result of a time loop the two of them are locked in. If Lucifer is freed and defeats Satan, then Lucifer the Lightbringer will be the aftergod of the two. If Satan wins, then Satan will be the aftergod. And which one prevails is the crucial linch pin of this entire war — and that job is now a young god's who when on earth was called Duj Pepperman. If Duj can't get Lucifer out of Satan's prison, that's it for the human race, the loyal angels including Lucifer, and God Himself.

God explains that He, Himself, is in fact vulnerable. He can lose. The outcome of this war isn't a sure thing, much as human writers would like to think so. God had to allow himself to be vulnerable as a condition of setting the events in motion that created the possibility of His victory in the first place. God had to die on Earth as a man in order to make resurrection of embodied humans possible; but when He did so, God was incapacitated for three Celestial Days. During these three Days, He is completely vulnerable to attack — and if the angelic guard fails, God can be captured and imprisoned forever, just like a Genie.

There is one minor catch, from Duj's point of view. Every human Duj recruits for the mission must be a willing volunteer whom Duj is convinced will be both effective and loyal. Then Duj must kill them, and resurrect them a few days later.

This is bound to draw attention, both from the enemy angels, and from earthbound police authorities.

Duj goes to work, looking for recruits. One of his first recruits is a living woman he falls in love with, lead singer of the rock band, Seminal Lunch. Her name is Caulinn Helms. After getting to know her, Duj reveals himself to her at a hotel in Culver City, California, asks her if she wants to join God's army, and when she says yes, he makes love to her tenderly then smothers her to death with a pillow.

Duj's next recruit is the Culver City police detective who's investigating the murder, "Manchu" Ellins. Duj recruits and kills him, too.

As the TV news starts reporting on a new serial killer operating in Los Angeles, Satan — who's better known on Earth as evangelist Sun Amen Chill — detects what Duj is up to, and Duj's only chance is to play double agent, convincing Satan that he's really on his side and that he's really spying out God for Satan. Satan might believe this, because Duj is right on the margin between whom he believes. And God's troops aren't supposed to go around murdering living people anyway — even the bad ones, much less the good ones.

The real danger is that this silver-tongued Satan just might convince Duj that Satan's side is telling the truth, that God is crazy.

At just the right moment, Duj makes his way into the morgue

at the medical examiner's, and pulls a resurrection.

The clock is now ticking. The beginning of celestial Easter has begun — the three days God is out of action. Duj can't uplink to the Tree of Knowledge without revealing his whereabouts to the enemy. And now that he's resurrected the people he's killed, Satan can probably guess which side Duj is fighting for. Even if Satan's not sure, he's not likely to trust Duj with anything important.

Duj gives his commandos a short course on their new powers, then takes them onto the raid. The concentration camp where Lucifer is being held prisoner is both well-hidden and well-defended, but through courage, logic, and more imagination than I have writing this at four o'clock in the morning, Duj and his commandos make it into the prison, liberate Lucifer, and help in the final mano y mano duel between Lucifer and Satan.

Return to Heaven. Sweet victory. All heroes reunited. John Williams music here. Thank you all very, very much for coming.

They all live happily forever after.

ESCAPE FROM HEAVEN
Writing Samples

THE OPENING
There's an old saying that everybody wants to go to Heaven, but nobody wants to die.

That's how it was for me, anyway.

I drove a Volvo because I was told it was the safest car around. And it was a smart choice. I was killed by something else.

I owned a gun so I wouldn't die at the hands of a burglar. I was right about that, too. The burglar who broke into my bedroom ran like hell when he saw the .45 I was pointing at him ... and I was killed by someone else.

I quit smoking, lost weight, worked out three times a week,

ate a low cholesterol diet, and practiced safe sex, because I didn't want to die of cancer, heart disease, AIDS, or emphysema, and it paid off: I died of something else.

You see, that's the part they forget to mention. No matter what nasty ways of dying you avoid, there's always another one waiting for you. If one thing doesn't get you, another thing will. Sooner or later, you die of something else.

Everybody could have saved an awful lot of thought that went into bumper stickers and public service messages. All they would have had to say is, "Don't do that. Die of something else."

It would have saved me a lot of trouble, too. I was a coward most of my life, because I was afraid of dying.

My story begins the day I died.

WHEN DUJ JUST DIES

I used to have an infallible way of knowing when I was awake and when I was dreaming. In dreams, I could levitate myself off the floor at will; when I was awake, I couldn't. This worked even when I was asleep and dreaming. If I could levitate, I was dreaming. There were plenty of times in dreams when I told people that I knew I was dreaming — they didn't exist and were merely part of my solipsistic fantasy — because I was levitating. And since I could only do that while dreaming, this was just another dream.

So right after my death, when I found myself levitating a few feet over my body, I thought at first I was alive and dreaming.

But somehow I knew that wasn't the right answer. In the remake of *Heaven Can Wait,* James Mason is an angel, trying to convince Warren Beatty, who's walking around the clouds confused, that he's dead. Mason asks Beatty something like, where do you think you are, anyway? And Beatty answers something like, I'm asleep and dreaming. What James Mason says next is so true, I wonder how the screenwriter knew about it without having died himself. Mason says, in effect, that dreams are a part of life, and if you just think for a minute, you'll know that this is something different.

That's exactly how it is. Dreams are a part of life, and when you die and leave your body, you just know that however bizarre this experience is, it's not a dream.

The thing I felt most when I realized I was dead was utter joy at discovering that I still was. I existed! I hadn't been snuffed out. My memory was intact. I still knew who I was and who I had been. I'd always wondered how you could have consciousness and memory without a physical brain to put them in. Well, my RAM was being saved to that big Hard Disk in the sky. It looked as if I still had a chance to discover meaning for my existence. Death wasn't the ultimate banality. Maybe there was a point to it all, after all.

They say that your life passes before you right when you die. Well, for me it wasn't literal, like watching my life in a movie or anything, but when it happened something told me that you sometimes have a choice about whether or not you can stay or go. Obviously, if your body is damaged beyond repair, you're going and that's that. But I had a sense that I was being given a choice. If I really wanted to stay, I could climb back into my body and hang on.

So I thought about my life.

I'd always thought of myself as an underachiever. I was never able to do schoolwork that didn't interest me. I got A's in subjects I cared about and F's in ones I didn't. I was the kid in the back row who was reading comic books and science-fiction novels behind the textbook I wasn't interested in.

I quit college to become a writer, and became one for a while. Some of my stuff was damned good if I say so myself, but it was never a real living. The occasional sale I got in Hollywood was option money on projects that never got into development; my books never earned out an advance. This didn't encourage agents or publishers to want the next one. I was broke a lot of the time.

I tried starting a lot of businesses, and never made a dime out of any of them. All were harebrained schemes, disastrously executed. Finally, I stumbled into a job as a talk radio host, and that's what I'd been doing for the last eight years.

I married late, had one wonderful child, and divorced early. My ex-wife had remarried and moved cross country; I had to wedge my time with my daughter into phone calls and occasional weekends. I was lonely a lot of the time, and tried to handle it with stoicism.

When I considered the thought that my life was over, I felt unfinished. What was the point of my life on Earth anyway? To reproduce? Okay, I'd done that. But that merely pushes the necessity of finding a meaning for life onto someone else. What was the meaning of my life? What was its purpose? Why had I lived and what was I supposed to do with my life now that I was dead?

Right about the time that some lady came along, tripped over my body, and screamed, I saw the night sky blaze into a brilliant light, and I had an overwhelming sense of being drawn into the light.

I was being given a choice. I thought that above all I had always felt out of place during my life, as if I was in a foreign country, and now I was being given a chance to go home. I also thought that the mystery that had always puzzled me — the question of why we live in the first place — might be answered for me in a few minutes.

Life is a suspense story, and what makes it suspenseful is not knowing how it comes out. The biggest mystery — the one that has you lying in bed awake at night — is whether or not you die when your body dies.

All you know when you're on Earth is life within your body. You can't imagine living without it. For all your life you're in the dark about what you are. You read that you're a biochemical reaction trapped in a piece of meat, and when you die, the reaction fizzles and the meat rots. And, so, most of the scary images of death have to do with dead bodies in various states of disintegration: skulls, bones, meat lockers, graves, and the paraphernalia of the undertaker.

If that isn't enough, horror stories try to make it worse with three awful ideas: first that this rotting meat is all that's left of you when you die; second and worse: that after you die you're a disembodied ghost trapped in post-life impotence; or third and worst: that you're still conscious inside the rotting meat, and can experience the slow rotting. All the Halloween death images, ghosts, and goblins, are a conspiracy by people who don't believe in an afterlife anyway to scare the shit out of us.

It works. In that fear is a con game — and you're the mark. If we knew down deep — really knew, without fear of doubt – that we were going to continue living once we separate from the meat — and not as ghosts, either — our fear couldn't be used to stampede us.

I'd made my decision. I didn't even bother looking back to see what was happening to my body. As far as I was concerned, I cared about it about as much as clothes you leave for the Salvation Army truck.

I floated up toward the light. You hear about the light, and how it overwhelms you with a sense of joy. Let me tell you, it's better than anything. In specific terms, it'll be different for you. But for me, flying into the light was like making it with Sophia Loren in zero-gravity while eating a pralines-and-cream sundae and listening to Brahms' Third Symphony and cracking up at Sam Kinnison and getting that final piece in the puzzle and crossing the finish line. All satisfaction circuits on full Jack.

There is a dreamy quality in flying toward the light. Then you get to it, and your eyes — or whatever sight organs have replaced them — adjust, and things come into focus, becoming real again.

Religions make a lot of promises about what you win if you make it to Heaven. You're supposed to be reunited with your loved ones. You meet God. Some suggest that you yourself become a god. Some promise you rest, or peace. Some promise you a bigger playground to play in, and all the time you want to do it.

Yeah, that's what's on the contract.

RETURNING TO A HEAVEN UNDER ATTACK

I was startled by a voice that sounded as if it was right next to my ear: //Duj, can you hear me? It's Myron.\\

"Myron?" I said aloud, looking around frantically. I didn't see anyone. "Where are you?"

//Shhh!\\ I heard Myron say. //If you talk aloud the angels will hear you! And believe me, you don't want that. Just think clearly and I'll hear you — we've got a private channel.\\

I thought hard, //Can you hear me now?\\

//Perfect. Listen, I can't come to you so you're going to have to come to me.\\

//How?\\ I asked.

//I'll make a tunnel right in front of you. Fly into it and follow it to the end. Hurry! They've spotted you!\\

I saw a glowing hole in the blackness iris open a few yards in front of me almost at the same time I heard the shouts getting closer. I dove into the hole just in time; it irised closed behind me, just as I saw a glowing hand reach for my foot.

The glow was up ahead of me now. //Myron, you still there?\\

//Just fly forward. I'll be at the end.\\

The tunnel wasn't straight; it twisted around like a snake. But I managed to navigate through until I saw the proverbial light at the end of the tunnel. A few seconds later, I emerged into what looked to be a palatial hall, with a couch, a coffee table, and some upholstered chairs sitting in the center. Myron, dressed in jeans and a dark blue sweater, was standing next to the coffee table.

I floated over near to him and landed.

Myron put out his hand and we shook. "Duj, glad you could make it. You can talk again, now — we're safe here."

I looked around the room for the first time. It was sort of a mixture of Buckingham Palace and Superman's Fortress of Solitude. "Nice place. Yours?"

"Yep. Be it ever so humble. Listen, take a load off. We have a lot to talk about."

"That's the understatement of ... of eternity," I said. We sat down. "Myron, where are we? What's going on? What the hell's going on out there?"

"Short answers?" Myron said. "We're in my personal apartments inside the walls of the Heavenly Palace. Outside the walls are what's left of Heaven, a city in the middle of what you in the broadcasting business like to call 'civil unrest.' And that was a gang of angels who were sent to capture you."

"Why would they want to capture me?"

"Because they knew that if they didn't stop you first, you'd end up here."

"And why should they care about that?"

"Because God needs you to defeat them."

DUJ CONTEMPLATES HIS UPCOMING MEETING WITH GOD

You know, it's hard to read the *Bible* and not get really pissed off at God.

Take the Book of Genesis. Adam and Eve, practically born yesterday — and with no knowledge of good or evil — disobey their father as any child might, talked into it by a playmate. God curses them for it. They're run out of Eden because they might eat off the Tree of Life and become immortals, and are sentenced to a life at hard labor, followed by death.

Their son, Cain — a farmer — brings God some of his crops as an offering. Well, he's a farmer — what would you expect to get as an offering? God rejects it in favor of some barbecued lamb from Cain's brother Abel, a sheepherder. Then God lectures Cain on how he has no reason to be sullen for being rejected. Cain kills his brother in anger at God's unfair rejection; and God curses Cain.

There's no mention of God raising Abel from the dead, either. I guess God didn't learn that technique till later. Or maybe He didn't think all that much of Abel to begin with.

Even with these curses from God, the budding human race prevails. The angels think our women are beautiful and marry them. God disapproves. Does He impose sanctions on the angels? Nope. He cuts our lifespan from eight or nine hundred years, to a maximum of one-hundred-twenty — to make us less attractive to the angels.

But God isn't finished with us. Except for one human family, He floods the Earth and drowns the human race; then tries to make up for it with a promise that He won't do it again.

We're just getting on our feet again, and figuring out how to build a city with a tower — and God figures that if we're building skyscrapers in our racial infancy, nothing will be beyond us when we grow up. So does He praise us for our initiative? Maybe even lend us a helping hand? No, He does not. He curses us so we can't all speak the same language anymore, to set us at war with each other so we can't try it again.

He suckers Abraham into thinking that he has to kill his beloved son Isaac as a sacrifice to God — then sends a messenger to stop him at the last instant, with the lame excuse that He was just trying his faith.

Then there's Job, a good man who worships the very dust God kicks in his face. God turns him over to the devil on a bet, and lets the devil kill his children, take all his wealth, and plague him with illness. And when Job is tormented by his friends for not admitting that his cruel fate is the result of his own sins, and Job cries out to God for any relief at all — even immediate death — God gives Job a lecture about how much smarter he is than Job and how dare Job put his judgment up against God's on anything.

You can almost see God's guilt on that one: he does what any child-beater does the next morning — goes on a shopping spree and tries to make it up. The maximum human life span is supposed to be one-hundred-twenty years? God breaks his own limit and gives Job, already an old man, another one-hundred forty, and restores his property double. God even gives him replacement children.

But you're left wondering whether Job ever cries at night over the loss of his first kids.

Reading through the first five books of the *Bible* in one sitting is enough to convince any objective person that this God whom Moses is working for is a manic-depressive nut case. God frees the Israelites from slavery to the Egyptians only to prove Himself a slavedriver so awful that afterwards the Israelites, almost to a man, wish God had left them in Egypt. And the feeling is mutual: there is so little love and respect between God and the Israelites that God tells Moses that He should just kill everyone He's liberated, except for Moses, and make Moses's offspring his chosen people. For some perverse reason, Moses talks God out of it, and the two of them subject the Israelites to police-state regulations that even Orwell couldn't have invented. Talking wrong or thinking wrong is punished by death – burning to death if God is particularly miffed. Women's periods are lumped in with leprosy as "unclean." The rules for sacrifices, punishments, diet, and sex make the IRS code seem lucid and benevolent by comparison. And God's rules about how anyone who isn't physically perfect is to be kept out of his sight — any disability, even a scar or a broken leg — is enough to have the ACLU set up permanent picket lines.

We jump forward to the New Testament, when God incarnates himself as a Man. It seems God has decided He doesn't want us to be deaders after all, after taunting us for the first few thousand years about how we're going to return to dust. He's going to give us immortality after all. Okay, human beings get convinced that this Man really is God — and we strike. We've had enough of this drunken, pompous, bullying child-torturer of an abusive father — this cosmic Adolf Hitler on a coke binge. His battered children nail Him on the cross as fast as we can.

Speaking for the battered children of God — could you blame us? With a God like this, who needs a Devil?

This was the God I was being summoned by. I knew why the churches always talked about fear of God. This God was supposed to be all-powerful, and whenever He started talking about how much He loves us, it's always looked like a good time to duck and cover.

Our race had good reason to be scared shitless. So did I.

Of course there was another possibility: that all these stories about God were a crock. If the *Bible* was a pack of lies, then God might have got a bum rap.

But I was going to have to ask. And if God didn't give me answers to convince me that he was not only powerful and smart, but more importantly loving, kind, sane, and just, then I wasn't going to enlist.

On behalf of the human race, it was nice to be in the driver's seat, for once.

DUJ'S INTERVIEW WITH GOD

"You have some questions," God said. "Ask them."

"When was the last time you spoke to anyone on Earth? Directly, I mean; not through dreams or revelations."

"As myself? A couple hundred years after I died on the Cross, more or less."

"That was the last time you visited Earth?"

"Oh, no. I'm there right now. In disguise, of course. Got to keep my eye on things."

"Why have you been so secretive?"

"You get nailed up on a Cross, you wouldn't be so anxious to let people know who you were, either."

"That seems a particularly selfish answer, for a God who claims to be a loving father."

"From the way you were thinking about it before you came in here, I would think I"d be doing you a favor by staying away entirely."

"Well, was what I was thinking true? Did you do all those things the *Bible* says you did?"

"Let me ask you a question," God said. "The Book of Job" – He pronounced it "Eyob" — "it recounts a conversation I supposedly had with my adversary — the leader of the loyal opposition. 'Satan,' in the King James translation. So tell me. How is it that a conversation up here in Heaven gets reported on Earth?"

"You tell me," I said.

"It doesn't. Never happened. Hogwash from a political priesthood."

"Adam and Eve?"

"These first ancestors of yours — bad-ass kids. You still have the type in your century — phone phreaks, computer jackers, credit-card scam artists. Young Lex Luthors. Hacked their way into the Tree of Knowledge on a bet. Once they were augmented by the Tree, there could have been no stopping them. You've heard that knowledge is power? The Tree has a record of everything. How to genetically engineer a virus. How to make a sun go supernova. How to create a self-destroying time loop. I was easy on them, just kicking them out of Eden — taking away their powers. I thought about killing them on the spot. Sometimes I still think I should have. If I had, though, you and

I wouldn't be having this conversation."

A chill went up my spine. It's one thing to contemplate never having been born. It's another to contemplate your race's having been stillborn.

"Cain and Abel?"

I wasn't even around when this punk kid murders his brother. This business about my getting turned on by burnt offerings – barbecue smoke. Does that make any sense to you?"

"No."

"Never happened. Next."

"Abraham and Isaac?"

"Old man had Alzheimer's disease, starts thinking that I want him to sacrifice his son to me. Would've done it if I hadn't sent an angel to stop him."

"Noah and the flood."

"That story couldn't have been written any other way, because only the survivors lived to tell the tale. I told everybody on Earth about the upcoming flood. Earth's axis was going to have to be realigned — polar ice caps were going to melt. It was either that or lose the entire planetary ecology, anyway. Take my word — or consult the Tree to bone up on cosmological economics. Anybody who believed me built ships, took animals and family aboard. Those who didn't drowned. Hardly anybody believed me, except a few families. And for the record, there were eight arks, not one. Noah's the only captain who kept a ship's log."

"You could have saved everyone, if you wanted to."

"I didn't want to. I played fair. Gave a warning to those who'd listen. Evil and stupid go hand in hand. I can't see anything wrong with letting evildoers get blown up on their own petards. Be happy you aren't descended from the ones who died. You can't imagine what bastards they were."

"Their babies, too?"

"Those kids never had a fair chance. Their parents would

have made them go bad, and after the flood, there was barely enough to go around for the ones who lived. We're talking post-disaster times. Evolution has its own built-in logic. You show sympathy when you have to let weeding happen, all you do is make more misery later."

"You do sound like Hitler."

"Difference between me and Hitler is that he was a moronic lunatic with no knowledge of science, and I'm God. When I weed, I don't do it on the basis of national borders, or ethnic alliances, or religious beliefs. I don't even do it on the basis of sexual preference, much as your religious right would like to pin AIDS on me. When I kill a bloodline, it's to improve the overall breed. The job has to be done and I'm the only one with enough knowledge to do it. If I hadn't, your race would have murdered itself a hundred times over already, or died weakened by another thousand ills."

"I apologize," I said. "My comparison was uncalled for."

"No apology needed. You do a thorough interview. Next question."

"Cutting our lifespan because of the angels marrying our women."

"That's exactly backwards. Only reason your race continued living that long was because of angelic cross-breeding. Once I forbid them from raping your women, your race reverted to its design specs."

"Why weren't we offered immortality until your incarnation?"

"You were supposed to have it from the start — and would have if Adam and Eve hadn't pulled their little stunt. Remember, the Tree of Life was already planted in Eden. Think it was there for fun? Took me a few millennia to reengineer around the problems Adam and Eve caused by trying to steal what they weren't ready for. Evolutionary ecology is a tricky business."

"Tower of Babel? The curse of languages?"

"Come on, get real. You people invent jargon and dialects

to set yourselves apart. Amazing you understand each other at all."

"No curse?"

"No curse except being cut off from the Tree of Knowledge. A Berlitz course comes free with every uplink."

"The sexism in Leviticus?"

"Male chauvinist priesthood. Not my doing."

"How about the endless laws, rules, and regulations? Reading Leviticus and Numbers on the regulations for sacrificing animals, ritual purification, dietary laws — it's like reading Orwell and Kafka at their darkest. The least infraction is punished by death — sometimes burning to death. Death penalties for blasphemy, cursing, homosexuality. The list is endless. The ancient Israelites sound like the worst police state I can imagine, all centered around a homicidal religious cult."

"That's a fairly accurate description. I could point out, however, that most everyone else around them was even worse."

"And you approved of all this?"

"I did not. It was all done in my name, which makes me come across as an Oriental Potentate to any sane person who reads these accounts. But this is not accurate history of what went on, much less of what I said or did. It's part tribal myth, part rules set up by a fanatic priesthood to gain control of people's minds. Look, try to analyze this logically. Do you think I'm going to hang around in a box inside a tribal tent? And that if an animal isn't slaughtered in precisely the correct way, I'm going to throw a tantrum? Or that I'm so addicted to the smell of burning flesh that I have to have an army of priests just to keep whomping up batches of the stuff? Please."

"Then why didn't you make corrections to the *Bible*? Separate out the lies from the truth?"

"Why should I? It's human literature. Some myth, some bits of real history, some poetry, some genealogy, some how-to stuff, and a lot of political speechmaking. Anybody who wants to know what really happened can read the truth for themselves, once they're here, by doing an historical search in the Tree of Knowledge."

"Then the *Bible* wasn't supposed to give us the Word? Teach us morality?"

"Listen, nothing can teach you morality. I know from experience, having tried and failed numerous times."

"Well then how do you expect us to act rightly?" I asked.

"Trial and error, just like I did."

"What?"

"You want to be gods? You're gods. I made you to be gods. And the first thing a god needs to figure out is what to do with immortality. Immortality cuts out all the imperatives caused by striving for survival. You jump right off the end of the Maslow scale. So what's left?"

"You tell me."

"No, I tell Me. You tell yourself. As an immortal being, I am faced with a choice more fundamental than Hamlet's. Not 'to be or not to be' but 'to do or not to do.' Why do anything? I can lay back and watch for eternity, if I felt like it."

"Then why do you do anything?"

"Because no matter how good any vacation is, sooner or later any intelligent person gets bored. And if nothing is forcing you to do anything, then you learn to come up with reasons of your own to justify doing things. There's the beginning of all imperatives — the beginning of morality. The purpose of life – immortal or otherwise — is to avoid going insane, turning towards yourself and away from reality. Solipsism is the final boredom. Everybody should try it at least once, just to get past it. After a good dose of a universe with nobody but yourself as a thinking companion, you'll find out what loneliness is."

"That's why you create intelligent beings?"

"That's why. I started out solo. It worked for a while. Then I got to a point when I wasn't sure what was real and what was hallucination. That's a trap you can't imagine, if you've never been the only god in a universe.

"I thought you were a trinity. Didn't that give you someone to talk to?"

"Whether you want to think of my three parts as one person or three, it's still an internal dialogue. Given a set of facts, we'd reach one conclusion — no disagreements, no reality check. No different than you talking to yourself. I created other intelligent beings so I could have someone to talk with who didn't always agree with me."

"You seem to have more disagreements than you care for right now."

"So I do. I want others who can think for themselves. I don't want people who decide that they dislike me so much that they want to lock me up forever. I'm still the Eternal. I was here first and I'll be here last. I don't have to put up with that and I won't."

I thought for a long moment.

"Why should I fight for you?" I asked. "I don't mean what would you pay me — I'm sure it would be more than I can imagine. I don't mean gratitude for your having created me because I can't evaluate the worth of my own life to me or to you until I know what it's being used for."

"You don't have the perspective needed to value your own worth."

"Then you're going to have to lend me your perspective, so I can understand. I have to know before I can make a right choice. If you'll forgive me for saying so, this is too important for me to take it on faith."

"You would have to be Me to understand a full answer of what's at stake."

"I don't need a full answer. Just an adequate one."

"All right. Would it be an adequate answer if I convinced you that I, personally, am worth fighting for? That I'm perfect and have the perfection of all other conscious beings as my goal? That I have your race's best interests at the center of my heart?"

"That would do it," I said.

"All right. Tell me if any of this is over your head. The question you have to ask yourself is how you can know that I am perfect. Well, there's no such thing as a static perfection, but there is such thing as a process of perfection that can continue infinitely. For a conscious being, unlimited by disintegration, continued existence is an ever-increasing perfection of one's self and of one's surroundings. Every action you take is a risk and a test. The more you risk, the more you learn. If you believe anything of what I've said to you, then you can't avoid the logical conclusion that I'm the most perfect of all beings that exist merely by fact that I'm the only being with no beginning. You and others may join me in never ending; you can never join me in not having a beginning. By the nature of what I am, I have been tested infinitely more and perfected infinitely more. To all other conscious beings, I am an indispensable reference."

"You admit making mistakes?"

"If I hadn't, I wouldn't know so much. Because I've made more mistakes than anyone else, I know what works and doesn't work more than anyone else. My mistakes perfect me."

"And you share all of this knowledge without limits?"

"There are logical limits. I share all that I may without doing more harm than good."

"But you decide."

"No one else can."

"You've got yourself a boy," I said, extending my hand to God.

"I knew that already," said God, shaking it.

DUJ GOES ON A DATE

I made plans to meet Caulinn that night for dinner. Frankly, I was more than a little nervous. Not only was this my first date since my divorce, it was also my first date since I'd died.

If things went the way I intended them to, I was going to be doing something with my new body that I'd only done with my old body ... and I didn't have the luxury of uplinking to the Tree to find out if there was anything I'd better be careful about. I recalled a science fiction story called "Man of Steel, Woman of Kleenex" — which speculated fancifully on coupling problems between Kryptonese men and Earth women — and hoped Mr. Niven didn't know something about supermen that I didn't.

Well, there was only one way to find out for sure. I hopped into my Volvo, took a short drive over to a magazine store on Motor Avenue, and picked up a copy of a small digest magazine called Kinky Letters. Then I returned to my apartment, drew the drapes, and read through what purported to be genuine accounts of the correspondents' carnal experiences, letting nature — or should I say supernature — take its course.

It turns out that because I'd never got around to changing the defaults for sexual performance on my new body, I found no major differences between the experience of arousal and completion from that which I'd known in my old body.

Okay, yes, it felt better. Much better. And there was none of the lassitude that followed such an experience when I was human; I felt a priapic energy that would have allowed me to continue at will. It's good to be a god.

But my point is, the Kleenex was more or less intact at the end of the experiment.

#

Caulinn Helms was drop-dead gorgeous when I picked her up at her hotel that evening, and yes, that was the first thing I told her and she never tires of hearing it. There was nothing about her of the blatant sexual symbolism she used on stage, to create an impact reaching to the upper bleachers of a stadium: no exaggerated make-up, bustier, micromini, leather, chains, or spike heels. She merely wore a basic black cocktail dress that emphasized by its design that she was soft and curvy where men like women to be, and lean and muscular where men like women to be. She was also wearing a seductive perfume with a name like Heroin or Crack, or some other illicit drug.

Also, I've never understood what it is about long blond hair flowing silkily over pale, naked shoulders and black fabric that looks so sensational, and I don't think I'll ask the Tree to analyze it for me, either. You don't have to tell me that other color combinations of skin, hair, and fabric produce spectacular results, because I don't want to know how it works until I start designing my own species and have to know. There are some mysteries too enjoyable to end by explaining them away, if you don't have to.

Souplantation might have been a good enough place to meet God for dinner, but from the way she was dressed, it wasn't going to be good enough for Caulinn. Given the casual sportswear I was sporting, I was glad that even the fanciest Los Angeles restaurants didn't have much more of a dress code than, "No shoes, no shirt, no service." Nor did I think I'd impress Caulinn by pulling out my Entertainment Membership Card to get a "significant discount at the restaurants located in the Fine Dining Section of your book." This was definitely going to be a night for the old American Express card.

Maybe you wonder why, as a god, I just didn't wave a magic wand and materialize a few hundred gold Krugerrands, cashing them in as necessary. The first reason is that I didn't know how to do that without uplinking to the Tree, and I couldn't uplink without blowing my cover. The second was that even if I had a way to uplink, it might have tipped off the ever-watchful enemy that there was something different about Duj Pepperman, and maybe they'd better keep an eye on him.

"I didn't want to make reservations until I knew what you were in the mood for," I told Caulinn. "Sushi, Sicilian, or seafood?"

"Sicilian seafood," she said.

I headed over to the lobby pay phones and made a reservation for a private room at the Mobster Grotto on Sunset.

The earliest I could get was 9:15, a couple of hours hence, so I suggested to Caulinn that we drive up to Griffith Park Observatory. She'd never been there before so she wasn't hard to convince.

I've always enjoyed playing tour guide. "The observatory has always been one of my favorite places," I told Caulinn. "It's always looked to me like a temple devoted to the worship of science. Its placement high above Los Angeles offers spectacular views of the light-dotted cityscape on nights like this when the absence of smog allows it. Also, it has that magical quality of dramatic deja vu you get from frequent movie locations around L.A. The observatory was used as Jor-El's laboratory in the first episode of the Superman TV series, and in the scenes of James Dean mooing and knife-fighting in Rebel Without a Cause."

"Shut up, you wonk, and kiss me," Caulinn said, exasperated.

I've often suspected that women are less romantic than men.

SATAN HAS A DIFFERENT OPINION

The red Corvette pulled up to the curb. Satan was behind the wheel. He was wearing the white tuxedo he wore on TV that night as Sun Amen Chill. He motioned me into the passenger seat, then took off like a shot.

Satan didn't waste any time. "He sounded perfectly rational, right?"

I nodded.

Satan shook his head. "He has His good days and His bad days. You caught Him on one of His good days."

I fastened my seat belt, out of habit, I supposed. Satan chuckled.

The Sepulveda entrance to the 405 was up ahead. Satan turned into it, taking the diamond lane.

"Everything He said made perfect sense to me."

"Look, He's still God, even if He is crazy at times. What did he tell you, point by point?"

"The story about his bet with you about Eyob. He said it never happened."

"It happened. If anyone knows, I know."

"He said things that get talked about in Heaven aren't reported on Earth."

"Maybe He'd like to think so. My challenge to Him was in public — an open criticism session. You can't keep stuff like that a secret. Angels go down to Earth, they talk to people. It gets around."

"Well, if you knew He was crazy, why did you bring up the subject?"

"To show everyone what He was, how He really felt about his creatures."

"That's pretty mean-spirited of you."

"That's why I got the job as his Adversary. I never allow sentimentality to interfere with what needs to be done."

"Let's look at another case. Adam and Eve."

"You ever take the keys to your old man's car without his permission? Or go into his stuff when he wasn't home?"

"No."

"I can see why He likes you. Well, you have a daughter. Let's say when she's a teenager she did that. You going to curse her for life?"

"From what I hear about the Tree of Knowledge, it's more like going into dad's gun case and taking his elephant rifle out for a joyride. Not exactly a teenage prank."

"Depends on what the youngsters did with it. Did they take the Weatherby out to the desert for a test, or to the city zoo for a slaughter? Sure, they disobeyed his rules and had to be punished. But you need a little perspective here. God had lost His. Adam and Eve weren't bad kids. Just inexperienced. They showed poor judgment. God gave you his standard speech about how He's been perfected through eons of trial and error? Well, how were Adam and Eve supposed to learn if the first time they made a mistake, He expelled them from school? What else did He say?"

"The sacrifices, the rules for the Israelites. He said it was all the priests doing. He dismissed the idea that he would hang around in a box in a desert tent as crazy."

"Yes. Crazy. Exactly. During His sane periods even He can see that. Just look at the design specs for the Ark of the Covenant, if you need proof it was built for Him. It's a Faraday cage to prevent His electrical charge from leaking out and frying everybody. Even so, a couple of Moses's brothers bought it that way, going in unexpectedly. Look, God's a trinity, right?"

"Right."

"Wrong. There are four personalities, not three. He, Himself, only knows about Three — a painstaking craftsman, a creative genius, and a loving spirit. The fourth is a homicidal maniac, jockeying to be dominant. Number four is also a creative genius, but is an unstable manic-depressive artist."

I got really scared. Satan was making sense, and I was biased in favor of my race in the first place. On some level it was easier to believe that a crazy God was behind our ills than that we were doing it to ourselves. It's always nice to shove the blame off on someone else.

"Look," I said. "I have no doubt that you could sell refrigerators to Eskimos — you have that reputation. But I need proof."

"You asked Him for proof. What proof did He gave you?"

I thought back on the conversation. "A metaphysical proof. Logically, since He has no beginning, He has to be the most perfected being in existence."

"That would be true if God didn't go crazy occasionally.

Did he talk about solipsism at all? How He created other beings to avoid going crazy?"

"Yes. He made a point of it."

"Well, He did that in one of His lucid periods. He's smart. I keep on telling you, crazy or not, He's still God. It worked. He created other beings to give Himself a reality check. Well, here we are. The diagnosis is in."

GOD MEETS DUJ AT A 7-11

God was waiting for me, per previous arrangement, inside the 7-11 at the corner of Washington and Lincoln in Marina del Rey. He was black and wearing a Seminal Lunch T-shirt with a Dodgers cap on backwards, Nikes, and wrap-around shades.

God didn't bother with any preliminaries; He knew what was on my mind. "They don't call Satan the Prince of Lies for nothing," he said, pouring Himself a cherry Slurpee.

I shoved a red-hot bean burrito into the microwave and set it for two minutes. "You say you know about this charge that you have a fourth personality?"

"It's an old heresy — that both good and evil are within me. Well, for a God who has to act as a hunter occasionally – thin out the herd to improve it — it's an easy charge to believe."

"You deny it."

He took a draw off His Slurpee. "Of course I deny it."

"Satan said the design specs of the Ark of the Covenant were proof of what he was saying. That it's a Faraday Cage to contain your electrical charge."

"The Arc of the Covenant was a giant capacitor — a storage battery. The Israelite priests used it for special effects during their ceremonies ... and an occasional electrocution to send a message to troublemakers."

I shook my head. "How am I supposed to figure out what's true and what's not? I'm just a man."

"Not any more, you aren't. You're a god. Consult the Tree."

"Satan said you control the Tree, that you can rewrite it at will. That I can't trust it."

"Then there's the proof you need that he's lying. If the Tree isn't to be trusted because I've adulterated it — if its information is unreliable — then Satan wouldn't be working so hard to get back into it."

I laughed. "You know, I was sure that when it came right down to it, you were going to tell me that I was going to have to take your word on faith."

The microwave beeped. God took my burrito out, peeled it open, and handed it to me. "I don't demand faith, but you're going to find that you can't get along without it. I'll tell you when you're going to need faith. There's going to come a moment when you're in the middle of a battle, and you're going to have second thoughts about everything we've talked about. Satan's going to be at your elbow with a plausible reason to discount everything you think is true. And you won't have me there to counter his lies, because I'm going to be out of action – vulnerable. That's when you'll have to grit your teeth and go on, out of sheer faith."

God plunked some cash down on the counter for His Slurpee and my burrito. "My treat," He said.

WHAT DUJ HAS LEARNED BY THE END OF THE STORY

All things end. I remember when I learned this lesson. I was thirty-five years old, and it was one of three times — I know now — that God spoke to me when I was alive. It required a certain warping of consciousness for me to come to this realization, that all things end. I understand some people can get new understandings from drugs — hallucinogenic drugs in particular. But I was always too afraid of drugs to alter my consciousness deliberately. I craved control too strongly. So for me, the warped consciousness came upon me unexpectedly.

I had been a moderate coffee drinker, even though coffee acid gave me severe indigestion. The caffeine high was a necessary part of my writing at that time; I needed the rush to write. Then I got a mild chest cold and suddenly the indigestion was creating gas that was constricting my breathing, at the same time the coffee was quickening my pulse and making me breathe faster. The result was a threshold hyperventilation that kept going over the edge — and the more I hyperventilated uncontrollably, the more I became scared and hyperventilated even more.

In an instant, it stripped me of a lifetime of carefully built-up defense mechanisms. I was completely vulnerable – completely emotionally defenseless — to everything around me.

First of all, I thought I was going to die that night. That scared me senseless to begin with.

I tried watching TV. The thirty-second drama of a commercial was too much for me to take, in my emotionally labile condition.

Finally, as I lay in bed, thinking I was dying, God came to me and laughed at me.

"Why are you laughing at me?" I asked.

"Because you're afraid of death."

"Why is that so funny?"

"That you should be afraid of death."

It sounded like a compliment, but it was a compliment that I couldn't understand. Was I so brave that the idea of my being afraid of death was funny to God? I just didn't understand. Not until later anyway. God knew how I would think about it later before I did.

Then God asked me if I wanted to die. I felt God's hand on my heart, squeezing. I knew He could take me, that it was His choice, not mine.

I said "No, I want to live."

God said. "If you live, it will be without any promises. You have no claims on life. You will take what comes to you."

"I understand," I said. "Let me live."

"You understand. If you live long enough, you will see everything you love end."

"Yes, I understand."

And I did. But this understanding made me old that day.

Today I know that even for an immortal, all things end. Even if you go on forever, you die every moment and are reborn as something else. Every thought you have — every act you take – makes you into something different — and that which you were is left behind, dead.

The child who grows into an adult has died: that adult takes over the body and continues.

When we leave our bodies, we die as human beings. The human is dead while a new god is born.

The friend or loved one we see tomorrow has continuity only with our friend or loved one of yesterday: they are different, even if only incrementally different. If we are lucky, we find that which we love still alive in the new; but the old is surely dead by virtue of having been changed out of existence.

I realized that all my life I had both worshiped change and feared it. It was this dilemma — this paradox — that made romanticism wistful. Romanticism in intellect is the thought that we are growing and becoming better. Romanticism in emotion is nostalgia for every loved moment we leave behind.

In the name of all of us, we know it hurts.

But from such pain and paradoxes, we grow wise.

Such is the meaning, and the price, of eternal life and its countless changes.

About J. Neil Schulman

J. Neil Schulman is a novelist, screenwriter, journalist, publisher, filmmaker, songwriter, and actor.

His dozen books include his 1979 first novel, *Alongside Night*, entered in 1989 into the Libertarian Futurist Society's Prometheus Hall of Fame, and 1983's *The Rainbow Cadenza*, winner of the Prometheus Award for best libertarian novel. His third novel is the 2002 comic fantasy, *Escape from Heaven*. Other of his books include his short story collection, *Nasty, Brutish, and Short Stories; Stopping Power: Why 70 Million Americans Own Guns; The Robert Heinlein Interview and Other Heinleiniana;* and *Profile and Silver and Other Screenwritings*, which includes his original script "Profile in Silver" first broadcast prime time on CBS' *The Twilight Zone* March 7, 1986. J. Neil Schulman's latest book is 2013's *The Heartmost Desire*.

Schulman's articles and essays have been published in magazines ranging from *National Review* to *Mondo Cult*, and in newspapers including articles and Op-Eds for the Los Angeles Times. He's written for libertarian magazines including *Reason*, *Liberty*, and Murray Rothbard's *Libertarian Forum*.

He was a writer and editor for all of Samuel Edward Konkin III's *New Libertarian* magazines, and is considered with Konkin to be one of the original founders of the Agorist movement.

Schulman has written, produced, directed, and acted in two feature films, 2009's *Lady Magdalene's*, which won three film-festival awards, and 2013's *Alongside Night*.

His other awards include the 1993 James Madison Award from the Second Amendment Foundation, the 2009 Samuel Edward Konkin III Memorial Chauntecleer Award from the Karl Hess Club, and a Sovereign Award from Libertopia 2013.

www.ingramcontent.com/pod-product-compliance
Lightning Source LLC
Chambersburg PA
CBHW032014230426
43671CB00005B/76